DATE DUE

OCT 2 2 1996	
MAR 2 8 1997	
MAY 2 7 1997	
FEB 2 3 1998	
APR 4 1998	
MAY 6 1998	
JUL 2 1 1998	
AUG 1 7 1998	
JAN 2 2002	

GAYLORD   PRINTED IN U.S.A.

MANAGING THE
WORKPLACE SURVIVORS

MANAGING THE WORKPLACE SURVIVORS

Organizational Downsizing and the Commitment Gap

Marvin R. Gottlieb
Lori Conkling

QUORUM BOOKS
Westport, Connecticut • London

HD
58.8
·G67
1995

Library of Congress Cataloging-in-Publication Data

Gottlieb, Marvin R.
    Managing the workplace survivors : organizational downsizing and
the commitment gap / Marvin R. Gottlieb, Lori Conkling.
        p.   cm.
    Includes bibliographical references and index.
    ISBN 0–89930–922–4 (alk. paper)
    1. Organizational change.   2. Downsizing of organizations.
    3. Employee motivation.   4. Reengineering (Management).
    I. Conkling, Lori.   II. Title.
    HD58.8.G67   1995
    658.3'14—dc20   95–4247

British Library Cataloguing in Publication Data is available.

Library of Congress Catalog Card Number: 95–4247
ISBN: 0–89930–922–4

First published in 1995

Quorum Books, 88 Post Road West, Westport, CT 06881
An imprint of Greenwood Publishing Group, Inc.

Printed in the United States of America

The paper used in this book complies with the
Permanent Paper Standard issued by the National
Information Standards Organization (Z39.48–1984).

10 9 8 7 6 5 4 3 2 1

Contents

Appendixes

Figures and Tables

Preface

As this manuscript is being prepared to go to press, headlines in the business media continue to trumpet major layoffs. Merger and acquisition activity, which had slowed substantially in the first few years of the 1990s, has accelerated to the point that 1994 is second only to 1986 in the total amount of consolidation activity.

The changes that were and are rocking—and will continue to rock—the business community have reshaped the very nature of work. Nothing has been spared. Technology is rapidly changing not only the way work is done but also where and when it is done. Workers' attitudes have shifted away from affiliation and loyalty toward security and self-centeredness. At the eye of this storm is today's manager, and he or she has his or her own discontent. Managers are being called on to respond to the changing demands of a disenchanted work force. If they are unable to meet these demands, they will have failed their primary role and their organizations will suffer the consequences.

On the other hand, if they respond effectively, they can be the real champions of change and usher in a new era of high productivity and commitment. These goals require a new way of approaching management tasks and responsibilities. They require a new way of looking at the work force and accepting that things will never return to the way they were. Managers must deal with the fact that their success as managers may depend on their ability to discard many of the traditional management prerogatives in the interest of creating a new contract with their workers.

Halfhearted attempts at change are worse than no attempts at all. Such efforts only feed the growing demon of work cynicism and apathy and increase the "commitment gap." This book draws attention to what we call "survivors" in today's organizations. These are the people who are left after the rest have gone. They have special needs and concerns, and their view of reality has been altered forever.

In a sense, managers who are charged with the task of dealing with survivors are survivors themselves. So, many of the feelings and concerns attributed to the workers can be easily shared. The problem is to move beyond feeling, sharing, sympathy, and the like toward a plan of action that moves these survivors from where they are to something better—both for themselves and for the organizations they work for. We hope this book provides a springboard for such action.

The book is divided into two main parts: "Gaining a Perspective" and "Developing a Survivor Strategy." The appendixes are collectively nicknamed "The Manager's Toolkit" and contain some instruments and exercises that have proved effective in implementing the Survivor Management Model. Part I places more emphasis on who survivors are, where they came from, and what is happening to them. Part II shifts more emphasis to recommendations about what to do with them.

Much of what appears in this book derives from many years of consulting experience with a wide variety of organizations,—both private and public sector. We have purposely refrained from naming specific organizations, except as parts of quotes or summaries from other sources. In the rapidly changing universe we occupy, any specific company cited for good or ill will inevitably have altered course within minutes of the publication of this text, rendering our examples either irrelevant or questionable.

Our hope is that managers who read this book will understand the issues, perceive the opportunities, develop the competencies, and take up the challenge to lead their survivors to a new reality.

PART I

Gaining a Perspective

Chapters 1 to 4 provide historical, theoretical, and conceptual background relating to the creation of the survivor population. Chapter 1 summarizes the external factors that have forced organizations to downsize, merge, and reorganize. The emphasis in Chapter 1 is on understanding the critical issues—such as job insecurity, disappearing loyalty, shifting values, changing expectations, and displaced commitment—that are driving hearts and minds of both survivor managers and survivor employees. It introduces who the survivors are and lays the foundation for articulating the manager's critical mission and responsibility for managing and motivating his or her survivor employees.

Chapter 2 illuminates the changing attitudes, values, and beliefs held by survivors that affect both their ability and willingness to give their full effort in the workplace. The chapter also summarizes findings from a major survey, done by the Families and Work Institute, which highlights some areas for potential manager intervention.

Chapter 3 discusses the changing nature of leadership in today's workplace. It also discusses past and current role models and suggests an appropriate model for effective survivor leaders. Strong focus within this chapter includes the demystification of the teamwork panacea, which has insidiously infiltrated survivor organizations under the guise of empowerment and salvation.

Chapter 4 examines the evolution of organizations and the theoretical frameworks that have driven these organizational constructs. By recogniz-

ing the particular structure and the systems that are in place in his or her own organization, the survivor manager can more readily identify which organizational barriers he or she must work through in the process of reaching and enabling the survivor employee.

CHAPTER 1

The Survivor Syndrome

Historians are fond of naming periods of time to establish them as cogent entities—to give them a character, a cohesiveness. Once named, the time frame or era can be studied, making events appear as if they were contributors to or the result of the nomenclature. The "Age of Reason," The "Age of Analysis," and the like are representative of such attempts. In the business world, what will historians call this period? The "Age of Entrepreneurism"? This is a good candidate but unpronounceable. Besides, the term is out of control. It seems that everyone who, by force of circumstances or choice, is attempting to make a living outside a conventional corporate structure is an entrepreneur. The entrepreneurial range spans the distance between the housewife baking cookies for profit and the whiz kid stumbling onto yet another technology to process and move information much faster then any of us can believe.

THE AGE OF REORGANIZATION

If we are to name this period, let us call it the "Age of Reorganization." If your company is not involved in a merger or acquisition, the object of an unfriendly takeover, or restructuring its entire operation, then you are not with it. Corporate objectives read like the menu at a health club: *downsize, maximize, get lean, leverage*. These euphemisms generally translate into the same thing—somebody is getting fired (or perhaps "entrepreneured").

The widespread proliferation of job layoffs and employment reductions throughout the private and public sectors in the United States continues to foreshadow uncertainty and instability for both the American worker and the American economy. In July 1992, *Time* magazine reported that the

United States lost 117,000 jobs in the month of June alone. In the first six months of 1992, corporate America shed an average of 1,500 positions a day.[1] Nearly 547,500 jobs were eliminated by the end of 1992. New York City, long considered to be both a magnet for and the center of national and international business, has experienced a dramatic decline in both prestige and jobs over the past several years. The business press estimated that New York continued to lose jobs throughout 1992, although at a slower pace than the record-breaking 195,000 jobs lost in 1991. New York had already lost about 45,000 jobs by June 1992 and was forecasted by the WEFA Group, Inc., to lose another 55,000 jobs by the end of that year.[2]

The year 1992 is important as a watershed because the escalation of downsizing was responsible for creating the shock that led to the survivor environment. The 1992 roll call of company downsizings and employee firings included a litany of disheartening announcements which, despite their regularity, continued to shock and discourage most of us. A sampling of some of the more significant organizational changes in the United States in 1992 follows.

September 1992

International Business Machines Corporation (IBM) announced that a total of 40,000 jobs would be eliminated this year through buyouts. Since 1985, IBM has reduced its work force of more than half a million workers by 25 percent.[3]

August 1992

Manufacturing employment continued to drop by 97,000 jobs in August, capping three years of almost steady decline. Unemployment among adults reached nearly 7 percent during the month, its highest level since the early 1980s.[4]

July 1992

In a major setback for its subsidiary, Hughes Aircraft Company, General Motors Corporation (GM), as a result of its move into the defense business, took a $749.4-million write-off in the second quarter. This was expected to result in 9,000 more layoffs. The cuts, equal to 15 percent of the current work force, pared employment to about 50,000.[5]

Amoco, Unocal, and Mobil announced major business restructurings. Amoco said it would cut 8,500 jobs, or nearly 16 percent of its work force. Unocal planned to eliminate 1,100 of its 17,000 jobs worldwide, mostly in the United States. Mobil said that it would cut 2,000 salaried jobs, or 9.5 percent of that group.[6]

March 1992

Reporting a loss of $4.5 billion for the year, GM announced the closing of twelve plants—representing 16,000 jobs—a down payment on a previously announced plan to fire 74,000 workers by 1995.[7] Even once-considered recession-proof industries also began to see their foundations crumble. Between December 1991 and September 1992, six key defense-related industries—ordnance, aerospace, shipbuilding, missile manufacturing, communication gear, and navigation equipment—lost about 100,000 jobs. That accounts for two-thirds of the fall in manufacturing employment. Even the computer industry, once one of the nation's strongest, began shrinking fast. Between 1989 and 1992, it lost approximately 50,000 jobs.[8] We wonder how history will assess these years in human terms.

Daniel Yankelovich has named this era The "Age of Self-Fulfillment," and perhaps it is. The victims of "lean and mean," while initially traumatized, are free to follow the sounds of different drummers. Many, perhaps most, will do well—maybe better than ever. The need to be responsible has been replaced by the need to make ends meet, and the demand to fulfill basic needs tends to bring out the best in people. It is also its own reward. But what about the survivors?

BUT WHAT ABOUT THE SURVIVORS?

√There are plenty of support systems in place for the victim. The natural sympathy of family and friends, the drawing closer in shared experience, the growing body of examples in literature as well as real life to provide behavior models are all available to the person cast adrift from the organizational harbor. The very organizations that cause the problem offer solutions in the form of "outplacement" services designed to prepare the downsizees for a challenging new career at midlife.

The trend continued throughout 1993, when a record for job cuts was set. Although downsizing slowed somewhat in the first ten months of 1994, 460,063 job cuts were announced. According to the Challenger Employment Report, the majority of job losses were the result of restructuring. The largest cutback announcements in October 1994 were 6,000 from American Express, 5,000 from Syntex, and 4,000 from Ameritech.

When Unisys Corporation announced that it was eliminating 1,700 jobs in addition to the 3-percent reduction the year before because of restructuring, the announcement further revealed that worldwide employment would be further reduced by 7,000 to 8,000 employees by the end of 1990. To accomplish this, Unisys provided not only outplacement but also financial and emotional counseling. Kodak provided a $5,000 retraining allowance in addition to outplacement services when it eliminated about 4,500 jobs worldwide. Kodak called its approach "an enhanced separation plan." While the primary purpose of these services may be to minimize the number of wrongful dismissal suits, these counseling services are very helpful in getting a person through the early transition from trauma to trying something new. But what about the survivors?

They are a rapidly growing population in corporate America. Survivor pockets are cropping up like wildflowers throughout the United States, from automobile factories in Michigan and California to huge conglomerates housed in silver skyscrapers in New York and Chicago. They are part of the mainstream of business life.

Survivors are the people who are left when others are swept away. They were part of the company when the wave rolled in, and they are still part of the company after the wave carried others away. After the brow is mopped and the stomach has settled, after the goodbyes to old comrades and some antagonists, what then? Forget and go on? Not likely. Picturing a man with his head in his hands and a confused, haunted look on his face, the August 4, 1986 issue of *Business Week* heralded "The End of Corporate Loyalty" on its cover.[9] Amidst the general discussion of the erosion of loyalty (estimated as a 65% decline from ten years ago by a *Business Week/Harris Poll*), the article discusses the survivors of cutbacks and suggests that survivors feel a sense of distance between themselves and the company. The individual begins to focus on personal security rather than corporate loyalty.

More recently, a September 1992 article in the *National Business Employment Weekly* reported on a survey of thirty-one large companies by EnterChange, an Atlanta-based outplacement firm. It indicated that restructuring programs designed to improve efficiency and profits had the opposite result—at least in the beginning. Employees' nonproductive time increased from 1.8 hours per day to 4.8 hours, while managers responsible for implementing the changes reported feeling lost. During the transitions, 59 percent of the companies' managers were perceived as not being effective in communicating a rationale to employees, 72 percent were unable to build a commitment to the new organization, and 77 percent didn't raise employee confidence levels. EnterChange double-checked the data by interviewing 203 employees of a large organization undergoing a major change. According to the poll, 95 percent of employees reported having no specific job to perform during the transition. They also said they had difficulty completing their normal tasks because of distractions. Almost half said they had strong feelings of anger and bitterness, and 20 percent felt betrayed by the company. An estimate of company morale put it at 2.5 on a 10-point scale.[10]

While some attempts have been made to show survivors that the company is still committed to its people, most such efforts are greeted with the cynicism they probably deserve. Survivors are often terrified. Instead of recognizing an opportunity to mold a dynamic and creative work force, management often views these survivors as if they were still potential targets. "They should be grateful they still have their jobs!" and "They better buckle down or they'll be the next to go!" are often the messages management subtly or overtly communicates to their survivors. The survivors feel punished and often do not receive renewed encouragement to grow and thrive within the corporate structure.

If top management does not begin to invest in their most precious resource—their people—then we will truly be handing over our building and factory keys to those who can and will. Survivors can no longer be kept underground; they are the key to a reorganized or downsized company's new success or inevitable failure.

What is actually happening inside the survivor mentality? What thoughts, feelings, and actions translate into traditional productivity issues? By making a short-term financial gain, does an organization seal its long-term doom by losing the commitment of its work force? Survivors of organizational downsizing are subject to the same trigger for change as the victims. This change evokes feelings which are at once positive and negative about the self and the organization: fear and hope, relief and anxiety, loss of meaning and new meaning, a threat to self-esteem, and a new sense of value.

WHAT IS SURVIVING?

To survive means to remain alive or existent, to outlive and outlast. Bruno Bettelheim, in *Surviving and Other Essays*, copes with the issue of survival through his analysis of Holocaust survivors.[11] While clearly at a higher level of seriousness, there are some basic attitudes, behaviors, and beliefs culled by Bettelheim in his interviews and discussions with Holocaust survivors that can provide us with insights into organizational survivor behaviors. Bettelheim tells us that in order to achieve survival, one must successfully come to terms with one's own guilt. A powerful determination is involved in the act of survival. In the concentration camps, once people let go their grasp of determination, once they gave in to the omnipresent despair and let it dominate their wish to live, they were doomed. To survive, the prisoners had to help one another. To survive, a person had to be active in his or her own behalf. To survive, one had to want to survive for a purpose. Only active thought could prevent a prisoner from becoming one of the "walking dead (*Muselmänner*)," those who were doomed because they had given up all thought and hope. Of course, to successfully survive, the feelings of guilt needed to be managed—guilt for having felt glad that it was not oneself who perished. Bettelheim quotes Elie Wiesel: "I live and therefore I am guilty. I am still here because a friend, a comrade and unknown died in my place."[12]

⚔ Guilt is a feeling frequently mentioned by those who remain after an organizational transformation. Often one's close colleagues are let go, and certainly when this happens a personal assessment by those left behind is undertaken. Survivors start to ask themselves, "Why am I the lucky one to remain? Why have I been chosen not to have to deal with a dramatic dip in my income and the task of finding a new job?" From these observations can emerge a different perspective: After the outplacement and counseling, the string pulling, and references, former employees are often perceived to wind up with better and more challenging positions. Those left behind, who are frequently still in contact with those let go, hear statements such as, "Being fired by XYZ Company was the best thing that's ever happened to me. I was able to get a position with a more prestigious company with a bigger salary, with a bigger office," and the like, or "The severance package provided by XYZ Company provided me with the capital I needed to own my own business, something I've wanted to do but never could afford."

Survivors start to feel like the unlucky ones, those poor saps who are left to clean up the corporate mess. They are left with reduced resources, less staff and more work ahead of them than they can see their way around. Some survivors do let go of their determination and give up, causing the company to carry along a disloyal, dissatisfied, and marginal employee who either flees on his or her own or must be let go at a later date.

It is our contention that the vast majority of companies that are in a downsizing or restructuring mode are failing miserably in their attempts to retain and successfully motivate their survivors. On their part, the survivors are also failing to effectively come to grips with their new reality and convert their surviving into thriving.

ORGANIZATIONAL PARADIGMS IN LATE
TWENTIETH-CENTURY AMERICA

In a way, I feel like I'm preparing for doomsday. I mean . . . it's not like I'm hoarding canned food or building a bomb shelter in the back yard. But, I'm going to be forty next year and I have worked for GM for almost twenty years. Don't get me wrong, I want to hang on to my job. But, I'm starting my own little business on the side, because, the way things are going, I have to think about a future without GM. It seems like every time you turn around a plant is being closed, people are being laid off. I have some friends who have been out of work a long time.

—Frank R.

Calling today's work force "defensive entrepreneurs," *The Wall Street Journal* (May 25, 1994) in a front-page article, "Eye on the Future," discussed the growing trend among current employees to prepare for a future outside of the organizations they currently work for—"people who, while continuing in their regular jobs, are developing new careers—for psychic as well as financial reasons. They're sacrificing weekends and vacations to moonlight as small-scale landlords, innkeepers, studio photographers, mechanics and owners of hardware stores and hair salons."[13] While acknowledging that people have always moonlighted, *The Wall Street Journal* pointed the finger at the tremendous restructuring that hit corporate America in the 1980s as the major factor that brought a new sense of insecurity to the work force at all levels. People who began careers twenty years ago tended to feel that they had a lifetime contract if they performed well. Now, these workers no longer trust their companies and are willing to make the sacrifices and take the risks necessary to allay their anxiety. With all of the attendant problems that come with trying to start and run a small business, particularly while still employed full-time elsewhere, many are accepting the challenge.

The Wall Street Journal discussed three workers who had opened small businesses while employed and said the risks were a small price to pay for gaining some measure of control over their future. The insecurity at their places of employment was evident from some numbers: The three employers—GM, American Telephone and Telegraph Company (AT&T), and IBM—had reduced their work forces by a total of at least 87,000 jobs, counting those who left through early retirement programs.[14]

IBM, GM, Hewlett-Packard (HP), Control Data Corporation, Salomon Brothers, Exxon, General Electric (GE), AT&T, Apple Computer, Du Pont, Eastman Kodak, Union Carbide, Intel—a roll call of but a few of the numerous companies in late twentieth-century America who, through the result of downsizing, restructuring, or reorganization have laid off employees and, as a result, have created the new job–social class of the survivor, which many companies find to be, at best, a displaced and unpredictable group.

Downsizing includes reducing the work force, letting people go, doing more with less, flattening corporate pyramids, and becoming lean and mean. Why? Why are companies downsizing, restructuring, and reorganizing in late twentieth-century America? There are several reasons.

The Result of Corporate America's Effort, Begun in the 1970s, to Cope with the Recession

Although it was predicted that once the economy recovered people would eventually regain their jobs, this is not what happened. In fact, many companies discovered that staff reductions had not significantly hurt productivity but had significantly improved profits. For a long time, there had been a large amount of personnel "fat" taking up a lot of room in offices and cubicles all across America. Partly as a result of the post–World War II covert promise of full employment and partly because organizations were used to and expected to do business this way, corporate

America was emerging with an awful lot of flab around the middle. It is no wonder that as we Americans started to have to seriously tighten our belts economically (as well as physically witness the beginning of our national obsession with health and fitness), we started to cast a cold and unsparing critical eye at the way our companies were structured and conducting business. After all, Japan was becoming a national source of embarrassment because of its technological and work force breakthroughs.

Perhaps we did not really need five, six, or seven layers of management protective flab separating our chief executive officers (CEOs) from our workers. What were those middle managers doing anyway? Internally, companies, in order to stave off spiraling costs—partly from domestic inflation and partly from increased competition from abroad—began a series of restructurings, downsizings, and staff reductions that are still continuing today. A strange phenomenon began to happen. The survivors (although they probably had no idea early on that they were part of a new and special work force category) began to learn new ways of managing their companies and working with one another. People who had spent most of their management days chairing endless meetings and task forces and shuffling innumerable reports were now being asked to accept the mantle of responsibility. Their performance did matter. Their productivity mysteriously did improve. The company actually needed them.

Cost Containment

Increased benefits, pension, and compensation costs, with no corresponding increase in revenues, were draining companies dry.

Rising International Competition

Inexpensive goods filtering to American consumers from abroad threw many companies out of the game; competition became intense.

Mergers, Acquisitions, and Divestitures

Combining corporate entities typically have layers of duplication in management functions, and this factor brings about the need to eliminate redundant positions.

Threat of Takeovers

This often leads companies to downsize. It costs a lot of money to defend a company in the face of takeover attempts, and work forces are often reduced as a direct result in order to keep the company afloat.

Technology

As offices and factories become increasingly automated, many jobs have been and will be phased out.

Maturation of the Baby Boomer Generation

As the baby boomers continue to climb the corporate ladder, they often find themselves blocked because of their predecessors and their colleagues. With the former, we now see that the population is leading longer and healthier lives; and mandatory retirement policies are disappearing. A major challenge for corporate management will be to make room for those rising through the increasingly crowded ranks, hence the proliferation of early retirement packages, parachutes, and employment contracts.

The October 1987 Stock Market Crash

The crash has directly and indirectly transformed our economic barometer. All industries, along with the way in which we conduct business, have been severely affected; and unfortunately, into the 1990s and beyond, more problems will emerge.

Where are the survivors in the midst of these changes? How are they reacting to the external and internal turmoil? They are left confused, angry, and resentful toward the corporation and, paradoxically, are possessed with feelings of guilt for having been chosen to be survivors. The survivors realize that corporate loyalty is a joke and a sad substitution for the "good old days" of corporate paternalism. "The corporation is just in the business to make a profit! They are not going to take care of my family and me for life! They betrayed me!"

These survivor reactions are commonplace and most troublesome for the individual. How does the survivor emotionally come to terms with the need to make a living and the necessity to realign oneself with a company that has shattered his or her secure world? Leonard Greenhalgh and Todd D. Jick, in their article, "Survivor Sense Making and Reactions to Organizational Decline: Effects of Individual Differences" identify the following as contributors to a survivor's success or failure in managing organizational change:[15]

- Individual tolerance for ambiguity
- Individual sense making related to that situation
- Reality construction

Greenhalgh and Jick note that personality creates the psychological environments individuals develop from their objective environments. They claim that individuals who have low tolerance of ambiguity and a high need for security see a better picture regarding the ambiguities of their jobs and the organization's future. They also react more positively to their job situations, having fewer health problems, remaining more satisfied and involved with their jobs, and reporting less likelihood of leaving the organization. The process of sense making does, indeed, seem to be an important factor.

Communications concerning the work situation present the employee with ambiguous stimuli. Response to the stimuli involves projecting a definition of the situation compatible with the individual's personality characteristics. Individuals who have a basic aversion to threatening ambiguous situations evidently make sense of ambiguous stimuli by constructing a reality that is free of aversion-producing information. Perceptual defense mechanisms appear to be mobilized that, in effect, deny or distort objective ambiguities, thereby enabling the individuals to cope with their objective predicament.[16]

A young middle manager in an international company put it this way:

The truth is, like most organizations today, particularly those with ties to the financial and Wall Street communities, we're in trouble. We're scrambling. Products are late, sales are down, the stock is plummeting and no one is exactly sure just why. So, what do we do? We reorganize, restructure, or, as my company likes to couch it, we "rationalize." Every six months, like clockwork. People are let go, and people are hired every day. The scary realization is that we are the company, the people who work here. Our identity is the company's identity, but the reflection is transparent because we stand on shaky ground. In the last three years, I've moved my office four times, I've had three different job titles, two bosses, and have been in two separate departments. I just found out we're going to reorganize again.

While using a defense mechanism such as denial or distortion can provide temporary relief and a false sense of corporate security for the survivor, the healthier and more rewarding tactic for the survivors is to come to terms with the objective reality of their situations and shift their loyalties to their careers and toward self-actualization. A recent *Business Week* cover story entitled "I'm Worried about My Job" picks up and enhances this theme. It advises workers to develop marketable skills and to view all jobs as temporary.[17] As individuals, survivors need to develop strategies for transformation into thrivers.

Career Thrivers

Survivors need to renew their dedication and commitment to their individual strengths and talents and to developing an inner security core. Survivors will realize that no one person or organization can take this away—unless you let them.

Organization Thrivers

If the survivors have a well-developed loyalty to their careers, they cannot help but be successful players in the organizational arena. They have come to grips with the realization that they have contracted to provide expertise and loyalty to the corporation for a specified or unspecified period of time. They can contribute the best of their talents to the success of the organization because they are the best they can be.

Personal Thrivers

Ultimately, thrivers feel, act, and think as winners in all aspects of life. Above all, loyalty to one's career will save the individual in the 1990s and beyond, as John Naisbitt and Patricia Aburdene assert in *Megatrends 2000*:

A recent survey confirmed what executives have complained about for years. Seventy percent of managers report employees—especially young executives— do not exhibit the same loyalty to their companies that was the norm in the 1950's, concludes a study by Egon Zehnder International, a Zurich-based consulting firm with offices in New York City.[18]

On the other hand, *Success* magazine, which surveyed the young people themselves, found they thought loyalty was important, but never as important as personal growth.

"Have skills, will travel" seems to be the motto of the job-jumping baby boom generation, conforming to the stereotype of the selfish yuppie. On the other hand, the fast pace of social and technological change has forced young people to adapt and change. The average American entering the work force today will change careers—not jobs, careers—three times, according to the Labor Department. Private experts tell people to count on five different careers.[19]

Michael Maccoby, author of *The Gamesman* and *The Leader*, postulates a new corporate archetype that tracks well with the *Success* executive profile. "A 'self-developer,'" he says, "is an individual who values independence, dislikes bureaucracies, and seeks to balance work with other priorities like family and recreation."[20]

In *Why Work?*, published in 1988, he describes a new generation of professional engineers whose main corporate objective is self-development. He points out that they recognize that corporations cannot be trusted to take care of their workers. Security lies only in the skills an employee can take to his or her next job.

If you are a manager, a leader (and also a survivor) in an organization, how do you motivate and lead your work force? "Paradoxically, people who are difficult to supervise and free to leave, people who think for themselves, who question authority are a leader's best source of information and only hope for achieving organizational goals."[21]

The new work force will help the company achieve objectives if it can achieve its own personal goals as part of the bargain. An effective leader creates a vision that tells people where a company is going and how it will get there and becomes the organizing force behind every corporate decision. Will this action help us achieve our vision? More important is selling that vision to the people who will actualize their own goals—for achievement, security, and creativity—by achieving the corporation's goals. Without their energetic participation, little can be accomplished.

MANAGING THE SURVIVORS

In 1984, Noel Tichy and David Ulrich, writing in the *Sloan Management Review,* saw "fat and flabby" U.S. companies engaged in a gradual decline in the increasingly competitive world economy. They called for a new brand of leadership to *transform* organizations and head them down new tracks. Further, they charged their leaders of the future with the responsibility of making major changes in the basic political and cultural systems of the organization. Much of what they had to say about the role of leadership maintains its validity today, with some modification. Tichy and Ulrich were tied to the basic hierarchical model. Although they used phrases like "lean and mean" they did not foresee (or at least describe) the flat matrix structures that are emerging today. They placed their hopes on the CEO as the initiator and modeler of change. Their idol was Lee Iacocca.

This bailout came with a stigma, thus Mr. Iacocca's job was to change the company's cultural values from a loser's to a winner's feeling. Still, he realized that employees were not going to be winners unless they could, in cultural norms, be more efficient and innovative than their competitors. The molding and shaping of the new culture was clearly and visibly led by Mr. Iacocca, who not only used internal communication as a vehicle to signal change but also used his own personal appearance in Chrysler ads to reinforce these changes.[22]

In fact, it has not been transformational leaders but the hard realities of a faltering economy that have had the major effect on cultural change in organizations. A subsequent wave of change in the form of increased work force diversity is about to hit the beach with full force. While Tichy and Ulrich's view does not reflect today's reality, the basic model they suggest for managing change has considerable application. Separating the major targets for change into organizational dynamics and individual dynamics, they constructed a model that took into account trigger events, forces resistant to change, potential interventions, and the results of such interventions.[23]

Using their model as a springboard, the model in Figure 1.1 was created to demonstrate the process of moving the survivor through various stages

Figure 1.1
The Survivor Management Model

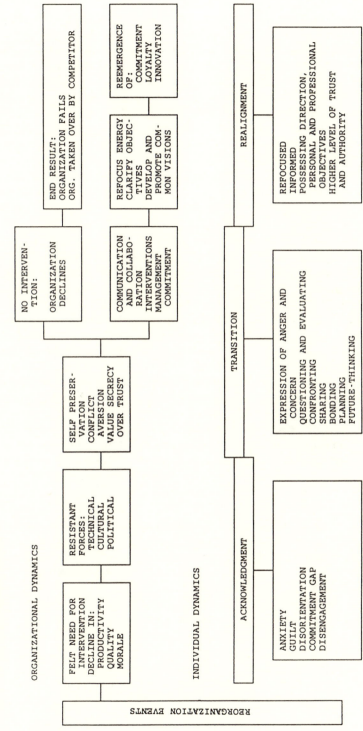

toward what we call "realignment." In the initial phase, there is a "reorganization event." This can be stimulated by economic conditions, a change in the market, new technology, a takeover, or because the organization wants to take advantage of the general economic climate to eliminate some "fat." The organization experiences a decline in productivity, quality, and morale. The individuals experience anxiety, guilt, and disorientation, leading to a commitment gap.

As with all change, forces within the organization move to maintain the status quo. Here, we borrow Tichy and Ulrich's resistance categories: technical, cultural and political.[24]

Technical resistances include habit and inertia, fear of the unknown or the loss of predictability, unwillingness or inability to adapt to new technology, and focus on the investment already made in old approaches (sunk costs).

The culture of the organization creates selective perception and tunnel vision. It inhibits the ability to employ innovation as a means for adapting to change. Also, there is a comfort level already attained with the current culture that is hard to give up. There is a security in the past and a general feeling that "if we just wait this out, we'll get back to the 'good old days.'"

Political coalitions draw tighter lines around their boundaries. Tendencies for territoriality become overt competition for dwindling resources. Managers are reluctant to rescind decisions or abandon objectives they have only recently made. Everyone becomes more acutely aware of their perception within the organization, and much time is spent "covering backsides."

On the organizational side, these resistances lead to a preoccupation with self-preservation, conflict aversion (except to protect territory), and the valuing of secrecy over trust. The individuals express these feelings through cynicism, anger, sabotage, and the withholding of effort. If something is not done at this stage, the organization will most likely decline.

In the midst of all these forces interacting, there is one factor that remains within the control of managers at every level—that is, how much and in what form they are willing to communicate. Managers who succeed in maintaining high levels of quality and productivity during periods of retrenchment are those who proactively deal with the feelings and information needs of their subordinates. In the absence of solid information, rumors fill the vacuum.

To be successful, any interventions developed to help the survivors should have three parts: an acknowledgment phase, a transition phase, and a realignment phase. Managers and subordinates must face squarely that they are living in a new order; that, while the future is uncertain, there is no going back to the past; that those who are gone will find their way; and that the grief they feel is more about the uncertainty of their own future than the futures of the ones who left. Managers must believe and project that there is a future and that what the future is will become clear in time. They must be self-disclosing about their own anxieties but also provide a model of commitment that others can see and emulate.

CHAPTER 2

The New Work Force

It is difficult, if not impossible, to pick up a newspaper, magazine, or any other business-related media and not be confronted with at least one announcement about workers losing jobs or about added concerns and burdens for those who remain employed. While considering the plight of those 50-year-old managers, one does not have to think back too far to conjure up pictures of an entirely different world. The world of the past is gone, and has changed so radically as to be unrecognizable in present-day terms. Think of the concerns that these men and women were facing in their early, formative years.

There was a time—and, we emphasize, not too long ago—when the major issue of discussion and debate at colleges and other places where the future shapers of the world would meet and discuss issues was what we were all going to do with the inevitable leisure time that we saw developing on the horizon. Some of you may recall having taken part in those debates. Shorter workdays, four-day workweeks, and the like seemed to be the future, along with the accompanying benefits and social problems that were projected to arise within a leisure society.

As Juliet Schor relates in her book, *The Overworked American: The Unexpected Decline of Leisure*, "It was projected that economic progress would yield steady reductions in working time. By today, it was estimated that we could have either a 22-hour work week, a six-month work year, or a standard retirement age of 38."[3]

Having bought into this notion, hundreds of thousands of upwardly mobile workers in all categories, firmly convinced of a straight-line projection of leisure into the future, began to reshape their approaches to work and their concerns about self-fulfillment. They purchased second homes, boats, and other leisure-related toys in extraordinary amounts.

In essence, workers—and, in particular, managers—who felt that they were keeping their side of the bargain by going to college in ever-increasing numbers and trading off portions of their newly coveted personal freedom for corporate concerns believed that they were in the driver's seat. They believed that, unless they seriously screwed up, they would always have a job; and if one job did not please them, they could readily find another.

They further believed that the organizations they worked for, since they made up the organic material of those organizations, would have to bend to suit their developing needs. In short, in the early 1980s, as the economy continued to grow, workers—and, in particular, educated workers—believed that they were in control of their destinies. They certainly did not envision a future that would reposition them as victims.

WORK AS A RIGHT, NOT A PRIVILEGE

As recently as 1983, Daniel Yankelovich presented some extraordinary findings and conclusions about changes in the work force in his book, *New Rules: Searching for Self-Fulfillment in a World Turned Upside Down*. In many aspects, Yankelovich foreshadowed the survivor culture of the 1990s. While these new perspectives were the result of a myriad of interwoven extrinsic and intrinsic factors—including a rapidly changing American (and world) economy; the civil rights and women's rights movements; and the post-Woodstock adoption of a wider range of choices, values, and lifestyles—they all pointed to a radical change in the self-identity of the American worker.

Tens of millions of Americans have grown wary of demands for further sacrifices they believe may no longer be warranted. They want to modify the giving/getting compact in every one of its dimensions—family life, career, leisure, the meaning of success, relationships with other people, and relations with themselves . . . to the efficiency of technological society they wish to add joy of living. They seek to satisfy both the body and the spirit, which is asking a great deal from the human condition.[4]

Yankelovich saw people engaging in a new social ethic gradually taking shape. He called it an "ethic of commitment" to distinguish it from the traditional ethic of self-denial that underlies the old giving–getting compact and also from the ethic of duty to self that grows out of a defective strategy for self-fulfillment.

In 1979, Yankelovich's company—Yankelovich, Skelly and White—set out to survey nearly 3,000 Americans employed either full time or part time in the United States. Yankelovich's methodology for culling the essence of these new rules included conducting several hundred life-history interviews and drawing on a number of large, previously published national surveys of the American work force.

Yankelovich's findings were startlingly revealing of our personal values, largely as a result of these open-ended life-history interviews. People were asked to describe what *self-fulfillment* and *success* meant to them in the most personal sense of these terms. The people discussed their values, moral convictions, and life goals and contrasted their own personal feelings about success and self-fulfillment with how their parents felt about those matters and pursued them in their own lives. The respondents were also asked to recount the risks taken for the sake of success and self and the risks each had chosen to shun.

Two significant statistical entities emerged from these studies:

One of the larger changes we discovered in the research was a sharp drop in the number of college students who believe that "hard work always pays off." In the mid-sixties, 72 percent of college students subscribed to this view. By the early seventies its adherents had been almost cut in half—to 40 percent. . . . In the decade between the late sixties and the late seventies the number of Americans who believe "hard work always pays off" fell from a 58 percent majority to a 43 percent minority.[5]

The research also revealed that one group of working Americans placed their personal self-fulfillment high above all other concerns about money, security, performing well, or working at a satisfying job. This group constituted about 17 percent of all working Americans (approximately 17 million people at that time). They were younger than average, and more of them were professionals than among average Americans. When surveyed, fewer had married or owned their own homes than average Americans, and their politics leaned more toward the liberal than toward the conservative wings of the Democratic or Republican parties. They were also the best-educated of five groups, with more than half (51%) having received at least some college education. Also, their parents had much more college education than the rest of the working population (42% compared to 21%).

A most important phenomenon that emerges from these dynamic shifts in American values and attitudes and shows up in the contemporary workplace is referred to by Yankelovich as the "commitment gap." Many of these young workers of the 1970s grew up to be the survivors of the 1990s.

In order to understand some of their plight today, we must understand the climate of tension and rebellion the young workers of the 1970s participated in. Nothing could have been further from the values of these self-fulfillment seekers than the class-conscious, hierarchical, authoritarian, adversarial attitudes that characterized the managerial outlook in many American industries at the time. Workers engaged in the search for self-fulfillment rebelled against the status quo by holding back their commitment, if not their labor. They were struggling to revise the giving–getting compact in the workplace. In return for giving themselves unstintingly to the job, they demanded important psychological incentives as well as economic ones. These demands made them troublesome to work with—as a condition of their commitment, they were constantly demanding things for themselves. Yankelovich foresaw that the work style they preferred was potentially far more productive in today's service–information–high technology economy than in the work relationships of the past.

From the organizational perspective, work is perceived as a privilege rather than a right. The single choice that is offered to today's work force is to earn and re-earn, sometimes daily, the right to continue to be employed. The only other option—that is, to dive or be pushed overboard—is a terrifying prospect to a vast majority of essentially risk-averse people who began their work lives with the assumption that they would be taken care of.

Schor's research testifies to the cold reality of our losing battle with preserving our leisure time by asserting that, over the past twenty years, our actual working hours have increased by the equivalent of one month per year.

"When surveyed, Americans report that they have only sixteen and a half hours of leisure a week after the obligations of jobs and household are taken care of. Working hours are already longer than they were forty years ago. If present trends continue, by the end of the century Americans will be spending as much time at their jobs as they did back in the 1920's."

It may be an exaggeration to say that all the second homes in America are currently on the market; but, as we approach the end of the century, the overriding concerns of a leisure-oriented society sound as a distant echo in the caverns of today's reality.

The "new work force," as we term it in this chapter, is an entity caught up in the flow of rapid and continuous transition—transition to what, we do not yet know. However, one thing is certain: The work force of today and what it will become in the future is starkly different from both what was and what was expected only a few years ago.

Today's work force is grappling with a distorted perspective of time and its value as a personal commodity, largely as a result of the uncertainties of job security and economic growth. Those employees who are lucky enough to be herded into the survivor population of an organization experiencing downsizing, restructuring, or reengineering are finding themselves putting in a marked increase in work time, partly because of the fact that they are now assuming two or three other jobs which have been "rightsized" out of the corporation.

A recent *Fortune* article examining family-friendly companies notes, "As employers bolt from life-time commitments to employees and seek to renegotiate that contract, they're sending mixed messages. While waving their family-friendly banner with one hand, they are tossing out the chicken soup with the other."[6]

In a response to a *Fortune* poll, more than two hundred CEOs (almost 80% of the respondents) said they will have to push their people harder than ever before to compete in the 1990s. That is particularly true at companies experiencing layoffs, since fewer people do just as much work.

Many of today's survivor employees are also burning the midnight oil, because of their employer's short-sighted belief that work is getting done only when an employee displays his or her undying commitment to the organization by pushing papers around the desk after 5 P.M., no matter what is actually being accomplished.

According to the *Fortune* article, face time counts. You must put in long hours. Even if you are not being productive, putting in time is still viewed by many bosses as a sign of loyalty.

Marcia Kropf, a vice president at Catalyst, conducted focus groups with up to two hundred people at a dozen major companies. "We'd hear it over and over," she says, "that men who take off in the afternoon from 3 to 4:30 to play squash but stay at their desks until 7 are seen as more committed than women who work nonstop but leave at 5."[7]

Those employees who find themselves abruptly severed from the survivor population as the result of an organizational downsizing, restructuring, or reorganization, find themselves caught in a paradoxical bind with the sudden surplus of "free" time available to them. This "free" time becomes anything but that, and the unemployed worker often unknowingly misuses this once-sought-for commodity.

Because a good number of white-collar and some blue-collar long-term employees are often booted out with generous severance packages, extended health benefits, maturing stock options, unemployment insurance, and supportive outplacement services in hand, the "ex-survivors" experience tremendous difficulty in redefining their sudden gift of free or leisure time. It is no wonder they are frequently envied by those who have been chosen to stay with the organization. The severed ones appear to be the winners, the ones who have been given a second chance to start their lives again, the thrivers of tomorrow. In fairness, this does work out well for some displaced workers. However, for others, all is not what it appears to be.

Many people, when confronted with the shocking reality of having been "outsized" by a corporation, feel an immediate sense of relief and an overwhelming hubris in their personal freedom and liberation. Most workers who have taken a number and stood in line awaiting the downsizing guillotine have already experienced incredible emotional and physical stress and personal hardship during the agonizing waiting period; these terminal events never really come as a complete surprise. Downsizees somehow psychically, intuitively, or blatantly know that they will not be staying—which is not to say that they do not go through a significant trauma once it happens.

For many, this newfound sense of time and its implications for new beginnings and a chance to reclaim egos and self-worth become prized

possessions to which they fiercely cling. The first month or two after experiencing a severance is often a fulfilling time of personal reflection and
growth for the newly unemployed. Since the downsized person now con-
trasts his or her present surplus of time with the previously long, hard, and
grueling hours often expected of employees whose company wields the
reorganization blade precariously over their workers' necks, they are often lulled into the illusion that this overabundance of time is how life
"ought to be."

While most newly unemployed people diligently attend outplacement
sessions, send out resumés, network with industry contacts, and go out on
any interview that could yield a paying job, they start to, almost simultaneously, begin to develop a fear of suddenly losing this free time once
again. The prospect of having to surrender their personal freedom and
quest toward self-fulfillment to another corporate demon creates, for
some, the image of once again being devalued, used, chewed up, and spit out.

The illusive sense of ample free time becomes an unattainable reality; as
one's financial base begins to steadily erode, the interviews become less
frequent and the once-free time transforms into an existential cell.

What about the workers who stay? For the most part, during the period
before the ax falls (or does not fall), they have lived the same uncertain
experiences as everyone else. They have felt the anxiety, the frustration,
and the anger. When they discover that they have been selected to remain
with the organization, the residual effects of all of the previous feelings do
not just disappear. Also, they get to add one more powerful ingredient—guilt.

For most survivors, it is not business as usual. Those who remain with
the corporation find themselves coming in earlier, leaving later, working
weekends, and cutting vacations short to get the work done. Many find
themselves handling two and three additional jobs, not out of any sense
of zealous ambition but out of fear of losing what little they have. Job security has vanished. It becomes quite clear as one survives wave after
wave of downsizings that anyone could be next—and so they wait for
another spin of the wheel.

Schor talks about the increased work load:

The average employed person is now on the job an additional 163 hours or the
equivalent of an extra month a year. . . . The breakdown for men and women
shows lengthening hours for both groups, but there is a gender gap in the size of
the increase. Men are working nearly 100 (98) more hours per year, or $2\frac{1}{2}$ extra
weeks. Women are doing about 300 (305) additional hours, which translates to $7\frac{1}{2}$
weeks, or 38 added days of work each year.[8]

Both survivors and those looking for or having found new employment
cling tenaciously to the importance of personal time. The tangible economic, prestigious, and security rewards once associated with steadfast

commitment and loyalty to an organization are just no longer there. Self-reliance, personal development, and fulfillment become overriding concerns. The organization is viewed as offering, at best, a temporary respite from financial, career, and personal insecurity and, potentially, a launching pad to something better.

As a work force, we are undergoing a transformation. This is coming in the form of awareness. There is growing public awareness of the need for change. Schor reports that, for the first time since such surveys have been systematically conducted, a majority of Americans report that they are willing to relinquish even current income to gain more family and personal time. In a 1989 poll, almost two-thirds said they would prefer to give up some of their salary, by an average amount of 13 percent; fewer than one-fourth were unwilling to give up any money at all. "Although still only a trickle, the stream of 'downshifters'—those who reject high-powered demanding jobs in order to gain more control over their lives—may be the latest trendsetters."[9]

THE ILLUSION AND REALITY OF CHANGE

We do not pretend to be social historians and, therefore, apologize in advance for perhaps overstating the case to make a point. However, it seems that every massive social upheaval, from Christianity to the American Revolution, has had relatively little impact on the way the vast majority of people supposedly impacted by those changes go about their daily existence. Despite all of the media focus on organizational change, if we were to take a snapshot of the attitudes, values, beliefs, and lifestyles of a cross section of today's workers, how are they really being affected?

TODAY'S WORKERS: THE FAMILIES AND WORK INSTITUTE STUDY

Daniel Yankelovich's groundbreaking surveys and studies of the American work force of the 1970s and 1980s prophesied the dramatic shiftings in the nature of work and its significant role as a self-fulfillment focus in the mid to late 1990s. By 1993, the New York City–based Families and Work Institute articulated the dynamic landscape of worker perceptions, values, and meanings as they pertain to our complex relationships with our work. Embracing a holistic viewpoint on the positive and negative effects of late twentieth-century work on both our professional and personal lives, the Institute's findings prove most revelatory to the person seeking to reclaim worker loyalty and commitment in survivor organizations.

The nonprofit research and planning organization conducted a nationwide representative study in 1992 of almost 3,400 workers to capture and articulate how professionals in today's corporations and large organizations feel about our dynamic relationships with our work. To some extent, the level of support for this research is indicative of the importance companies are beginning to place on a clearer understanding of the work force. The participating companies and organizations, who were also responsible for the funding support of the project, included the following:

Allstate Insurance Company	Levi Strauss & Co.
American Express	Merck & Co.
AT&T	Mobil Corporation
Commonwealth Fund	Motorola
Du Pont	The Rockefeller Foundation
General Mills Foundation	Salt River Project
IBM	Xerox
Johnson & Johnson	

Additional support was provided by Philip Morris Inc. and Ceridian Corporation. The information was collected through hour-long telephone interviews with randomly selected participants from those participating organizations. There is a built-in follow-up mechanism in the design of the study which calls for the Families and Work Institute to revisit surviving members of the original sample every two years, along with the flexibility to add new populations of young workers as time progresses.

Although the study is a most comprehensive reporting of a variety of attitudes and behaviors related to and affected by the nature of work in the late 1990s in America, ten dimensions in particular are of significant interest to us as we attempt to define a model for effective survivor management among contemporary organizations. The ten dimensions are as follows:

1. Effects of downsizing and reengineering efforts in worker organizations
2. Perceived demands of present job
3. Attitudes toward job burnout
4. Attitudes toward current job
5. Perceived autonomy on job
6. Control over work schedule
7. Personal definitions of success as related to job
8. Loyalty and desire to help employer succeed
9. Reasons considered "very important" in deciding to take job with current employer
10. Perceived task and work–family supportiveness of supervisors on job

Effects of Downsizing and Reengineering Efforts in Worker Organizations

It is most remarkable that a great majority of survey participants are, by definition, victims of a downsizing or reengineering process initiated within their corporation, or organizational survivors. Forty-two percent of the workers recently experienced a downsizing or permanent cutback of their work force; 28 percent reported cutbacks in the number of managers, 24 percent experienced a change in top organizational leadership, and 18 percent survived a merger or acquisition.

While Yankelovich—in the collecting and interpreting of his research on changing definitions of work, self-fulfillment, and commitment—correctly mirrors the internal psychological shifts we have made concerning what is of value to us, the data gathered for the Families and Work Institute study extend this perception and merge it with external dynamisms in organizational structures and economic occurrences.

Survivors bring a special challenge to the workplace today, since their previous extrinsic definition of job security has all but evaporated from our modern vocabulary. Ten or twenty years ago we could say that we were dealing with a work force that was questioning their importance and contribution within a relatively stable organizational framework; as long as their work contribution was what was at least expected of them, the "security contract" between employer and employee remained.

Today, a survivor's inner focus for development and fulfillment necessarily strengthens and becomes almost all-encompassing as the implicit contract rapidly erodes. Self-reliance and independence become survivors' cornerstones of self-integrity. No longer can the corporation or organization hold up its end of the bargain. The entire foundation for the individual–work relationship as we knew it has ended. A new paradigm begins to form.

Perceived Demands of Present Job

Today's work force reports information reflecting the downsizings, cutbacks, and restructurings of recent years. Eighty percent of the study participants assert, "My job requires working very hard"—28 percent strongly agreeing and 52 percent agreeing with that statement. Sixty-five percent of those surveyed confirm, "My job requires working very fast," with 20 percent of those participants strongly agreeing and 45 percent agreeing with that statement.

These extremely high percentages indicate that many survivors are assuming tasks and responsibilities abandoned by their once-employed colleagues. While increasing work challenge, diligence, and attention to high-performance standards are most important in a competitive economy, one wonders how long the skeleton crew of survivors can withstand the heavy and consistent demands being required of them. While most people are willing to assume extra work and expend increased effort within a limited time period, their willingness and ability to continue that pace indefinitely becomes questionable.

Attitudes toward Job Burnout

When a survivor is subject to constant physical and intellectual demands with little respite, the specter of job burnout becomes an ever-increasing detrimental presence. When asked about their feelings concerning job burnout, those surveyed gave disheartening responses. Within the past three months of being surveyed:

- Seventy-five percent report feeling used up by the end of the work day, with 33 percent of that group agreeing sometimes with the statement, 22 percent agreeing often, and 20 percent agreeing very often.

- Seventy percent feel tired when they get up in the morning and have to face another day on the job, with 30 percent agreeing sometimes, 21 percent agreeing often, and 19 percent agreeing very often with that statement.

- Sixty-one percent feel emotionally drained from their work, with 34 percent of participants agreeing sometimes, 14 agreeing often, and 13 percent agreeing very often with that statement.

- Sixty percent of those surveyed feel frustrated by their job, with 31 percent of them agreeing sometimes, 15 percent agreeing often, and 14 percent agreeing very often.

- Fifty-nine percent report feeling burned out or stressed by their work, with 29 percent agreeing sometimes, 15 percent agreeing often, and 15 percent agreeing most often with that statement.

These findings hold critical implications for the manager and any other concerned party wanting to rebuild employee loyalty. What is interesting about current reengineering efforts being implemented by many downsized or restructured organizations is that individual employees are often given more tasks, increased responsibilities, and (sometimes) greater authority; yet there are limits. The popular notion of empowerment carries with it a touch of enslavement. What choice does the average survivor actually have for saying, "No! Enough!" to his or her employer?

Attitudes toward Current Job

Additional survey information reveals a slightly different perspective on people's relationship with their work and their employer; for, despite the limits on individual capacities to work ourselves to death, we like work. It is important for us as both a fulfiller and a motivator. Sixty-one percent of the survey participants strongly disagree with the statement, "I don't care how well I do my job; I just want to finish it." Fifty-seven percent of those surveyed strongly agree and 42 percent agree with the statement, "I always try to do my job well, no matter what it takes." Fifty-four percent of the participants strongly agree and 43 percent of the participants agree with the statement, "When my job requires it, I work very hard."

The research has uncovered a stone to build with: People's strong need for achievement and self-actualization, and their belief in work as a prime self-identifier, holds many clues for rebuilding commitment within the survivor population.

Perceived Autonomy on Job

Some good news about current workplace practices and procedures shows that, as managers, we are giving survivor employees more room to accomplish their job tasks and responsibilities. Seventy-eight percent of the survey participants assert, "I have a lot of freedom in deciding how I do my work," with 23 percent strongly agreeing and 55 percent agreeing with that statement. Sixty-eight percent of those polled assert, "I have a lot of say about what happens on my job," with 17 percent strongly agreeing and 51 percent agreeing with that statement.

The danger lies in that fine balance of individual autonomy and bottom-line accountability. With increasing autonomy comes the possibility of the widening of Yankelovich's "commitment gap" and the use of discretionary effort in self-management in the workplace. Workers today have even more reason than those surveyed by Yankelovich to mismanage their discretionary effort in performing their jobs, particularly if an undercurrent of bitterness and burnout pervades the work environment. Also, it is necessary to raise the question of whether workers have more freedom by design or because there are fewer managers.

Control over Work Schedule

The majority of survey participants, 57 percent, say that they have considerable control over their work schedule, with 27 percent indicating some, 14 percent indicating a lot, and 16 percent indicating complete control in scheduling work hours. This is a surprisingly high percentage of workers who decide when and how their work gets done. While this is what should be expected of most professionals, given the current business climate, the "commitment gap" has the potential to expand. What is the quality of the work done within those self-imposed time frames? More important, how satisfied are those workers with their produced work? How motivated and committed do they feel toward their organizations?

Personal Definitions of Success as Related to Job

Survey participants give managers obvious, yet often overlooked, strategies for rebuilding a positive, strong survivor work force. The following are stated motivators and accompanying percentages of respondents asked, "What does success mean to you?":

Personal satisfaction from doing a good job	52%
Earning the respect or recognition of supervisors and peers	30%
Getting ahead or advancing in a job or career	22%
Making a good income	21%
Feeling my work is important	12%
Having control over work content and schedule	6%

The results of this survey inevitably hearken back to Frederick Herzberg's Theory of Motivators and Satisfiers, widely publicized in the 1950s as the result of his research with large manufacturing companies.

Despite the enormous changes between the workplace of the 1950s and the high-technology work environment of the 1990s, it is still those motivators which matter most to us as people and workers, those factors such as intrinsic personal satisfaction and gaining the attention of our supervisors and colleagues. While these satisfiers—such as making a good income and having control over work content and schedule—are important, long-term commitment and motivation still emanate from within, from individual internal needs and values; here we have the most potential for success.

Loyalty and Desire to Help Employer Succeed

An overwhelming 93 percent of the survey respondents indicated their feelings of loyalty toward their employer, with 27 percent feeling extremely loyal, 37 percent very loyal, and 29 percent somewhat loyal. The bedrock is certainly in place for positive recommitment in the workplace, even if the actual reasons behind the respondents' seemingly selfless statements on loyalty might be arising more out of fear of unemployment and economic insecurity. When one factors in the possible suspicion that may influence some of the responses to this question, it is striking that 36 percent reported being only somewhat loyal or less. Workers still want to be able to commit and contribute to the success of an organization, even though the employee–employer relationship might be charting some choppy waters at present.

Reasons Considered "Very Important" in Deciding to Take Job with Current Employer

Additional data on very important factors in considering reasons for choosing the current employer confirm the importance of the presence of long-term motivators in the contemporary workplace. The reasons given, and percentages of survey respondents indicating this reason as significant, are as follows:

Reasons	Percentage of Respondents Indicating Reason
Open communications	65%
Effect on personal and family life	60%
Nature of work	59%
Management quality	59%
Supervisor	58%
Gain new skills	55%
Control over work content	55%
Job security	54%
Coworker quality	53%
Stimulating work	50%
Job location	50%
Family-supportive policies	46%
Fringe benefits	43%
Control of work schedule	38%
Advancement opportunity	37%
Salary or wage	35%
Access to decision makers	33%
No other offers	32%
Management opportunity	26%
Size of employer	18%

While a personal favorite is "no other offers" (32%, itself partially reflective of a tight market), we are soon struck by the importance of providing a highly participative working environment where people perform meaningful and interesting work, where they feel they are significantly contributing toward a higher goal, where they can achieve a healthy balance between their work and their personal family life, and where career development and growth are valued and encouraged. As managers, we can cull important, practical strategies for survivor recommitment from these results.

Perceived Task and Work–Family Supportiveness of Supervisors on Job

Perhaps the most significant and revealing data for our purposes of effective survivor management relate to the direct relationships between employees and their supervisors (see Table 2.1).

The implications for almost immediately positive impact and change in the survivor workplace are highly apparent. By focusing in on the quality of day-to-day supervisory practices and activities, we can build and maintain a more committed work force. In fact, most managers today seem to be taking concrete steps in that direction. Certainly the employee–supervisor relationship is a key linchpin in the Survivor Management Model and its implementation in a changing organization.

Briefly, the Families and Work Institute summarizes their study's findings as follows:

The most powerful predictors of work attitudes and behavior are workload, job autonomy, work schedule, control, social relationships at work, workers' percep-

Table 2.1
Relationship with Supervisor

My supervisor:	Total	Strongly Agree	Agree
Keeps me informed	82%	33%	49%
Has realistic expectations	89%	32%	57%
Recognizes when I do a good job	84%	32%	52%
Is supportive when I have a work problem	87%	34%	53%
Values differences in employees' cultures and backgrounds	79%	25%	54%
Is fair	79%	28%	51%
Accommodates me when I have family or personal business	93%	42%	51%
Is understanding when I talk about family or personal matters that affect my work	88%	31%	57%
I feel comfortable bringing up family or personal issues with my supervisor	65%	21%	44%

tions of equal opportunity in the workplace, and supportiveness of their culture. Additionally, this study reveals that workers want to shift their focus to devote more time and attention to their personal and family lives. . . . These findings argue for expanding the issues that are typically considered in workplace improvement effort to include the question of how these initiatives will affect family on personal life. They also argue for broadening the definition of work family efforts from dependent care to including the ways jobs are structured and designed.

Since better work does seem to promote more job satisfaction, more commitment, more loyalty, harder work, and more initiative, as well as a better work—family balance, there is an opportunity to align workers' needs with workplace goals. What helps workers also seems to promote workforce productivity.[10]

Studies such as this one provide a basis for analysis of work force attitudes. What we do not know is how survivors respond to questionnaires. Do they tell the truth, or have they become wary and distrustful of any attempt to examine them for fear it will ultimately be used against them? These are the challenges of leadership. In Chapter 3, we will examine what type of leadership works in the survivor's world.

CHAPTER 3

Reengineering
Corporate Leadership

Gerald Czarnecki, a high-ranking IBM Corporation executive who abruptly resigned Tuesday, quit under pressure because he wasn't making fast enough progress in cutting the workforce and remaking IBM's culture, according to industry executives familiar with IBM.[1]

There is something fascinating about major climatic disasters, like tornados or hurricanes or even bad thunderstorms, not only because of the devastation they tend to leave in their wake—the changes to the landscape, the toll paid in both property and human terms—but also because of the dynamics of the storm. There are times during the storm, sometimes preceding it, sometimes virtually in the middle of it, when there is an eerie quiet, something foreboding or threatening. The storm that is, or was, or will be is not in evidence. "Will it pass us by?" "Will it land on us with full force?" "Will it change everything around us to the extent that we will be affected indirectly?" These questions can only be answered after the storm has passed, and its effects surveyed and analyzed.

In a sense, we are in the middle of a storm. The storm is change; and like other irresistible forces of nature, the results, effects, and damage—the reshaping of the landscape—can only be assessed after the fact. Ten, maybe even five, years from now, we will be looking back and making judgments from the comfortable perspective of history of what has happened, should have happened, should have been done, and so on. The problem is that we live in the present. Our reality is change. Decisions and judgments must be and are being made every moment of every day. Who are the people making these decisions for our companies? Who are the leaders? Do they have a sense of what is happening? Or do they live in the eye of the hurricane, feeling the foreboding, realizing that something probably should be done, bracing themselves and waiting for the storm to pass?

Robert Eccles and Nitin Nohria, in their excellent book, *Beyond the Hype*, Describe the reaction of managers to what they call "a time of rapid and discontinuous change." They make the case that the factors driving the "present frenzied search for better management practices" have always been with us; but the erosion of our competitive advantage over Japan and, to a lesser extent, the European Community, has created a "sense of urgency about the need for good management." They point to the dramatic rise of MBA graduates, executive training programs, training firms, consultants, and business books and ironically suggest that there might be a "causal relationship" between the decline of American business and the proliferation of available advice.[2]

Although intended as a joke, this may not be that far off the mark. One thing is certain, based on demographics alone. The observation can be made that we have an entire generation of management who came into their maturity during "good" times and have little or no experience with adversity. When you compound this with the fact that the most likely people to be fired or packaged out of the organization are the older managers, there are few left to react with at least some of the wisdom gained from past economic downturns and other factors that impact the shape of organizations.

LEADERSHIP FOR TODAY

Leadership has always been an elusive quality to define. There always seems to be a need for a dollop of charisma along with an identifiable point of view. As the needs and temperament of the troops change, so do the subtleties of those who lead them. In the 1980s, we had the image of corporate leaders who were larger than their companies. CEOs like Chrysler's Lee Iacocca, GE's Jack Welch, and American Airlines' Robert Crandall seemingly reshaped their organizations in their own image and single-handedly rescued them from ruin. Whether it was the iron fist or the pitchman's tongue, the balance sheets seemed to respond to their initiatives. In their wake, however, they left pretty much the same company they started with; and none of them nor their employees were spared the ax.

Another problem with any discussion of leadership is that we tend to gravitate to those figures like Iacocca and Welch, who, for one reason or another, have become larger than life and unreliable as role models. Or, worse, we are presented with examples in the media who are, at best, megalomaniacal and, at worst, psychotic abusers of power characterized as leaders because they have made large amounts of money.

If we are to develop an approach to organizations that is at once realistic—responsive to the needs of a changing business climate—and humanistic—a place where people will be willing to provide a regular and continuous quality effort in exchange for some consideration and quality of work life—then we need to look at leadership as a phenomenon that takes place throughout the organization, not just at the top.

Rightly understood, leadership is part of the total pattern of behavior regulation that takes place in organizations. In this context, leadership can be identified as a means for behavior regulation suitable to the overall behavior-regulation patterns of the organization. All organizations regulate both formally and informally, directly and indirectly. Indirect regulation occurs as a result of the culture and the political climate. Direct regulation occurs as a result of directives or, more important to leadership, through exertion of influence.

One way to define *leadership* is as the exercise of interpersonal influence. The useful thing about this construct is that it helps separate traditional management prerogatives ("Do this or I'll fire you") from a pure form of leadership that can exist anywhere in an organization. The employee may have a stronger power base than the supervisor ("The union contract says that I don't have to do that; and if you fire me, we'll walk out"). Many otherwise excellent initiatives have failed in organizations because no effort was made to bring the "opinion leaders" on board.

Another important factor in leadership was pointed out by research done by French and Raven in the late 1950s and holds true today. They showed that power of one person over another was the result of the *perception* of power, not necessarily the reality; that is, John Smith has power if Jack Jones thinks he can provide rewards, punishment, or information, regardless of whether this is true.[3] This focus on perception forces us to define leadership from the perspective of the follower. Why do some people follow others? There are three basic reasons that apply to the business setting: fear, personal profit, and common vision.

Fear

There is an apocryphal story that is attributed variously to Lyndon Johnson or to a high official in the Nixon administration (perhaps Nixon himself) who, when asked about leadership, is purported to have said, "When you have them by the balls, their heads and hearts will follow." In a cover story for *Fortune*, Brian Dumaine profiled some of the "toughest bosses" in American business. *Fortune* selected seven notables including Steven Jobs of NeXT Computer; Linda Wachner of Warnaco; T. J. Rodgers of Cypress Semiconductor; Herbert Haft of the Dart Group; Jack Connors, founder of Hill Holliday; and Bob and Harvey Weinstein of Miramax.

To make the list, candidates had to show a "penchant for psychological oppression—an especially sadistic way of making a point."[4] They maintain unrealistically high and unattainable expectations and are angry with themselves and others for not being able to achieve them.

Why do they survive? "Because they make pots of money." Also, they balance their tyranny by hiring a small group of very talented people and paying them enough to put up with the abuse. As the article goes on to say, this balance of rewards is not passed on to middle-level managers.

Fear, closed communications, and obvious lack of control have infiltrated these lower-leadership ranks and, according to Lee Smith writing in *Fortune*, have led to the creation of a cadre of "Burned-Out Bosses":

Another reason for managerial angst is that midlevel bosses face two incompatible assignments. Be a cold-blooded cost-cutter and be liked. Notes the Menninger Clinic's Dr. Rosen: "He has been told that the new management style of the Nineties is to think of himself and his people as teammates. But in front of his subordinates the manager has to play contradictory roles: He is their friend; he may also be their executioner. The strain of reconciling these personas fans the flames of stress and resentment. In firing longtime employees, managers feel that they have violated a trust.[5]

Fear is a powerful motivator. If your employees fear you, they will follow you. This factor is enhanced by the dynamics of the survivor environment. Employees look around them and see heads being lopped off on a regular and systematic basis. Despite the fact, as we have mentioned earlier, that they might be better off in the long term if they were fired, they prefer the devil they know. They keep themselves in check, stay low, and do nothing they perceive will enhance their candidacy as a downsizing target.

For the survivor employee who is also a manager, the pendulum often swings to the extreme; and the manager finds himself or herself swirling in a frenzied tornado of seemingly unlimited activity. It is no secret to anyone who manages staff within today's corporations and organizations that they are overworked, undercompensated, and often struggling to assume the responsibilities of former colleagues who have been deemed expendable to the organization. While human capital may be superfluous, the work load remains the same and often increases, gaining in sophistication and complexity and leaving today's survivor managers with a perpetual stream of frustration, weariness, and unfinished tasks.

One of the many corporations that has downsized, streamlined, and reengineered its operations and its human resources within the past decade is NYNEX. In a recent *Business Week* article, Nancy P. Karen, NYNEX's Director of the company's Personal Computer Network, describes the quality of her managerial life and points out that "working smarter also means working harder—much harder." She once directly supervised twenty-six people; now it is seventy-nine. She used to work more normal hours as well; now she claims to put in fifty to sixty hours a week, from 8 A.M. to 7 P.M. every weekday. She also carries a beeper and a cellular phone and checks her voice mail every hour. "It's a different mentality," she says.[6]

Having counseled one top manager on the negative effects of layoffs with little or no communication, we felt we were making headway when she took note that a great deal of otherwise productive time was being spent by employees discussing the company and what was going on rather than working on their tasks at hand. She decided to take action. Walking out into the hall, she screamed (so that she could be heard on two floors), "Any of you who have nothing better to do than waste time talking about what's going on here will be the next to go!" She walked back into the office and asked if that covered the communication issue.

The problem with motivating by fear is that it could become divisive. It forces the development of subgroups that over time can gain in strength and split the organization into factions. As factions grow in a company, the focus shifts from external to an increasingly internal preoccupation; and this is bad for business.

Both the survivor employee and survivor manager often develop preoccupations with an internal locus of control, tinged with bitterness and cold reality. Brian O'Reilly, also writing in *Fortune*, observes that companies that make explicit the new rules discover that they can demand a new form of commitment and hard work from employees at the expense of good relations and loyalty. He quotes a young project manager at Prudential in central New Jersey:

We're cold and calculating and looking out for ourselves. If the economy picked up, I'd consider a job elsewhere, much sooner than before. I wouldn't bat an eye. . . . The message we're getting now is that the company doesn't owe you anything. . . . Everyone is shocked. The drones are panicking and looking for somebody to tell them what to do. The better ones are looking for opportunity. . . . The people who will survive have realized we have to look out for ourselves.[7]

Personal Profit

People will follow when they believe that they will profit from following. The key here is that they perceive the ability to achieve desired goals more quickly by following someone else than they could by doing it for themselves. When people follow for personal profit, they are generally more productive and less divisive. Managed effectively, they are more creative and have more initiative.

Leading through greed has its downside. If people are following you primarily because of what they stand to gain, you may find yourself abandoned when your followers discover that (or develop skills to a level where) they can accomplish the same goals for themselves.

This lack of followership is especially acute within the survivor culture of today's organizations. Expanding the definition of personal profit to include not only financial- but career- and prestige-related goals, any survivor employee clever enough to have remained employed within a downsizing organization learns early on that the key to remaining emotionally and psychically intact while all is swirling about is to find either a leader/manager who will provide support, a clear purpose and tasks that are of value to the changing organization, or (hopefully) both in a winning combination.

At this point, managers in downsizing organizations should abandon all illusions they still cling to regarding employee loyalty. This is particularly true if the organization's leaders are providing little or no information about the plans for future layoffs. This is also the case if people are being let go incrementally, in sudden spurts of corporate axing followed by periods of seeming calm, leaving each survivor employee wondering if he or she will be the next to go.

Given these circumstances, the employee is on the corporate battleground for one reason only—personal profit. The survivor has quickly and rudely adapted to the harsh inequities of downsizing. The rules of the game have changed. We are no longer working for the corporation. We are working for ourselves. Brian O'Reilly points to certain companies that are forging a new contract with employees. Sometimes it works for a while. Stripped of the camouflage, it goes something like this:

There will never be job security. You will be employed by us as long as you add value to the organization, and you are continuously responsible for finding ways to add value. In return, you have the right to demand interesting and important work, the freedom and resources to perform it well, pay that reflects your contribution, and the experience and training needed to be employable here and elsewhere.[8]

Common Vision

The most enduring form of leadership derives from a perception of common beliefs and shared values. Common-vision leaders identify and articulate a common or shared vision in what the organization could be. They strengthen followers' beliefs that this vision can be achieved through their individual and collective efforts. They mobilize the energy and resources of others through appeals to their hopes, values, dreams, and aspirations. They are able to capitalize on the strength derived from a feeling of "groupness."

The common-vision leader appeals to the emotions as well as the intellect. He or she articulates the exciting possibilities that are inherent in an idea or a project. The focus is on a better future with which all can identify. On the world stage, this form of leadership was seen with Churchill, Kennedy, and Gandhi. It was also seen with Hitler, Mussolini, and Napoleon.

Fear and personal interest are still very much on the scene as leadership styles and scenarios. If we are going to reengineer leadership to work within the parameters set by the demands of competition and the displacement of change, however, we need to examine the atmosphere in which such leadership must survive.

The fact is, despite much evidence of their continuing existence, there has been somewhat of a decline in authoritarian styles of management. This is, in part, because of the less hierarchical organizations resulting from the wholesale downsizing of middle management. In order to get work done, companies have increasingly turned to "matrix" approaches and the use of project teams. In order to get their jobs done, project and team leaders need the cooperation of those in functions over which they have no direct authority.

The New Leader

Leadership for today's companies cannot depend on relationships built on coercion, dependence, and obligation. The new leader believes in being supportive. He or she is willing to share power if it means getting the job done to everyone's satisfaction. The new leader derives power and influence from being trusted and by being able to develop collaborative behaviors in diverse groups.

How are these results achieved? They are achieved in the following ways: by being open and direct, as well as candid without malice; by establishing standards and ground rules for everyone, including themselves, to follow; by being "consultative" in their working relationships—asking for and understanding everyone's wants and needs, and contracting with everyone to deliver them; by being open to ideas and innovation, demonstrated by a willingness to try alternative actions to their own; by being consistent whenever possible in the changing environment and openly discussing inconsistencies and the reasons for them; and by being accessible and actively listening to others, demonstrated by paraphrasing, sympathizing, and empathizing with team members and subordinates as each situation dictates.

The most effective models for leadership currently exist in the "informal" networks within an organization. Every company has one or several people who, despite their lack of direct authority, manage to get things done. They are using their access, experience, knowledge of the company (and the people), and their ability to put individuals together in productive relationships.

The new leader for dynamic, turbulent organizations must possess the flexibility and tenacity to guide and manage an anxiety-ridden work force through the choppy waves of change. He or she must have the ability to provide employees with a focus, a direction which will revitalize the department; directly contribute to the success of the organization; and, most important, empower individuals to take charge, initiate change, and create a new organization that will have ownership from top to bottom on the organizational chart. While older models of leadership theory, such as Blake and Mouton's Managerial Grid and Hersey and Blanchard's Situational Leadership paradigm, provided a two-dimensional perspective on leadership—where the style of leadership could be altered depending on whether the focus was on the people, the tasks, or varying combinations of both—today's leaders benefit more from a version of the transformational approach, articulated by Noel Tichy, which assumes a larger, more integrative, and holistic organizational dynamic.

The transformational leader is highly sensitive to internal and external forces of change affecting the organization and uses his or her ability to orchestrate positive change through changing the behavior and attitude of employees. What distinguishes the transformational leader from his or her colleagues is, first, the leader is able to formulate and articulate a vision of the future organization. Second, by being able to share that vision with his or her employees and facilitating their ability to translate that vision into achievable tasks, goals, and objectives, the leader reenergizes the group. Third, by valuing individual differences and understanding the need to sensitively guide employees through the change process, the transformational leader rebuilds trust, encourages teamwork, and values continuous feedback and communication as cornerstones for future success. Although unable to offer unlimited job security, the transformational leader becomes a catalyst for facilitating individual self-esteem and internal motivation.

The employee working with the transformational leader begins to develop an inner career security, a lessening of limiting dependence on the paternal organization, and increasing job satisfaction and productivity. The leader who assumes a transformational approach understands that change is now a constant within today's corporations; standing still, or what we used to call stability, is to be avoided at all costs. As Pepsico's CEO Wayne Calloway points out:

A static company has no opportunity for gifted managers to build anything; they either leave or end up focused inward, struggling among themselves for a bigger piece of the same-size pie, instead of looking out toward the competitive horizon. Or, just as destructive, they focus on the trivial and bureaucratic, turning an organization into an impotent mandarin court, where no promising young person would want to work, and the future is lost.[9]

Leadership and the Mystique of Teams

In a recent article, Louis S. Richman says that what will replace the old idea of what will help you get ahead is "knowing how to thrive on ambiguity in an environment of perpetual change—the very talents that moving up the ladder discouraged."[10] He goes on to say that employers are replacing management layers with "fast-moving teams."[11] But how about at the top? Peter Senge writes in his book, *The Fifth Discipline*, that the concept of a "management team" is a myth. Management teams are supposed to be a collection of knowledgeable veterans representing various functions within the organization who, collectively, are supposed to solve problems and issues facing the organization. More often they spend their energies "fighting for turf, avoiding anything that will make them look bad personally, and pretending that everyone is behind the team's collective strategy."[12]

One of the key challenges in the survivor environment is to work through the competitive dynamics created by the struggle for diminishing resources. To a large extent, the development and utilization of teams can work in the company's favor. If teams are going to be effective, though, they must follow certain caveats.

Teams Must Be Led

At first glance, it may seem obvious that teams are not a substitute for management and that they do not function without leadership and direction. Yet organizations all over the country, anxious to get on the bandwagon with the "latest" strategic initiative, are busily aligning people on paper, spending millions on off-site meetings, subjecting employees to team-building sessions where they must engage in activities ranging from walking around blindfolded to repelling steep cliffs in the hope that back at the office these workers will just dig in and solve all of the company's problems while leaving their managers alone—except for taking the credit.

The fact is that no team functions well without a leader. It is the nature of teams both to thrive on and engender leadership. Too often, when leadership begins to emerge in a designated team, it is viewed as empire building—a reactionary act by a player who has not "bought in" to the new way of doing business. Rather than subversive, the attempt to establish some structure and control is probably the result of frustration, confusion, and the inability to get anything done.

As critical as the notion of teamwork and its publicly hailed place within the corporate culture of many organizations might be, it is no replacement for creative and focused leadership, particularly when stakeholders zero in on the balance sheet. In a revealing article ostensibly about "America's

Smart Young Entrepreneurs" but, in actuality, about the behaviors and passions associated with successful leadership in the 1990s, *Fortune* magazine encapsulates the importance of risk-taking leadership styles over democracy-bound teamwork:

What's the most important lesson these young entrepreneurs have to teach? Just this: To make it big in a hurry, you have to be different, to push forth with a radical vision that everybody knows won't work. Says Trip Hawkins [CEO of 3DO and Electronic Arts]: "The most brilliant ideas are not going to be understood by most people, are they? If you wait around to make decisions by democracy, you end up with a boring company and, eventually, it's going to kill you." That's one idea you can't afford not to understand.[13]

The manager must take an active role in team leadership. Somebody must be the quarterback, call the plays, set the objectives, establish standards. In short, the manager who uses teams needs to militate against the natural tendency to use compromise as a form of conflict resolution and create the parameters within which the team will function.

This may require being directive. While this notion may be considered heresy by some, others believe you must be tough with your teams. Survivors need direction. Many would be just as happy to have someone simply tell them what to do, by when, and according to which standard. They long for some objective evidence of their worth, some specific job-related tasks that reveal a direction, a strategy, a vision as to where the organization is going. They want to know what the future is and, more important, their part in that future.

We are reminded of a popular group exercise that continues to appear in classrooms and training rooms everywhere. It goes under various names; but, with some variations, the object of the exercise is the same. It seems that a passenger ship has had an unfortunate accident and sunk, leaving fifteen people adrift in a lifeboat. The premise is that there is only enough food and water for eight, so some criteria need to be established for tossing nearly half the group overboard as rations get scarce. Lacking a clear leader, the group sets about evaluating the survivors based on characteristics provided on the instruction sheet—short biographies that are designed to ignite a variety of biases and prejudices. The exercise rarely fails to instigate a lively discussion as the pros and cons of each person are hashed over.

There is no doubt that this is a good way to learn something about group process in a laboratory setting. We wonder how it would go if each person were assigned to actually be one of the survivors or, better still, if it was in fact a real disaster. The problem with teams operating in a vacuum is that they focus on themselves. No matter how thoughtful and justified based on some set of measures, they will inevitably set about cannibalizing each other. There is no one there to say, "Why don't we just put some oars in the water and go north."

So it is with our organizational survivors. Cast adrift on an open and changing sea, they need admirals, not facilitators.

Make Sure It's a Team You Need

While many managers with ambitions for leading the corporate warriors through reengineering and downsizing transformations will enthusiastically herald teamwork as the catalyst for effecting change, they are erroneously perpetuating the belief that a team is the most effective mechanism for producing results. In their excellent article for *Harvard Business Review,* "The Discipline of Teams," Jon R. Katzenbach and Douglas K. Smith differentiate between the form and function of a team and a working group. Teams become critical when an organization must assemble a group of complementary-skilled individuals who will collectively share similar performance goals, purpose, and commitment. The result of the team's output will be what Katzenbach and Smith term "collective work-products." Teams function within a reality of shared leadership and strive for a tight synergy, which can lead to exemplary organizational results.

A high-performance organization also must nurture and recognize the importance of the working group, a more prevalent formation of employees who gather together to share skills and expertise but whose output is produced under the guidance of a strong and purposeful leader. Working groups are committed to the goals and strategies of the overall organization, and their end results are individual rather than collective work products. Performance accountability remains with the individual, whereas teams emphasize both individual and mutual accountability. With responsible and sensitive leadership at the helm of the survivor organization, one which is still undergoing the change process, the promotion of effective working groups can optimize maximum productivity and direction. As Katzenbach and Smith affirm:

Most of the time . . . if performance aspirations can be met through individuals doing their respective jobs well, the working-group approach is more comfortable, less risky, and less disruptive than trying for more elusive team performance levels. Indeed, if there is no performance need for the team approach, efforts spent to improve the effectiveness of the working group make much more sense than floundering around trying to become a team.[14]

The Life of a Team Is as Long as Its Key Objective

Not too long ago, we consulted with a major technology company in Canada. Their problem was that they needed to develop a new software package within a very short time frame. At the inception of the project, there was one thing that all of the groups agreed on—it could not be done. The teams and subteams were built, and the project was completed on time. It was an unqualified success. The people involved were excited, motivated, and learning a new set of skills. When the project was complete, several of the team members were either transferred or fired. The survivors were particularly bitter, since they had committed themselves and succeeded—fertile ground for cynicism.

The main problem was not that the team was disbanded and some jobs were lost but that team members were allowed to believe that the team would last forever. All teams are temporary and should be styled as such. No guarantees beyond the immediate objective should be promised or implied.

The basic tenet of group dynamics is that several people (up to a point), working together, can accomplish more of certain things than individuals working alone. However, these groups do not necessarily constitute "teams."

If you and your organization have bought into the notion that hierarchies are bad and teams are good—and if, as is happening in so many companies, the process does not work—do not be surprised. In many ways, ramming team concepts down the throats of employees is just another way for managers who do not know what they are doing to avoid the consequences of responsibility.

In a recent article in *Training Magazine,* Jack Gordon makes a crucial point about why teams fail. He points to a paradox in the advice being given to organizations: "Even as the business advice industry speaks of the diminishing need for managers, it insists as never before on the crucial importance and burgeoning skill needs of managers." He goes on to say that while they are not called managers (instead, leaders or coaches), they require abilities bordering on the supernatural in order to be effective:

supporting, guiding, counseling, developing, foreseeing problems and changes before they occur, knowing precisely when to speak and when to remain silent, when to ask and when to tell—all to create and maintain the precarious group dynamic, fragile as a rose petal, that allows the team to function on the knife-edge of effectiveness.[15]

Survival Leadership Strategies

Today's survivor corporations and organizations engulfed in the turbulent waters of change hold the seeds of tomorrow's vital and profitable companies. Without clearly defined and innovative leadership, however, the foundations for future growth and success remain precarious. Nowadays, managers cannot afford solely to assume the traditional role of planning, organizing, delegating, and controlling. While these functions comprised the hub that kept the corporate wheels turning, in today's dynamic organizations, the rational approach is just not enough. Successful managers in survivor organizations are also effective and creative leaders. Their perspective is simultaneously present and future oriented; they know that motivating an anxiety-ridden work force is key and that reengineering organizational processes, products, and profits is foremost. At the same time, a third eye must remain firmly focused on the future position and viability of their corporations within the expanding global marketplace. Leader/managers must also pay close attention to the training and nurturing of tomorrow's corporate leaders. Both for themselves and their protégés, certain personal attributes and organizational focuses are necessary.

Probably the most important characteristic encompasses a leader's ability to remain flexible and positive to the potential of change. He or she needs to be a catalyst for the organizational change process, and that requires a whole-hearted belief in its essential value. A broad-based source of diverse skills, experience, and expertise gives today's leader the credibility needed to mobilize change efforts within the organization. He or she must thrive on uncertainty; be adept at problem solving, decision making, and analyzing; and maintain an optimism in the face of frequent adversity. One of the most frequently cited and sought-for attributes for present and future leader/managers is vision—the talent for creating a present and future perspective on what the organization can and should be. This vision should relate to all aspects of organizational life and ignite the motivational fires within the organization's work force.

For a leader to stand up for something he or she believes in requires courage and commitment. Today's organizational leaders will often find themselves at odds with the mainstream. While this probably always was the case, it is worth reasserting that today's leaders are required to take a large measure of interpersonal and professional risk. In order to take these risks, the leader must begin with a clear idea of what is important to him or her personally.

These questions must be asked frequently during the course of any action designed to effect meaningful change:

- Why am I doing this, and what am I getting out of it?
- How will I know when I have achieved my goals?
- In the context of what I am trying to do, what are the critical few components that are worth taking the greatest risks for?
- What, if anything, in my vision or the actions that I plan to take is not negotiable or subject to compromise?

Using these factors to create a direction, today's manager must develop a leadership philosophy that can be articulated and shared with others. All workers, and especially survivors, expected as they are to make major changes in the way they relate to the organization, require a clear under-standing of the forces that are driving leadership decisions. A good way to begin formulating your philosophy is to ask this simple question: When I leave this organization, what are the things that I would want to be re-membered for?

The manager's philosophy will determine the values he or she finds most important or compelling. Adhering to those values is the quality that creates both the potential for interpersonal risk and the potential for suc-cessful leadership. A manager who succeeds as a leader is one who mea-sures each decision against his or her values and looks for situations that provide opportunities to take a stand to support these values.

Leading in this manner requires courage. It also generally negates the possibility of being an ongoing winner of the "popularity contest." Almost any action a manager takes in the survivor environment is going to create resistance and negativity from a variety of quarters. However, survivors are looking for leaders who will support them when they are put in the position of making tough choices. They want leadership that attacks the major issues directly rather than ignoring or hiding from them or hoping each issue will resolve itself. Perhaps the worst behavior a manager can exhibit in the current climate is being tentative. However, along with not being tentative comes the necessity of having the appropriate background and support materials that provide the rationale for your decisions.

Many managers fail as leaders because they have not adequately dealt with their own reluctance to change. Leaders recognize the inevitability of change, even when the necessity of change runs against their grain.

An often-heard complaint in corporate corridors is that certain indi-viduals who have made mistakes in judgment or have implemented deci-sions that have been unsuccessful seem to be retained and valued even more highly by the organization. While this is not always the case, most organizations today have learned to value their risk takers. An individual who is willing to take an action and accept the consequences demonstrates the kind of leadership quality necessary to survive in the future.

Organizations that have management made up primarily of yes-people will ultimately fail the competitive challenge. In the face of a difficult de-cision, today's manager must face the fact that the outcome could cost him or her the job. This is what we call "looking over the edge." Managers who either will not or cannot look over the edge and accept the worst-case sce-nario will not develop into substantial leaders.

Clearly, a manager cannot go to the wall for every issue on the agenda. However, identifying the critical few issues is relatively simple when the following points are considered:

- Does the issue run against my philosophy or values as a manager?
- How does this issue impact the group?

- Does the issue impact on the group's ability to complete objectives necessary to meet organizational goals?
- Will the issue have negative impact on either external or internal customers?

Certainly, the ultimate decision about which issues are critical lies with the manager. However, gathering input from a variety of sources can enable the manager to make more informed decisions about which issues need to be addressed. Keeping an open line to direct reports, networking with peers, and surveying internal and external customers all provide valuable information for leadership focus. In addition, a simple force-field analysis should be conducted to determine the major factors both driving and inhibiting your group's performance.

Another determinant involves future thinking. More than ever before, successful managers need to anticipate how current issues will impact on future performance and what future issues may grow out of current actions.

Managers will not find their survivors eager to make difficult decisions. However, a successful leader/manager will resist the temptation to take responsibility for all of the decisions. Rather, he or she will provide the necessary resources and expertise to enable workers to make their own decisions. Survivors also require a large measure of commitment and, at least initially, some guarantee that taking certain types of responsibility will not hasten them to their demise.

This combination of providing expertise, resource, and commitment helps to develop lower-level employees and focuses their attention on the potential role they may be able to play in the future. Even when workers make poor decisions, they need to be rewarded for their initiative.

The process of reengineering, downsizing, and restructuring has left the ranks of middle management fairly thin. The leader/manager must be able to manage a large group of direct reports, often reflecting people of diverse backgrounds, skill levels, and degrees of motivation. He or she should enjoy being a juggler of many projects and learn to live with the certainty that a good number of them will be as abruptly abandoned as they were initially embraced.

Openness to communicating frequently with staff and the skill to marshall them as a team or work group, as required, are also most important. Successful leader/managers understand that one no longer manages people and leads organizations in a vacuum. Proactive partnerships with customers; competitors; and a myriad of business, industry, and governmental organizations are necessary for future professional and organizational growth.

Leading toward Independence

Perhaps one of the most obvious differences between contemporary and traditional leaders is the compact between employer and employee in the current work environment. No longer is lifetime employment or even job security a given factor for any employee in any organization. While intellectually understanding the economic, social, and technological reasons for this shift, many employees harbor longings for "the way it used to be" and carry a great deal of anger and resentment into the workplace. This can present a tremendous challenge to the leader/manager who is often himself or herself undergoing a similar emotional tug-of-war. To motivate both oneself and one's employees, both parties must work toward gaining control over their careers. All of us, employers and employees alike, must be involved in a lifelong learning journey to upgrade and expand constantly upon present skills, abilities and knowledge. In their article, "Toward a Career-Resilient Workforce" for a recent *Harvard Business Review*, Robert H. Waterman, Jr., Judith A. Waterman, and Betsy A. Collard describe the new work force contract. They affirm that it involves entering into a "new covenant" under which the employer and employee share responsibility for the individual's development and employability inside and outside the company. This opportunity to develop is provided by employers in exchange for better productivity and some degree of commitment to company purpose and community for as long as the employee works there. While the employee is responsibile for managing his or her own career, it is the company's responsibility to provide the tools, the environment, and the opportunities for assessing and developing their skills.

And it is the responsibility of managers at all levels to show that they care about their employees whether or not they stay with the company. The result is a group of self-reliant workers—or a career-resilient workforce—and a company that can thrive in an era in which the skills needed to remain competitive are changing at a dizzying pace.[16]

While career independence and constant learning will contribute to an employee's ability to remain employed within a variety of organizations within his or her lifetime, the other side of the compact requires that focused and caring leadership be pervasive in thriving organizations. Let us hope that the reign of corporate bloodletting will be put to rest so that a more integrative and mature employer–employee relationship model will serve as a paradigm for the emergence of responsible leadership and organizational growth.

CHAPTER 4

Organizational Structure
and Change

One might ask, "What comes first—the structure of the organization or the management philosophy?" One major factor that enhances our ability to study organizational structure is that, unlike so many other things that are historically bound, there are excellent examples of a variety of structures in existence simultaneously today. There are classical examples fostered by the assembly line and perpetuated in the sewing rooms located on second floors throughout urban New York, Puerto Rico, and the Caribbean; and there are still assembly lines. There are organizations where the employees exist in virtual space, interacting electronically without any face-to-face personal contact. The one thing they all have in common is that they are peopled by survivors.

All organizations are displayed on a spectrum from highly structured and autocratic, on one end, and loosely or randomly structured and egalitarian, on the other end. One could begin developing a perspective by reviewing philosophical positions put forth in antiquity by Aristotle and Plato. Aristotle believed that the many were better governed by an aristocratic few. Plato, in his writing, showed a concern for people as individuals and believed in equality of opportunity.

In a sense, these seemingly bipolar points of view represent the anchors of a continuum that organizations display themselves across, with most clustering in the middle. It seems axiomatic that as soon as a company has initiated a plan to decentralize (or centralize), plans are already being shaped to do just the opposite.

The current notion of decentralizing authority with its attendant lexicon—matrix management, empowerment, and so on—was written about extensively in the 1920s. Mary Parker Follett writes about the need for "cross-functioning" and the replacement of "vertical authority" in order to improve communication in organizations.[1] There is nothing new about the way organizations configure their internal and external relationships. Technology has enabled enhancements both to the ability to decentralize and tighten centralized controls. There is no real difference in the way companies do business and compete with each other either. As Eccles and Nohria put it,

> The decentralization of authority is only one example of a "new" management theme that turns out to have been quite common throughout this century. Others include producing quality products, providing responsive customer service, formulating strategy in a way that takes into account distinctive internal capabilities, rewarding performance fairly, and running a socially responsible enterprise. Who could argue with such advice? When did managers think—let alone say— they were doing otherwise?[2]

They go on to point out that the shift in emphasis is a matter of rhetoric rather than substance. Today's survivors are particularly cynical about shifts in emphasis. When surveyed, they provide comments such as those that follow. On the paradox created by double messages,

> The financial reports for the company indicate a company that is doing well under the circumstances of the economy; however, employees are continually told that raises will be lower and personnel requisitions are on hold because of bad times. In the meantime, large sums of money are being spent on reengineering meetings in expensive locations. Are times really bad, or is the state of the economy a very convenient excuse?

On communication in general,

> Tell us honestly and directly what is going on—the good, the bad, and the ugly. Look at us as adults—talented, interested, informed adults—and don't patronize. Don't couch things in ineffective verbiage—don't cover up. Don't make long-winded speeches; cut to the bottom line. The point is, don't hesitate and don't equivocate. We like our management straight!

On focus and direction,

> Is there a company business and organization plan? If so, it has not been communicated. It seems, over the past five years, senior management keeps experimenting with the organizational structure to find out if it works. There isn't any sound organization plan as to where we are going.

It is interesting to note that the issue that continually comes up is communication. We will return to this theme throughout the book. For now, let us look at the organizational continuum or, to put it another way, the options that have always been—and continue to be—available to managers as they shape the relationships between themselves and the people they need to produce the goods and services that spell success for the organization.

Theories of organization derive from the necessity of finding ways to coordinate technology, people, material resources, and the environment to compete effectively in the marketplace. We would like to reiterate that, in our view, there is no "best" theoretical approach to management practice. When something works well, it is because of a blending of the organization, the circumstances, the products, the personnel, the marketplace, and the personality characteristics of the individual manager. The review of organizational theories that follows begins with "Bureaucracy" and ends with "Unit Interdependence." These theories are presented in chronological order based on the primary theorist(s) who identified and defined them and the period of their research. Organizational theory concerns itself with three basic issues:

1. Structure—levels of authority, task allocation, interdependence
2. Management—work processes, decision making
3. Behavior—human needs, participation patterns, culture

PRIMARY THEORISTS

Max Weber—Early 1900s

Max Weber was a German sociologist who concerned himself with the study of the division of labor. His name is usually associated with the term *bureaucracy*. He believed in a hierarchy or stair-step distribution of power. He felt that to be successful all organizations needed standardized approaches for processes and procedures. Each area of the organization should have a specialization that contributes to the overall goals and objectives of the total organization. Level of authority is determined by technical competence. Communication takes place along strictly defined avenues that reflect the hierarchy. Every employee should have a clear definition of tasks and responsibilities. Individuals' concerns are of secondary importance to the concerns of the organization.

Today, the term *bureaucracy* is considered pejorative; but one does not have to look very far to find examples of this approach in full force. The most compelling example is government. At its best, the approach is very effective. It assumes a multileveled structure, peopled by experts who know their place in the hierarchy and abide by the rules. Most of us never experience bureaucracy at its best—only at its worst.

Frederick Taylor—Early 1900s

As might be expected, the aggressive capitalism of this era spawned more than one theory. Frederick Taylor has become associated with the "Scientific School" of organizational theory. He is also the father of time and motion studies. Simply put, Taylor sought ways of accomplishing the greatest amount of work in the least amount of time. In this approach, people are viewed purely as economic units. Taylor's objective was to discover, by detailed analysis, ways of cutting costs per unit and thereby increasing productivity.

Taylor demonstrated exceptional benefits from his approach. In his book, he discusses a study done for the Bethlehem Steel Company. It seems the standard practice was for coal shovelers to bring their own shovels to work. These varied in size and were used for all shoveling regardless of the job. A group of shovelers was selected; and various sizes of shovels were tried, along with methods of shoveling. Taylor discovered that the most efficient weight of a shovelful of coal was twenty-one pounds. Each worker was given a standard shovel with a 21-pound capacity and was provided with some training on the best way to shovel. The results were that the average amount of coal shoveled per day increased from fifteen to fifty-nine tons. Costs dropped from 7.3 cents per ton to 3.2 cents per ton. Also, a common result associated with the scientific approach, Bethlehem Steel was able to lay off more than 250 workers.[3]

Taylor believed in testing workers to determine their suitability for the job. He promoted objective measurement of organizational achievement, a notion very much in line with today's emphasis on quality assurance. In his view, there was a definite line between managers and workers: Managers planned; workers worked. Because he saw workers as purely economic units, he felt that they were motivated by financial incentives alone and did not need a great deal of humanistic involvement.

The durability of Taylor's ideas is extraordinary. While some of his contemporaries, like Henri Fayol, enhanced his views by generalizing them to a common set of principles (plan, organize, command, coordinate, control), we see Taylor's basic precepts coming through in the most contemporary attempts to manage labor efficiently. An example is the concept of "de-skilling" being employed in the fast food industry and elsewhere. Place an order at McDonald's and the cashier will push a button on the cash register that has a picture of what you requested, thus eliminating the time-consuming and error-prone activity of adding and subtracting.

Elton Mayo—1920s

The human relations approach to managing people and structuring organizations traces its behavioral roots to Elton Mayo's infamous lighting experimentation at the Hawthorne Western Electric plant in the 1920s. Mayo and his associates at the Harvard Business School set out to understand the relationship between working conditions and worker output. Some of their assumptions included that as working conditions improve, so should the productivity of those affected by them. Curiously, a divergent effect occurred, most notably in the lighting of the plant. Mayo and his group brightened the lighting. Not surprising, worker output increased. They then continued to raise the lighting, incrementally, to its highest voltage. Again, positive productivity resulted. Then, the lighting began to be incrementally dimmed; worker output remained high. As the lighting was reduced to near-zero visibility, still the productivity increased. Mayo concluded that the external lighting conditions actually had little effect on the number and quality of outputs produced by each worker. What employees were responding to positively was the incredible amount of attention given to them and their working environment. Yes, they were human guinea pigs; but this was probably one of the most exciting and prestigious events to have occurred within their working lives. It was not every day that a cadre of Harvard Business School professors microscopically examined you and your work output.

Mayo's findings and the subsequent development of the human relations approach to organization were to have profound effects on the twentieth-century workplace. Mayo reminds us of the following:

1. Employees need and appreciate attention from management.
2. Motivation can be created through a sense of community and teamwork.
3. Channels of communication between employees and management should be two-way and enable a working dialogue; employees should be able to participate in the shaping of their goals and outputs and management would do best to listen to them.
4. Ultimately, the best organizations are those who are people driven; who put the needs and the skills of their employees foremost; and who believe that maximum motivation, cooperation, and productivity will result from a humanistic climate of organizational life.

Organizations and survivors within those organizations today inherently know that a human relations approach is a sound foundation for rebuilding productivity and growth, yet we are remarkably unsuccessful in applying these principles to achieve the strategic objectives of corporations. Take, for example, IBM Corporation, probably the best-known example of a company that took care of its employees. Fledgling managers fresh out of business school signed on for life. Benefits were generous; education and training resources plentiful. The working environment was more than comfortable. Systems and opportunities for two-way communication between employees and managers were well designed and frequent.

Then it all came crashing down. It was not enough. Through a classic case of hubris, Big Blue failed to foresee imminent technological changes and gave the bank away to their global competitors; and yet, to the end, many employees downsized by the corporation which had once promised life-long employment were humanely treated, through generous severance packages, outplacement services, and retraining assistance.

We know now that successful organizations need both humanistic management and a strong and dynamic strategic business plan to survive into the twenty-first century. Yet, we naively try to motivate both survivors and new employees (who were abruptly thrown out of previously "caring" organizations) with proclamations of teamwork, family friendliness, and diversity for all. It is no wonder that they do not trust us as far as they can throw us. While employees are willing to work hard to be personally and organizationally successful, they know that giving up their loyalty and commitment to a paternalistic organization will never happen again. Increasingly, employees have learned to take care of themselves and, through much pain and searching, have developed what it takes to be survivors.

Chester Barnard—1930s

With the publication of Barnard's *The Functions of the Executive* in 1938, a shift in perspective was broadened and the world of work was viewed through a systematic and integrative lens. According to Barnard, organizations run at their optimal levels when the importance of executive functions is stressed. These include the formalized coordination and communication systems which enable work to take place and reach completion.

Barnard makes a distinction between the executive and nonexecutive functions of an organization, with the nonexecutive functions concerned with the effective management of people and the executive functions with the smooth coordination of systems, work output, and formal communication relationships. For Barnard, the executive functions should include a critical emphasis on the recruitment, selection, and retention of personnel within an organization. Not only do organizations need to attract talented and experienced people with diverse and complementary abilities (Barnard warns against the dangers of "inbreeding" when an organization hires personnel of similar backgrounds and mind-sets; this can lead to groupthink mentality), but they also need to pay close attention to the quality and quantity of the work output they expect of well-hired personnel. For Barnard, there must be a "goodness of fit" between the hired individual and the host organization. If an organization can achieve this compatibility, then the employee can accomplish maximum role performance, which can lead to employee satisfaction, commitment, and employer loyalty.

An additional key aspect of the distinction between executive and nonexecutive functions is that the executive function is concerned with strategic, long-range formulation of organizational purpose and goals. For Barnard, managers then take those goals and translate them into specific objectives and their corresponding work processes.

Today's survivor organizations would do well to listen to the importance of the executive functions, which are often overlooked in the name of reorganization and change efforts. While a long-term strategic plan is critical to the eventual rebirth of a restructured and downsized organization, many downsizings have been spurred by attention to short-term results to the profitability of a company. Although most downsized organizations have shown significant initial improvement, the long-term view shows that the upheaval of human capital and the subsequent organizational climate of demotivated, angry, and fearful survivors puts the reorganization in a doubtful light.

A focus on how to both recommit organizational survivors and commit new employees to strategic and intelligent long-range goals and objectives should be critical to the changed organization. As Barnard emphasizes, we must take care in the recruitment of new hires to the organization and make sure that a complementary fit is achieved both with existing employees and with the entire organization.

Last, the value of establishing a system of formal and informal communication mechanisms to ensure the successful completion of organizational purposes and goals cannot be overemphasized. Too frequently, survivors become most concerned with generating activity—work activity—without much direction or sense of long-range purpose, most of it a smoke screen for warding off the downsizing demon. If we can begin to build formal and informal communication systems that encourage the reciprocal dialogue so necessary to the reemergence of successful organizations, survivor satisfaction and organizational effectiveness will greatly improve.

Herbert Simon—1940s

The organizational theory of bounded rationality is attributed to Herbert Simon, as well as to James March and Richard Cyert, who, at different times, were instructors for the Carnegie Institute of Technology. Also known as the Carnegie School approach, bounded rationality starts with the assumption that human beings are imperfect in their ability to solve problems and make decisions. Simon believed that this was because of our limitations of knowledge and information-processing abilities. Although contrary to contemporary findings on the capabilities of human intelligence, Simon argued that we can only process information serially and not simultaneously and often make incomplete and imperfect decisions based upon our limited rationality. Simon recommended that, for effective functioning of an organization, upper-echelon personnel, since they are more able to skillfully use a variety of communication and problem-solving skills, should focus on broad-based, nonprogrammed decision-making techniques and opportunities for interaction with each other. Middle- to lower-echelon personnel should deal primarily with programmed (i.e., specific) decision-making skills relative to their job functions and work processes. Upper-echelon executives should pay close attention to their use and frequency of downward communications.

This elitist perspective has been widely perpetuated throughout many organizations, and it has contributed both to the breakdown of open communications and the lack of employee participation and commitment to the strategic goals of the companies. While many downsizings were speedily implemented because the key decisions were made by a very privileged few, these same survivor organizations cannot regain their market competitiveness and employee commitment without a radical redesign of the use and dissemination of critical information throughout the organizations. All levels of employees need to become accessed to and empowered with both information necessary for innovation and the problem-solving and decision-making techniques which, in a participation-focused environment, will enable those breakthroughs necessary for organizational survival.

Eric Trist and K. W. Bamforth—1950s

Trist and Bamforth's sociotechnical systems approach to organizational theory has as its groundings their research on the British coal-mining industry. With the advance of new technology, workers were forced to give up their previous team-centered way of completing tasks so that each might become a specialist in only one particular task. This predictably led to a remarkable drop in productivity, motivation, and morale. Conflicts increased; employee satisfaction markedly decreased.

Trist and Bamforth pioneered the sociotechnical approach to work by attempting to integrate the social and psychological needs of the workers with the technical demands of a new era. An integration of man, machine, and environment was achieved when each worker became fully trained in all components of the new technical equipment. The new technology was now viewed as another job aid to get work completed more quickly and effectively and not as a threat to individual capabilities. Workers could now rotate their tasks, since all were trained in the various aspects of the technology; and the group became responsible for the setting of production goals and outputs, as well as how they were going to be achieved. The sociotechnical approach works because there is serious consideration given to achieving compatibility of human resources with nonhuman technology.

Ideally, a balance between social/psychological and technical needs results. When designed carefully, the sociotechnical approach contributes to group autonomy and responsibility, enhances individual control over end products, increases both individual and group skill levels, encourages creative problem-solving and decision-making techniques, instills group stability and solidarity, and achieves a higher-quality product as a result.

We can look no farther than the American automobile industry debacle of the 1980s to see the superiority of the Japanese sociotechnical approach to manufacturing cars, in terms of team organization, product quality and design, and company profitability. Self-directed teams of technicians were responsible for building a new car in the Japanese culture. Employee commitment to the varied work and pride in the final product were high.

By contrast, the American assembly line was producing defect-laden automobiles, incredible employee boredom and dissatisfaction, and plummeting profits. By the time American management caught on, it was too late. Now we are beginning to experience an upswing in the American automobile industry, not without much downsizing and not before we adopted a team-centered, individually empowered, sociotechnical approach to automobile production.

Joan Woodward—1950s

The contingency theory of organizational design was developed and articulated by Joan Woodward in the late 1950s. Based upon her research with one hundred manufacturing firms in England, Woodward began to classify the companies according to their technological complexity. She determined that each organization's technology, markets, size, constraints, and the external environment shape to what extent that organization must be in a state of adaptation. Contingency theory recommends that as organizations experience dynamism, flux, and change, the management and organizational structures should remain as open as possible, encouraging participation and role exchange among their employees. The more stable the organization, the more the need for standardization, systems, and role specialization become apparent and necessary.

Survivor organizations have already undergone tremendous change efforts that have radically changed the nature, structure, and purpose of those organizations forever. Many of the companies that experienced particularly wrenching downsizing and restructuring activities had bureaucratic organizational systems and autocratic management, leading to especially painful and disorienting times for both the survivors and the "downsizees."

Now, knowing that it was those very structures and management styles which contributed to a company in need of restructuring in order to ensure its survival, those companies are now engaged in a frantic race to reengineer their processes, products and systems. Today's organizations must remain constantly adaptive in the face of constant technological, economic, and market changes and innovations. Survivors must possess the skills, expertise, and acumen necessary to perform their jobs at optimal levels in order to remain valuable contributors to their companies. Adapt or die seems to be the current corporate battle cry.

Chris Argyris—1960s

Argyris focused on the interrelationships between the organization and the individual and concluded that there are many incongruences between the demands and structure of an organization and individual employee needs. As a result, frustration, failure, conflict, and hostility become dangerous by-products of the employee–employer relationship. The organization's need for control can stifle individual productivity and creativity. Argyris recommended that the nature of the organizational–individual interrelationships must shift. Organizations should let the human capital shape the purpose and direction of an organization, and active employee participation in determining individual and company goals is crucial. If employees can achieve greater need satisfaction, the organization will benefit from their increased commitment and output.

Companies struggling to remain competitive are realizing that it is important to include employee participation and input in the shaping of company strategy, both in the long term and daily. A good number of organizations are also investing in the constant upgrading of their survivor employees' skills and abilities through training and development programs and activities. Not only is the skilled employee a valuable employee, but presumably, the level of organizational guilt will be lessened when and if that employee is downsized or reengineered out of his or her job. Employability at another organization becomes a greater possibility when the ex-survivor possesses up-to-date knowledge and skills.

Rensis Likert—1960s

Likert's theories hold the view that organizations practice either job-centered or employee-centered management. With job-centered management, the primary emphasis is on task accomplishment, jobs are highly structured and delineated, and the supervisory style is authoritarian. Employee-centered management keeps the needs of the employees at the forefront and emphasizes open communications, teamwork, and supportive working environments. Likert developed a system of management that describes four basic styles: exploitative/authoritative, benevolent/ authoritative, consultative, and participative. Participative management, for Likert, was the superior of the systems and stresses joint communication, goal setting, decision making, and participation among employees and their organization.

Participative management has become an ideal to which most survivor organizations strive to achieve competitiveness and profitability in the 1990s and beyond. The downside to continuous participative management is that, unless leadership is actively developed and supported throughout the organization alongside the teamwork concept, companies tend to expend a great deal of time and energy trying to create a "feel good" organization, often at a price.

Daniel Katz and Robert Kahn—1960s

Katz and Kahn articulate an open systems view of organizational life and emphasize a constant input–throughput–output cycle: The organizational systems take in energy from the external environment, that energy is processed and transformed within the organization, and an output is expended back into the external environment. Katz and Kahn emphasize the importance of both homeostasis—the ability to achieve organizational stability and balance—and dynamic homeostasis—the ability to adapt and change in response to environmental change factors.

Katz and Kahn recommend the importance of frequent communications among the participants in these organizational systems, since each unit is constantly influencing the others around it, whether directly or indirectly. They advocate the importance of using communications as a feedback and evaluative mechanism that can ensure dynamic homeostasis within an organization.

As survivor organizations are striving to include participation and open communications as driving forces for achieving stability, the use of communication opportunities as critical feedback and evaluative tools can be overlooked. A great amount communication is not always quality communication. Survivor organizations need to develop evaluative and critical models of communication in order not only to get things done in a timely fashion but also to get the right things done. Employee communications must become strategic and be linked more directly to the achievement of organizational goals and outputs.

James Thompson—1960s

Thompson looks at three ways in which we produce work and contribute to an organizational output; these three methods are both a product of and influence the nature of the organizational structure. *Pooled interdependence* describes a situation where individuals operate independently and separately contribute an organizational output. *Sequential interdependence* exists when an individual or unit is dependent upon another individual or unit's output for their input so that they, in turn, can produce an output. The most complex process is *reciprocal interdependence*, which emphasizes multi-individual and multigroup collaboration so that organizational outputs may be produced. Thompson points to the importance of the communication channels both when one is sequentially contributing to another's output and, more specifically, when the output is the result of multiple individuals and units. He emphasizes a highly interactive process of organizational communications which should flow upward, downward, and laterally.

Structurally, most survivor organizations are faced with communication systems that are complex, multiple, and ripe for confusion. Interdepartmental and project teams are the norm; and survivor employees frequently find themselves reporting, matrix-style, to a multiplicity of bosses, team leaders, and project directors. Managers must pay close attention to their responsibility of providing clear and focused leadership and direction to the employees of an organization. Strategic coordination of the multiplicity of projects and initiatives needs to be constantly monitored to ensure its viability to the end results of the company; if not, wheels are spinning and little is being accomplished.

Organizational Culture and Systems Theory—1970s, 1980s, and 1990s

We group the last twenty years or so of organizational theoretical development together for several reasons. First of all, no one or two individuals stand out as having provided a central theoretical focus. Second, most of the points of view expressed by theorists during this period have been variations on the same theme. Third, most academic research on organizational structure and behavior has moved away from the conceptual and theoretical toward limited empirical experiments.

In practice, by the mid-1970s the issues of formal structure and interpersonal human relations had been accepted as an inseparable combination rather than bipolar alternatives. During the 1980s, researchers and practitioners began to focus on the processes that employees use to make sense out of their work environment. The result was an understanding of cultural processes at work within individual organizations.

What comes down to us today as contemporary organizational theory was built slowly, piece by piece, as models were proposed, tested, modified, and retained. In fact, when we look across the whole spectrum of theoretical perspectives in the 1900s, organizations have changed relatively little. What has changed, primarily, is the degree to which we now understand the interrelations between the worker and the workplace, the manager and the managed.

The common approach that appears to be driving much organizational activity today derives from general systems theory. Systems theory is based on three key concepts: wholeness, boundary, and process. It asserts that every system is composed of a number of separate and interdependent parts (subsystems). Each subsystem simultaneously influences the other subsystems and the larger system. This happens because each subsystem monitors information provided by the actions of the other subsystems. We call this "input." That input is then processed; changed in some way (throughput); and, as a result, some action or product is produced (output). The basic tenet of systems theory is that the whole system is much more than just the sum of its parts.

Every grouping with some set of boundaries yields to analysis by systems theory. Whether it is a complex organization or the human body, within the existing boundaries of that system there is a number of subsystems—departments, in the case of the organization; organs, muscles, the cardiovascular system, and the like, in the case of the human body. At any given time, the actions of any of the many related elements of the organization may be influenced by the actions of any of the other interrelated subsystems. Although this is not a simple construct, it allows the simultaneous consideration of a large number of complicated interrelated factors in a single holistic model.

An important example of the boundary dimension of systems theory can be seen in the current emphasis on customer focus. What we are learning is that, in order to be competitive in today's global economy, organizations need to be open to influences occurring outside the identifiable barriers of the organization. In order to survive, organizations need to have permeable boundaries that allow a substantial amount of information to flow between their subsystems and systems located outside of their boundaries.

Open organizations have either a large number of people who maintain communication with outsiders or a small number of active people who perform this function. This boundary-spanning activity results in the collecting of information about the organization's inputs (such as raw materials, personnel, and strategies) or outputs (such as changes in consumer tastes, competitors' pricing, or advertising strategies). Based on this information, the organization can make better decisions.

The third leg on the systems theory stool is process. What systems theory tells us is that, within organizations, employees naturally develop processes that meet what they perceive are their needs and the needs of their organizations. When these patterns are repeated again and again, they become stable parts of the organization. When situations change, the patterns also change temporarily as people adapt to new pressures; but eventually, the patterns return to much the same circumstance as before. While systems are constantly adapting, they are doing so in such a way as to remain pretty much the same.

This need for both adaptability and stability is a major factor in the survivor environment. Organizations make serious mistakes in their attempts to realign their survivors by suggesting or representing, through both word and deed, that the entire process of the organization is being changed. The insecurity and confusion produced by such an approach is very destructive, especially when added to the other factors impacting the survivor environment. If we once accept that change is a constant in contemporary organizational life, we need to acknowledge it as such and then find and promote ways of systematically reintroducing stability and predictability into the organizational environment.

ACTIONS AND REACTIONS BASED ON
SYSTEMS THEORY

As we are catapulted forward through enormous organizational changes in the 1980s and 1990s, we prepare ourselves for discarding time-tested and outdated paradigms of what is work, how it should be structured, what the work force should look like, and what work should ultimately mean to the person performing it. We can look to two future-thinking yet strategically divergent theories and practices of work and their striking dynamics in the 1990s—Michael Hammer and James Champy's reengineering process and Tom Peters's crazy/chaos concept of contemporary work life.

In their seminal work, *Reengineering the Corporation*, Michael Hammer and James Champy outline a transformative method for improving efficiency of work processes, eliminating duplications of effort, increasing global competition viability, and ensuring responsiveness to customers, while maintaining a precarious realization that this transformation has no fixed end result—it is ever changing. For them, "Reengineering is the fundamental rethinking and radical redesign of business processes to achieve dramatic improvements in critical, contemporary measures of performance, such as cost, quality, service and speed." Reengineering involves rethinking outdated configurations of how work is structured and managed, and focuses attention on the global, economic, and work force changes that have impacted our productivity and profitability as the driving forces. Reengineering takes the corporation and compels it to look at the work and the products and services it produces as a series of processes, not a series of tasks, as work has been traditionally structured since the Industrial Revolution.

Some of the key results of reengineering are purported to be the following:

- Several jobs are combined into one.
- Processes have many versions.
- Decision making is thrust downward to the people performing the processes.
- Excess monitoring and control mechanisms are eliminated.
- Organizational structures shift from hierarchal to flat.
- Delivery time of the product or service from the start of process to its completion is noticeably decreased, and productivity enjoys healthy gains.

The implication for the worker is that he or she not only must undergo conceptual attitudinal and intellectual changes toward his or her work and its self-identity characteristics, but also must totally abandon previously rewarding methods of work generation and completion for new models and new interrelationships. For Hammer and Champy, the new business processes forever change a corporation's jobs and its organizational structures; the new jobs and structures transform the role of management and measurement systems; and, ultimately, new values and beliefs are embraced and assimilated into the corporate culture.

Peters believes that not only are we living in crazy, chaotic times where change is expected to remain a constant, but that, in order to survive, we must be willing to continually push ourselves to our creative limits and produce the best innovative products and services for our customers. For Peters, a sure sign of organizational burnout and decline is an organization's desire for homeostasis. Secure and stable organizations will not survive because of their built-in insularity against change, for change is the driving mechanism for business success. Companies and individuals must never be satisfied with the way things are—even if the customer was satisfied as late as yesterday. Because of the rapidity of change, new products and services burst upon the market continually, causing our customers to constantly crave and seek new, better, and different ways to meet their needs. Peters also takes a dim view when considering reengineering business processes to respond to change:

I recently ran across *Autumn Rhythm*, a Jackson Pollock painting . . . which to me looks the way a corporate organization chart should look . . . a total intertwining of people without regard to rank or function or location. *Autumn Rhythm* goes far beyond reengineering. . . . The "engineering" part of that increasingly popular word worries me because it smacks of neo-Taylorism. In linking up functions, reengineering substitutes a horizontal bias for Taylor's vertical one. That's great as far as it goes. Yet I worry that reengineering is just the latest "one best way" approach—different, but still engineering. I think we've got to move instead toward work as conversation, corporate talk shows, ensembles of interconnected communities of practice, Pollocking our way to growth and profit.[5]

Most of us are quickly realizing, both from the organizational and individual perspectives, that we must be more responsive to our external markets, improve the efficiencies of our work, and strive to be the best we can be. One factor distinguishes this latest wave of reshaping organizational structures and work—the fact that, unlike efforts in the past which needed an existing work force to be successful, new initiatives appear to deemphasize and devalue the permanency of that work force. As William Bridges, in a recent *Fortune* article entitled "The End of the Job," asserts, "We are told the only way to protect our jobs is to increase our productivity, but then we discover that reengineering, using self-managed teams, flattening our organizations, and turning routine work over to computers always make many jobs redundant."[6]

New organizational structures and work expectations are not only requiring a more flexible and more intelligent worker but are also forcing individuals to take maximum control over their work life and their careers. Not only has corporate loyalty become a quaint value, reminiscent of a quieter, gentler time, but the notion of employee commitment requires individual dedication to continuous retraining, upgrading, and selling of individual skills and expertise. The question remains if, over the long term, companies—both large and small—can sustain initial growth and increased productivity gained from new structures. By replacing the idea of working together for a common goal, product, or service with the resolve of working for one's own security, career, and life-meaning, we are toying dangerously with basic motivational values and theories. We are throwing out previously successful models of employer–employee contracting and accountability. We are cutting the heart out of the organization and replacing it with a superbrain.

As corporations and organizations are reengineering processes and redefining structures, it is becoming more prevalent that the new American worker will remain on the periphery of those new structures. Increasing trends toward outsourcing, part-time work, and temporary staffing, as well as the more all-encompassing downsizings, give rise to a new pioneer individualism, with survival of the fittest once again becoming the rule of the game. The problem is exacerbated when we take a look at recent statistics on the growing contingent work force: "A quarter of those employed today do so on a temporary, part-time, or contract basis. The number of Americans working part-time has grown by 2.2 million since 1973—entirely a function, according to the Economic Policy Institute, of more involuntary part-timers who would rather work full-time."[7] Two additional statistics point up the acuteness of a burgeoning "Lone Ranger" work force:

Job security has virtually vanished, as the pain of downsizing continues to rip through the U.S. Over the past year, almost 600,000 new job cuts were announced—

and this in an economy growing at a buoyant rate of 4% annually. . . . Americans are going entrepreneurial with a vengeance, with the rate of new business incorporations hitting an annual rate of 737,000 in the first four months of 1994—the highest rate ever."[8]

We have embarked on a precarious adventure. Our jobs, our careers, our financial security, and our self-identities are not only at stake but are very much in question.

PART II

Developing a Survivor Strategy

Chapters 5 to 11, though not abandoning the perspective-building activity of the text, focus more attention on developing strategies for dealing with the survivor situation. Chapter 5 provides background on various types of communication networks and discusses the effects technology is having on the way organizations communicate. Strategies are suggested for managers to develop networks that will support the transition from past to future.

Chapter 6 examines the critical part that the human resources department must play if companies are to effectively and humanistically manage organizational change. Unlike the personnel departments of years past, today's human resources department is becoming a strategic ally in assisting managers, in motivating and retaining employees, and in facilitating increased productivity and bottom-line profitability. For the reader who is a human resources professional, this chapter provides both professional-competencies and personal-profile checklists to ensure that he or she has the appropriate skill set to take on the human resources challenges of today's corporations.

Because of the impact diversity is having and will continue to have on organizations, special attention is given to understanding and dealing with diversity issues.

Chapter 7 examines various motivational theories and proposes a new motivational track. The chapter provides the survivor manager with meth-

ods of reinvesting in his or her human capital, such as redesigning individual work; maximizing increased productivity, autonomy, and responsibility; and increasing internal and external training and development opportunities.

The issue of discretionary effort is revisited, and strategies for assisting survivor employees in taking charge of that discretionary effort in order to close the commitment gap are explored.

Chapter 8 provides the reader with targeted methods for increasing motivation, productivity, and renewed vitality in the survivor employee. The focus in this chapter is placed clearly on the manager and his or her competencies for dealing with the situation. It emphasizes that a survivor manager cannot go forward to manage successfully and confidently his or her business unless he or she has a team of competent, committed individuals willing to provide the necessary support for the goals and objectives of the organization.

Chapter 9 provides the survivor manager with a step-by-step management plan for reforming, revitalizing, and recommitting his or her department staff members. The chapter provides a method for taking an inventory of the surviving employees: Who are they? What can they do? Since the survivor manager cannot thrive in a vacuum, the chapter also discusses how a manager must sit down with the surviving employees; reinterview them to determine their new responsibilities and future challenges; and most important, identify their thoughts, feelings, and plans for coping with the organizational change. It is here that the manager becomes also a career counselor and needs to develop creative approaches to career tracking employees in situations where many of the conventional tracks have disappeared.

Chapter 10 specifies an approach to coaching individual survivors, both to improve performance and to facilitate the opening of lines of communication that will be beneficial throughout the survivor transition process. The pragmatics of establishing contact and managing dialogue in a coaching situation are covered in detail.

Chapter 11 chronicles a case study where the authors applied the Survivor Management Model within a particular survivor environment. Each stage is discussed, and strategies are delineated.

CHAPTER 5

Making Communication Work

The new CEO argues that a good hard shakeup is the only way to get competitive juices flowing again. "You're gonna get exactly what you demand as a manager," he says. "When you liberate the good people, you create an electricity and they recommit to their jobs."
—Al Dunlap, CEO, Scott Paper[1]

To a large extent, the structure of an organization will determine many of the communication patterns that exist within it. Traditional or scientific structures focus most of the communication on work-related issues, while human relations–oriented organizations emphasize person-related communication. Types of organizations can be displayed across a spectrum that has work orientation on one end and person orientation on the other. Cummings, Long, and Lewis in their text, *Managing Communication in Organizations*, select three types of organizations to illustrate this point and display them as in Figure 5.1.

Figure 5.1
Types of Organizations

```
WORK-ORIENTED----------|------------------|-----------------|-----------PERSON-ORIENTED
               Manufacturing      Family       School
                   Firm         Business
```

Reprinted, with permission of publisher, from H. Wayland Cummings, Larry W. Long, and Michael L. Lewis, *Managing Communication in Organizations: An Introduction*, 2nd ed. (Scottsdale, Ariz.: Gorsuch Scarisbrick, 1987).

This book is not about schools, although much can be said about managing and motivating survivor teachers. We can determine that most of the communication that occurs within the business organizations that are the focus of this book tends toward work orientation rather than people orientation. In spite of this, many companies like to style themselves as "families" and their workers as "owners," although this is far from the case.

Regardless of the type of organization, workers have both personal needs and work needs. If their personal needs are not being met, a morale problem is usually the result.

Another factor that determines communication patterns is the division of labor. If the tasks of an organization lend themselves to people working alone, you will have different communication patterns than if the tasks call for people to work together. It is useful to take an inventory of how your organization fits within these various patterns. Ask yourself a series of questions:

- Would I classify this organization as people oriented or work oriented?
- Do the tasks of this organization require individuals to specialize in some ways while coordinating their work result with others?
- Do the people in this organization change roles depending on the situation and the need?
- Is the work of the organization complex?
- If the work is complex, how is the complexity influencing the communication patterns?

As task complexity increases, workers tend to be more specialized and channels of communication become more narrowly defined.

Another factor influenced by the type of organization is the communication flow. Some organizational structures create a one-way pattern of communication flow. Organizations built around a bureaucracy assume that communication follows a chain of command, as from manager to supervisor to subordinate. More participative management designs encourage the flow of communication in all directions.

In the survivor environment, change cannot be affected in the organization through one-way communication flow. That is not to say that an organization must first alter its structure before it can make meaningful change. We do not deal in absolutes. Any organization, regardless of its composition, can open the door to constructive feedback. To look at the other side of the coin, organizations that are too open to the flow of communication have an equal difficulty affecting meaningful change. There are points when people just need to be told what to do and by what standards their work will be judged. Collaboration becomes tiresome when there is no perceived direction or purpose for the organization's activity.

One of the most influential intraorganizational factors that shapes the nature, function, and complexity of communication patterns is the radical restructuring process transforming numerous corporations and other organizations since the late 1980s. Reengineering and redesigning companies so that they are prepared to withstand the imminent onslaught of the future is causing abrupt shifts in how survivors communicate within the organization with managers, peers, and support staff and how they interact with external customers, suppliers, vendors, and the larger business–economic environment.

When an organization suddenly reengineers around core business processes, individual, task-oriented functions are often eliminated. "Excess staff"—those who either are performing tasks and activities which were eliminated as a result of the reengineering or those who, based upon assessed skills, abilites, and knowledge, are deemed extraneous and expendable—are downsized from the organization.

The survivor employees find themselves in a maelstrom of rapid-fire change storms, often wildly orchestrated by external consultants with results, not people, as the frequently desired target. We do not intend to give the impression that all change efforts are heartless. Many of America's corporations and organizations needed to alter the way they did business drastically in order to revive their viability and profitability. Refocusing on a company's core business processes and strategically linking them to organizational goals, objectives, and vision make excellent business and economic sense in our ultracompetitive environment.

However, the survivors are frequently thrust into new roles and new patterns of communication and interaction with one another before the wounds have been allowed to heal. One day, a company does business as it always has, within a traditional hierarchical structure, with employees knowing exactly what tasks they are responsible for and to whom they are accountable. The next day, most of middle management is let go, the hierarchical ladder is flattened into a railroad track, survivors are quickly told to discard their old jobs and their outdated ways of working while being introduced to colleagues on their new "self-managing teams," and they are unreasonably expected to exchange one communication and work structure for another.

MANAGING INFORMATION

The organization and dissemination of information is perhaps the most important element in managing the survivor population. Efforts must be made to connect all of the workers by communication networks so that the organization as a whole can adapt to its environment and solve its problems. This is not an easy task. Cummings, Long, and Lewis point out that if you have only 10 people working in an organization, the number of possible communication links is 45. If you have 20 people in the organization, you have 190 communication links.[2]

In order to manage the complexity of exchanging information among a large group of people, organizations are segmented into departments. In most cases, departments differ in the type of information they have. The marketing department has marketing information. The technical services department has technical information. Organization charts not only reveal the structure; they also illustrate information priorities.

An alternative to departmental segmentation of information is the matrix organization. In a matrix organization, information is arranged according to both the function and the relationship that function has to a certain task requirement. Matrix organizations fail most often because functional and project managers become competitive over who actually commands the worker's time and effort, or the worker becomes overwhelmed from trying to serve two masters.

The communication patterns and flow of information within the new reengineered organizations become radically transformed. One of the key concepts underlying the switch from a vertical organizational structure to one which is a flattened, horizontal configuration is that information which was previously privileged to an elite core is now liberated.

Since the customer who buys a company's products and services is paramount, the people who are most involved with producing those outputs which will satisfy that customer's needs must have the necessary information to serve that customer in the speediest, most value-added way possible. Without appropriate knowledge and training to manage the glut of the information flood, survivors can often experience difficulty with appropriately filtering key, critical information from the unimportant. This becomes especially apparent when, as part of a reengineering process, new information technology is given to employees with little or no instructions.

The communication interactions between employees within an organization which has reengineered its business processes are substantially changed, based largely upon the fact that traditional employee roles have been altered. Employees are asked to abandon old ways of structuring jobs and levels, that is, of identifying oneself as an individual specialist, belonging to a specific department, reporting to a particular boss, and being responsible for a certain amount of people or work. Rather, they are expected to think of themselves as team members, responsible for one of the key business processes, reporting to a team leader and responsible to each other. People who had previously equated information with power and guarded it jealously are suddenly given a new way of working. Identities are taken away, new ones are put in place, and relationships are altered forever. Information proliferates; influencing throughout your networks becomes critical; and new, hopefully more effective, patterns of communication emerge.

Charting a course for the best way to manage information begins with a review of the various options for managing the exchange of information. Examining four distinct characteristics of the organization of internal company information can provide us with clues to how an organization prioritizes and values certain types of information.

Traditional configurations of an organizational chart of any given company reveal that people, their departments and their relationships to one another, their managers, and their subordinates are organized to achieve subject-focused communication, decision-making prioritization, ease of information retrieval, and optimal transmission of information. When we consider subject-focused communication, it becomes obvious that we form separate departments dedicated to research and development, marketing, human resources, management information services, and so on because not everyone within an organization has the expertise or the time to be involved in all facets of organizational management. Also, from a traditional focus, it seems efficient to create departments of specialists and experts so that overall organizational standards of operation and quality can be set and that both the internal and external customers receive a consistency of corporate products and services while costs are contained.

Depending upon the importance of a particular functional department, companies frequently organize internal information flow according to a decision-making prioritization order. If, for example, a large pharmaceutical company has experienced difficulty in the release and testing of a new drug, and external media sources reveal that communication to the public arena has been less than adequate, it is not uncommon for that company to highlight its priority of speedy and effective external communications by creating or expanding its public affairs and public relations departments. Sometimes, if they previously existed, the importance of those departments to the overall organization can be elevated in relationship to their importance to organizational goals and objectives by having those departments report directly to the CEO of an organization or by having the heads of those departments promoted to senior vice president status.

An organization also manages its information by examining the ease of information retrieval. With the explosion of information technology in the latter part of the twentieth century, companies have both heavily invested in computer technology—to manage and disseminate internal and external information—and created specialized departments to handle the management of information, the upgrade and maintenance of hardware and software, the creation of proprietary company systems, the training of employees in technology areas, and so on. A constant challenge continues to be the overwhelming speed and proliferation of all types of information and the task of prioritizing the importance of each information byte.

Last, an organization strives to achieve optimal transmission of information through its organization systems. Ideally, with new computer technology, for example, it should become easier and quicker for internal employees to communicate with one another directly as well as to their external customer base. With the emergence and expansion of the concept of the virtual office, that is, one where employees can work anywhere as long as they possess a computer, a modem, and a telephone hookup, barriers to effective transmission of important information should disappear. Interorganizational communications among all organizations should also experience improvements of time efficiency and quality of information sources.

As today's survivor organizations reshape the traditional hierarchical and bureaucratic structures of corporations past, they face the difficult assignment of maintaining internal and external communication systems for enabling subject-focused communication, decision-making prioritization, ease of information retrieval, and optimal transmission of information with a reduced work force. Certainly, we are witnessing the transformation of corporations and organizations as they de-layer bureaucratic layers of reporting, eliminate extraneous middle-management positions, create strategic frontline business units, and formulate horizontally rather than vertically structured, organizational configurations.

As employees become responsible for more and more functions and tasks, their accountability increases and their decision-making capabilities become more critical to the success of an organization. While increased employee participation in the outcomes of the organization can often produce higher-quality products and services with quicker production turn-around times, the support and resources accorded employees by their management become most crucial. An employee only feels empowered when he or she sees possibilities within reach. Most people are willing to consider new and more challenging ways of working if the appropriate assistance and reward mechanisms coincide with their increased efforts. Managers have a responsibility to support, train, and properly empower the increasingly overworked survivor employee so that the flow and transmission of internal and external information will succeed in achieving new configurations of communication and product and profitability success.

ESTABLISHING EFFECTIVE NETWORKS

The term *network* means different things to different people, both inside and outside the organization. Because of the currency of the term network, one might be led to believe that both the concept and the existence of networks are new phenomena. In fact, networks of various types have existed in all organizations since their beginnings.

We talk of global networks designed to increase our ability to compete in the emerging world markets. There are formal networks established within the organization for the purpose of ensuring the efficiency and effectiveness of the work being done. All organizations also share the existence of informal networks, through which employees of a particular organization acquire much of the information used to make judgments about the organization itself.

Workers talk about networking as a means both to enhance their ability to accomplish their tasks and responsibilities and to develop and maintain an awareness of additional job opportunities, both inside and outside the organization they work for.

Still another group within the organization talks about LANs (local-area networks) and WANs (wide-area networks). Their concept of a network relates specifically to technology that, among other things, enables communication to take place in ways and at a speed heretofore unavailable.

A useful method for assessing the nature, function, and impact of interpersonal networks within survivor organizations involves the examination of those networks from two perspectives. First, networks are often described according to the degree of openness and closedness of communication flow within the channels of those networks. The second dimension involves the degree of hierarchical- and horizontal-reporting relationships within those networks.

Open networks are often referred to as star networks (see Figure 5.2) and are characterized by the lack of restrictions imposed on the messages exchanged and on the channels of communication. Star networks work

Figure 5.2
Star Network

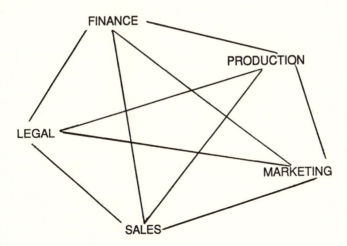

optimally among small groups of people where each employee is freely available to communicate with one another without protocol or censorship.

Closed, or controlled networks, are marked by the restriction of channels, messages, and people for exchanging information within an organization (see Figure 5.3). In controlled networks, the design of the organization dictates how certain information must flow, as well as to whom, on that organizational chart. Three common configurations of controlled networks are the chain, the circle, and the wheel.

When using a chain design, information is passed vertically or horizontally from one person to another. Protocol is followed; and, for example, the top person on a vertical chain does not communicate with the person at the bottom of that configuration. This chain-of-command network can produce impeded and distorted communication flow, since a particular message is open to a variety of interpretations as it is passed down (or across) the network.

The circle form of controlled networks is characterized by an information flow that is generated by one person then sent across channels to several other people in a circular format, eventually returning to the main source. Again, distortions of message as well as potential slowness of message flow can be detrimental to effective communications.

In the wheel configuration of controlled networks, communication is also risky, since the hub person is the only one who communicates directly with others, who form the spokes of the wheel.

Figure 5.3
Controlled Networks

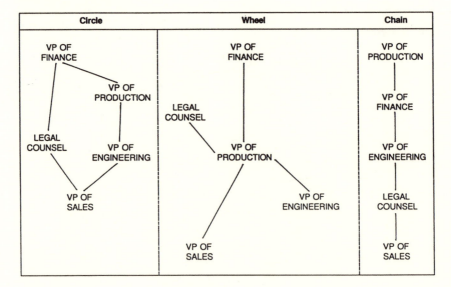

Networks in organizations can also be examined by their degree of hierarchy and horizontalness. A hierarchy-bound network (see Figure 5.4) emphasizes a vertical flow of information and a prescribed method as to whom people and departments must report and communicate. Messages must be passed through certain channels before reaching their final destinations. Hierarchical organizations are also marked by a closedness of information flow. Horizontal networks emphasize quickness and directness of communication flow from one employee to another. Lateral relationships are emphasized, and protocol is less important than message transmission and understanding.

Today's corporations and organizations are migrating from traditional closed, or controlled, configurations of networks arranged in a hierarchical design to more open, horizontal patterns of communications, reporting relationships and work responsibilities. Several new factors contribute to the construction of these emerging open and horizontal networks.

After a downsizing or restructuring, there are often less employees in a corporation, and those survivors frequently have the responsibility of assuming several jobs where they had one before.

Intense global-market competition and increased opportunities for international trade, as well as domestic pressures for quality and responsive products and services, require companies to discover more direct and quicker methods of communicating and doing business to succeed in the dynamic outer environment. Consequently, a company's internal communication systems need to find easier, quicker, and more effective ways to get the work completed and out to the external customer.

Figure 5.4
Hierarchical Network

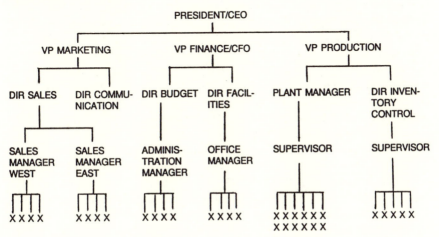

Last, the explosion of information technology in the American work-place, particularly the increasing proliferation of E-mail systems both within a company and between organizations, flattens and democratizes information flow and communications and delivers messages at the speed of light. Old hierarchies and protocols begin to crumble, and the artificial walls come down.

While survivors are equalized on the battlefield of work, their new re-sponsibilities for information flow put enormous strains on an already-overworked population. Traditional 9-to-5 designs of work beginnings and endings are disappearing as employees become more a part of the virtual office world. With laptop computers, modems, fax machines, cel-lular phones, and beepers, survivors are wired to a 24-hour marketplace whirlwind. They have become the ultimate network, but not without a price.

A useful framework for understanding the purpose and power of net-works is outlined by Thomas E. Harris in his book, *Applied Organizational Communication: Perspectives, Principles and Pragmatics*.[3] The significance of networks within survivor organizations, in particular, becomes height-ened when we adopt Tichy's view that the strength and uniqueness of networks lies in their essential transactional nature. Four media of ex-change travel over a variety of networks in an organization: information, goods and services, influences, and expressions of affect.

As an organization begins to undergo a total change process, the power of the formalized networks starts to ebb, largely because of the uncertainty of management authority and influence during this unstable period. People who were once key linchpins of several strong interorganizational networks get downsized or considerably reduced in power, and this pro-cess can instigate a domino effect of weakening and changing relationship ties throughout the entire network.

While the formal networks remain weakened and in a dynamic state during times of organizational change, the informal networks of an or-ganization often gain in strength and numbers, particularly as previously powerful members of the formal networks greatly diminish in force. While some of the informational and influential factors communicated across informal networks can be classified as rumor or gossip, and those particu-lar networks referred to as grapevines, a great deal of information be-comes critical to the survival rate of the remaining employee population.

As divisions and departments dissolve and word of layoffs and rede-ployment of personnel reaches remaining employees, a remarkable sur-vival instinct takes over. Those employees become quickly knowledgeable about the rationale and methodology for elimination of specific employ-ees and departments and can often adopt proactive behaviors and roles mimicking the characteristics prized in the new organization so that they and their departments are perceived as valuable to the new organization.

While their efforts to change instantly are usually unsuccessful and have little influence on management's already-made decisions regarding downsizing of personnel and restructuring of departments, these temporary informal survivor networks are most critical to the continued functioning of the organization and its people during the uncertainty of a change process.

Although employee–management relationships seriously deteriorate at this time, employee–employee relationships can strengthen and solidify during these times of crisis. People in a department as well as a network who previously had casual, passing contact with their peers suddenly become a united front against the oncoming troops of transformation. For the first time, the enemy has clearly identified itself and its motives. Employees begin to devise strategies for saving their jobs and the jobs of the other people in their department and network.

An informal system of outplacement is frequently initiated (just in case the worst-case scenario turns out to be true): secret resumé-updating meetings are held, flurries of "Help Wanted" ads arrive in interoffice mailers from concerned colleagues, and once-dormant rotary address files spin like the Wheel of Fortune in hopes of landing possible leads both for oneself and for others in the department and network.

The highly supportive behaviors and activities perpetuated by these informal survivor networks during organizational change are most critical for the psychological and social health of the survivors, the downsized employees, and ultimately, the organization itself. We must keep in mind that, as soon as employees understand that the stability of their organization is threatened and other personnel are being let go, a grieving process sets in with the remaining survivors. Survivors reach out to one other for comfort and compassion, not only to mourn the passing of a once-stable organization and the downsizing of previously valued employees but also to attempt to save themselves from the same fate. The supportive transactional nature of these informal networks supersedes any of its informational or influential properties so that the remaining survivors, the leaving employees, and the new organization can cope with a world and a life turned upside down.

All of these constructs—from the formal to the informal, from the interpersonal to the technological—must be consciously examined and strategically managed and executed within the survivor environment.

MANAGING NETWORKS

According to Ram Charan, writing for the *Harvard Business Review*, companies that are examining and strategically deploying networks are reacting to the need for developing a competitive advantage. They share in the belief that the traditional corporate structures, regardless of how "lean and mean" they may become after reorganization, reengineering, or downsizing, cannot develop and maintain the speed, flexibility, and focus that being successful in business today demands.[4]

Using networks effectively can reshape the process of decision-making. The objective is to acquire the necessary information, both horizontally and vertically, in the organization in order to make the best decisions from a competitive perspective—quickly and correctly. Managed effectively from both an interpersonal and technological perspective, networks enable the right people in the organization to converge faster and focus on the issues at hand. In addition to making the organization as a whole more effective and more competitive in its quest to offer products that satisfy customer needs and do so quickly, the effective and strategic management of networks provides additional opportunities for enhancing the relationship between the organization and its disaffected survivor population.

In the development of communication designs, managers need to consider certain questions related to both the competitive advantages that might ensue and the interpersonal or relational factors that can influence the entire organization environment, either positively or negatively. Here are some questions to be considered as part of an overall strategic communication network design:

- Which design will have the greatest impact on morale or job satisfaction?
- How can the establishment of networks improve productivity?
- What types of networks will or will not work because of the current culture of the organization?
- Which types of networks will or will not work because of the nature of the products and services the organization provides?

As part of the strategic planning process, the formation of communication networks must be taken into account, using three basic principles:

1. *Communication network designs change.* It is not a matter of setting up network patterns and assuming that the task is complete. The organization must continue to monitor what is happening in the communication environment. Any alterations in the communication flow within an organization will have a major impact on the psychological and social health of the workers.

2. *Communication network designs are created in conjunction with other factors.* Economic shifts, new product introductions, changes in corporate leadership, and the like all have a direct effect on the type of communication strategies that need to be put into place. Ideally, design decisions with regard to communication will be based on realistic assessments of the organization's short- and long-term goals.

3. *The communication network design is only as good as the population it serves.* Designs for communicating do not display themselves in a hierarchy. Selecting a design is not just a matter of picking the "best" one, since no one design is in-

herently better than another. The best design is the one that works within the culture of the organization to produce both productivity and effective interrelationships.

Networks formed strategically differ from informal networks. Informal networks will always arise of their own accord. However, much of the information exchanged on an informal basis can be influenced by what is taking place in the formalized approaches to networking information throughout the organization.

Building and managing effective networks begins with the managers themselves. As with most organizational initiatives, the rank and file can rapidly discern whether there is a real concern for change, based on their perception of the level of support provided by the people they report to. If managers are perceived to be taking part in formalized communication networks, workers will be more willing to participate in activities designed to draw them into the process.

Initially, managers' networks may not include every manager in the organization. When setting up such a network, members need to be selected by a variety of criteria, including business skills and decision-making ability; enthusiasm, or "buy-in" to the process; and the holding of positions that impact information flow to the rest of the organization.

Charan calls this manager network the "core network." The responsibilities of this core network are to hold regular meetings; form additional networks within their areas of authority; and to use all the means at their disposal, including conference calls, electronic mail, and computerized information systems, to keep the rest of their core network in the information loop.

Other characteristics of a core network, according to Charan, include frequency, intensity, and honesty of the information exchange among all members. In the best of circumstances, managers feel free to talk openly, candidly, and emotionally without fear. They are encouraged to test each others' motives and build trust and to individually and collectively evaluate the problems of the organization from the perspective of what is right for the customer and the company as a whole rather than focusing only on departmental or functional interests.[5]

Any formalized network must be distinguished from teams, task forces, work groups, or other collections of individuals for the purpose of solving a problem or making a decision. As we have already noted, most teams and work groups are temporary entities, established to accomplish a specific purpose. Networks are more permanent.

A core network of managers becomes even more important when one considers that managers in most organizations frequently do not understand the motives, priorities, and sometimes even the tasks and responsibilities of other managers and their departments. This lack of understanding among managers breeds territoriality and distrust. It creates an environment where managers attribute motives to one another that may or may not actually exist.

In our experience working with various organizations, it is not uncommon to find that people in research and development feel that people in marketing are totally arbitrary in the demands that they make for product development. People in administration have a perception that the sales department is never available to answer key questions, either for the needs of the organization or the customer, and that they spend their time primarily having lunch.

An exercise that we have conducted successfully with groups of managers from various departments who were in the initial stages of establishing a network calls for each manager involved in the forming network to take on the role and perspective of a manager in another department. The manager is then encouraged to make a presentation that illustrates his or her particular view and biases about the department he or she is putatively heading. It is astonishing how often this base level of understanding is missing among managers who are expected to collaborate effectively and achieve organizational goals.

Another factor that separates networks from other formalized organizational constructs is that they are proactive rather than reactive. Teams and task forces are provided with problems to work on, whereas networks generate new ideas and perceptions to accomplish the tasks and responsibilities of the organization.

Key to the success of networks is the level of support provided by the CEO. If top management insists on continuing to make all of the primary decisions, rather than focusing on building relationships among managers, the network will fail.

On the other hand, the CEO must be directly involved in the process of building and tending the core manager network. He or she must select the important influencers and key decision makers in the organization. This selection must be done without regard to seniority. Rather, those managers who are selected are the ones identified as most directly responsible for the success of the business.

Also, these managers must demonstrate the commitment and energy to make the network approach a success. Charan points out, from his research, that it is not important that the managers involved in the core network like each other, although outright hostility would not be a benefit. As he puts it, "Companies do not build networks so that managers will 'like' one another or behave like 'family.' Networks are designed to develop professional trust and empathy, and a richer and more widely shared understanding of the specifics of the business."[6]

As part of their role in developing and nurturing these networks, CEOs may have to deal with managers that, for one reason or another, are unable to adapt to this particular approach to doing business. The network, like any social organization, is very sensitive to negativity and can be hampered or destroyed by even single individuals who either cannot or refuse to adapt to the process. These managers will need to be either reassigned or dismissed.

The logical extension of the core management group is the creation, under the tutelage of each individual manager, of subnetworks within each manager's division of the organization. These subnetworks must emulate the objectives and actions of the core management group; that is, their focus must be on the broad exchange of information dealing with real business issues. In a sense, armed with the necessary information, everyone in the organization becomes part of the strategic planning process.

Networks are not formed simply to enable people to communicate better. They are formed in order both to provide and receive critical information to and from the people who are instrumental to the success of the organization.

We have already pointed out that the way information flows in an organization is one of the most important variables determining how the organization will respond in the competitive environment. In companies without formalized networks, information about the business flows down through the hierarchy and as such is subject to distortion and manipulation. When a network is working effectively, everybody who needs the information gets it simultaneously.

On the flip side, the instigation of networks throughout an organization can provide an atmosphere of added cynicism and distrust for the survivors. This is the inevitable result of organizations which, with great fanfare, announce and set up networks on paper and, at the same time, maintain hierarchical control of the essential information that everybody needs to make the networks function. When this happens, workers feel betrayed or put upon and resent what they perceive to be the additional work layered on their already overburdened schedules.

In order to harvest the gains to the organization that can grow within carefully nurtured formalized networks, managers at all levels must be willing to take the risk of sharing information openly and to respond to and evaluate support initiatives generated by the process.

COMMUNICATION NETWORKS AND TECHNOLOGY

Clearly, one of the driving factors behind the upsurge of interest in formalized networks is the availability of technology to support these initiatives. One estimate puts the expenditure on network hardware and software for 1994, among businesses around the world, at $3.25 billion. For hardware and software devices that sit at the center of computer networks, an additional tens of billions of dollars will also be spent for routers

and other networking gear, and for software such as Novell's NetWare or
Lotus Notes, or proprietary programs created in-house. In the United
States alone, organizations maintain some 28 million or more electronic
mailboxes.

This vast array of electronic support enables people within the organization to receive and send information to one another with extraordinary
speed and without the interposition of hierarchies. According to Thomas
A. Stewart, in a recent article written for *Fortune* magazine, electronic support for networks, in and of itself, changes the nature of the way organizations are managed.

In a wired world, fundamental management jobs, such as planning, budgeting,
and supervising, must be done differently. Tools like E-Mail, teleconferencing,
and groupware let people work together despite distance and time, almost regardless of departmental or corporate boundaries, which networks fuzz up or
even obliterate.[7]

Riding on the shoulders of this technological giant is the accelerating
potential for what Yankelovich has described, and we have referred to in
Chapter 2, as the commitment gap. As people become more independent
and responsible for managing their own work, organizations become
more dependent on the individual worker's willingness to provide the
necessary commitment to meet productivity goals. With increasing frequency, managers are looking out of the doors of their offices and seeing
empty rooms. The people whom they supervise are either directly responding to customers, located in satellite offices, or even working from
home.

It seems like only a few moments ago that one of the prevailing fads in
management was "management by walking around." Today, more and
more managers find themselves doing most of their walking by wire.

A by-product of the speed with which the new technology has exploded
on the scene is a generation of management that is not entirely comfortable with the emerging parameters, having been schooled in different and
more direct methods of supervision. According to Stewart, among the
major benefits to be derived from the network environment, one of the
most important is that, when handled correctly, electronic networks can
help the organization see and respond to its market in a more clear and
direct way. Rather than receiving information from reports that have been
handed down the line and edited along the way, it is possible for any
worker who needs raw data on any issue relating to the organization's
tasks and responsibilities to access the necessary information directly from
the network.

Supporting our contention about the mixing of approaches, Stewart
quotes Helene Runtagh, CEO of General Electric Information Services,

who tells us that in a network environment the worst thing you can do is hang on to hierarchical behavior while, at the same time, bringing in network-based communication.[8]

There are several dos and don'ts on the issue of managing in a technological environment. There are still many managers in organizations today who have opted out as far as the new technology goes. Stories have grown up around the resistance to technological change. One company supported the use of word processing by removing all of the pencil sharpeners from the desks in the office. A manager, upon being discovered in the supply closet sharpening a pencil, exclaimed when confronted, turning the handle on the sharpener with the pencil in the appropriate position, "I'm formatting a disk."

Another mistake managers make is trying to hang on to the old rules. Electronic networks both create and support openness. Managers committed to command and control styles will tend to limit people's access to the network. This merely defeats the network's purpose. Even though managers retain the power to hire and fire people, in the wired world, their authority is no longer associated with the ability to control information.

Managing effectively in the presence of an electronic network requires an environment of trust. As long as a manager feels that there are certain people in the organization who do not need to know certain kinds of information, he or she will find it difficult to manage in the networked arena. Cooperation as a concept outweighs obedience, and strong relationships are formed across nontraditional lines.

In the wired environment, the old adage, "Manage results, not activity," becomes a fait accompli. With workers operating at diverse locations and, in some cases, virtually on their own, it becomes impossible to know exactly what they are doing at any given point in time. Managers need to be concerned with overall performance and be adept at using project-management tools to ensure that objectives are being met in a timely fashion.

In short, today's successful manager is not focusing on making people work, but rather on creating a climate within which workers willingly provide the organization with a large measure of their discretionary effort. The relationship side of management outweighs the substantive side, in large measure.

A seeming anomaly is the need to interact face to face as much as possible with all of the people who are directly involved in accomplishing the work that the manager is responsible for. It is necessary to mount a sincere effort to work against the remoteness that resides inherently in the use of electronic networks.

CHAPTER 6

Human Resources Takes a Leadership Role

Among the many changes taking place in organizations throughout the world today, perhaps none are more pronounced than those changes occurring within the human resources function.

Now, as never before, human resources executives are being called upon to help the organization deal with strategic problems. No longer relegated to the back rooms to spend their time almost exclusively counting heads and processing benefit forms, today's human resources executives find themselves more and more in the front lines, dealing with mainstream issues and particularly those that arise as part of, or as a result of, a reengineering or downsizing initiative.

It used to be that an employee would have two primary opportunities to interact with a human resources executive. The first came when he or she was hired; was taken through a tour of the benefits, policies, rules, and regulations; and was issued the appropriate keys and codes. The second opportunity usually arose when the employee was being terminated. If the human resources executive was neither present nor conducting the termination interview, he or she would usually be involved in discussing the final bits and pieces of wrapping up employment with the organization.

The second scenario is still very much in evidence and provides an excellent example of how the role of human resources has increased. In today's work environment, the human resources executive, in his or her role as the facilitator of a downsizing operation, must develop appropriate and cost-effective methods for providing specialized benefits to the terminated employees, calculate severance and other types of packages as downsizing incentives, and monitor and assess the progress of the downsizing effort as it reaches toward the projected head count and fiscal goals.

For some human resources executives, their expanded role in the downsizing and reorganization process has been a suicide mission. We know of several cases where human resources executives have successfully met the challenges, as well as all of the corporate goals, for becoming "lean and mean," only to find that at the end of the process—or, perhaps, as a result of the process—the organization no longer had a need for an executive at that level.

However, our focus in this chapter is not on those executives who found themselves to be the last ones out the door but those who survive their own efforts and, and as a result, are afforded the opportunity to deal with the by-products of the downsizing process—the survivors.

NEW CONCERNS, NEW FOCUS

As we have noted in previous chapters, for a variety of reasons—including global orientation and the availability and use of electronic networks—human resources (the actual people in the organization) is playing a more strategic role in the accomplishment of business objectives.

The demands of the new workplace, combined with the issues and concerns of the survivors who people it, call for flexibility in human resources practices. In addition, the emergence of issues such as diversity, sexual harassment, and employee-assistance programs requires human resources professionals to be more actively and continuously involved in the day-to-day operation of the organization.

Being the executive responsible for people is arguably the most difficult and stressful task within the organization. Human resources executives today can find themselves responsible for a wide range of crucial activities, including recruitment and selection, benefits, payroll and other compensation programs, training and development, outplacement, and other outsourcing issues.

As a result of all of this activity and involvement, it is no wonder that human resources has become linked more closely to the competitive strategy of the business and also has become more directly related to the strategic choices for business growth or retrenchment.

Human resources practitioners agree that there are five primary issues that will shape the way human resources executives will focus their attention for the next ten years:

1. Increasing work force diversity
2. Increasing disparity between job requirements and necessary skills
3. Increasing globalization of competition

4. Changing technology

5. Continued mergers, restructuring, and downsizing

These same issues have direct impact on overall organizational objectives. It is this convergence between organizational objectives and human resources issues that places human resources in a central position within the total management process. In addition to what has been historically the human resources domain—that is, internal matters such as hiring, training, rewards, work design decisions, and monitoring compliance with employment laws—human resources executives are involved in formulating the mission, corporate objectives, and market strategies of the organization as a whole.

W. Wagel sampled human resources practitioners and academics in order to identify what they felt were key trends and issues for the next ten years. Following are the primary issues identified:

- Human resources forecasting will be used more frequently in the strategic decision-making process.
- Changes in federal regulations will affect employee benefits and retirement policies.
- Shortage of labor and problems compounded by functional illiteracy and cultural diversity will create problems that make education a continuing concern.
- Rising health-care costs will focus attention on national health insurance as a serious public policy issue.
- More organizations will have to address the issue of family and work conflicts through day care, family leave, dual career, flexible work scheduling, telecommuting, and other work force innovations.
- Global expansion and the continuing quest for quality will present significant challenges.
- The continued abuse of drugs and other substances will require employers to balance employee privacy with organizational needs for safety and productivity.
- Individual career planning will require the input of both employees and employers.
- Human resources will increasingly use computer technology to compile a human resources information system and analyze its data.

DRIVING FACTORS

George Milkovich and William Glueck, in their book, *Personnel/Human Resource Management: A Diagnostic Approach,* arrange the key factors into what they call the "diagnostic model."[1] This useful construct has influenced thinking and human resources development for many years. It considers four basic factors: external conditions, organization conditions, human resources activities, and objectives.

External Conditions

External conditions include such drivers as economic conditions, government regulations, and unions. In a typical force-field scenario, these factors can also be perceived as inhibitors; that is, while driving the organization to make decisions in certain directions, they also restrict the organization's ability to select strategy necessary to meet the ends. A change in economic conditions is certainly a driving factor behind the creation of the survivor.

As we stated earlier, not all organizations that are downsizing are doing so because of poor economic health; nonetheless, the vast majority of strategic corporate moves are geared toward improving the bottom line. As everyone knows, the quickest way to make an impact on overall profitability is to decrease payroll. Economic conditions also perform as an inhibitor, in the sense that managers are unable to hire people as they become necessary.

Government regulations also play the dual role of driving and inhibiting organizational decisions. Equal employment opportunity legislation has directly influenced the way organizations go about acquiring and eliminating personnel. Legislation and litigation surrounding the issue of sexual harassment has been a major driver for instituting diversity-awareness programs in most organizations. Also, today's human resources manager needs to deal directly with the irrevocable trend toward diversity in the workplace.

Unions are also playing the dual role of driver and inhibitor. Because of the language of contracts and other factors associated with union involvement, organizations with unions are restricted in terms of the choices that they can make to meet certain objectives. On the other hand, we are finding more often that unions are taking the lead in instigating meaningful change in the way of personal and professional development for the survivors in an organization.

In one such instance, at a major financial services organization, in exchange for certain trade-offs on hiring practices the union received a commitment from the organization to provide a new and comprehensive training program for both new-hire and veteran employees that is both innovative and employee centered.

Organization Conditions

Factors associated with organization conditions include the strategies and objectives of the organization, the kind of work that the organization engages in, and the type and configuration of the employees who do that work. Milkovich and Glueck include in this category strategies and objectives, technology, structure, and culture.[2]

By strategy, they mean the direction of the organization—what might, in other contexts, be called the vision or mission. The issue of culture is complex, and an examination of cultural influences goes beyond the scope and purpose of this book. However, it is worth noting that culture is extraordinarily resilient. The basic elements of an organizational culture will most likely survive the most vociferous attempts to alter or remove that culture.

Direct assaults on organizational cultures, either mounted from within or from external sources such as a merger or acquisition, usually result in the ultimate destruction of the organization when an attempt is not made to preserve the basic elements of the existing culture. The human resources manager, because of his or her unique position at the forefront of the human side of the organization, is the primary keeper of the culture.

On the more pragmatic side, strategic initiatives such as changing or adding to product lines or opening up foreign markets will also greatly impact human resources. The type of work an organization engages in is also a major factor. This has always been the case; however, in the survivor environment it becomes even more critical. As an organization downsizes, it loses its capacity to specialize job tasks and responsibilities. The argument certainly can be made that organizations had become too fat and overspecialized in the 1980s. However, in the survivor environment, employees and their managers are finding themselves fielding problems for which they have little or no preparation or experience.

Another serious concern that lies at the human resources manager's doorstep is how to maintain morale and motivation in the survivor climate. These issues are covered in much more detail in other places in this text, but it is worth noting that many of the initiatives that impact motivation and morale begin with human resources activities and interventions.

Human Resources Activities

With everything else that is going on, the human resources manager is still responsible for doing the traditional work of human resources; that is, he or she must still maintain adequate staff with the necessary knowledge, skills, and perception to fulfill the tasks and responsibilities of the various jobs. The human resources manager is also responsible, perhaps more than ever before, for the development of existing staff within the organization.

The training need becomes greater in the survivor environment for two primary reasons: first, because survivors are spread thinner across a wider range of competencies; and second, because opportunities for personal and professional development provide one of the key building blocks for developing, maintaining, and realigning employee willingness to provide more discretionary effort and close the commitment gap.

The need for employment relations is also enhanced in the survivor environment. Concerns about fair and equitable treatment, conflict between employees and managers, grievance procedures, assistance programs, labor relations, and the like present problems that have become exacerbated by the reconfiguration of the organization.

Compensation programs, the escalating cost of health care, the emergence of bonus-incentive plans, and other activities relating to fair and equitable pay all require initiatives that tend to put the human resources manager in the forefront of cost savings and the overall strategic plan of the organization.

Objectives

Objectives need to be set to achieve both organizational effetiveness and human resources effectiveness. They also become the standards for evaluating the success of the organization's managers.

STRATEGIC HUMAN RESOURCES MANAGEMENT INITIATIVES

Gone are the days when the human resources manager could afford to be buried in the details of head counts and health forms. Today's human resources professional is very much a part of the strategic landscape. What was once a back-room operational and administrative function has become an active, frontline, clearly visible function.

As we have pointed out elsewhere, managers of all stripes need to be aware of and sensitive to environmental issues, both outside and inside the organization. Nowhere is this more true than with the human resources manager. By building bridges and opening up links to the communities they both occupy and serve, organizations can enjoy benefits and support that will aid in their competitive survival. They also can gain access to services that will support the organization's efforts to realign their survivors.

Today's effective human resources manager steps across organizational boundaries and discovers areas for cooperation, collaboration, and synergy between the organization's resources and needs and the community's resources and needs.

The *Successful Manager's Handbook*, published by Personnel Decisions, Inc., suggests several ways in which today's managers can liaise with the communities they serve. We find many of these suggestions particularly appropriate for the human resources manager taking a leadership role:[3]

- Depending on the community the organization resides in, there may be community agencies that could provide a resource. These resources could include child care, family counseling, or drug and alcohol rehabilitation, in addition to the usual health and human services agencies. Using these resources as a springboard, the human resources manager can develop programs to interact with and complement the services.

- Lines should be open to political and community leaders to gather and maintain a good understanding of their issues and concerns.

- There may be opportunities to work with the local schools. The organization can provide speakers and other resources for classroom use, and offer tours of the workplace. Schools are also a good source for interns and for building relations through scholarship opportunities.

- Besides making himself or herself available, the human resources manager should start a Speakers' Bureau for the organization. This bureau would provide speakers for local functions and provide visibility for both the organization and the individual speakers.

- Major steps can be taken to account for work force diversity by making an effort to ensure that the organization's demographics are representative of the community. Connection with the community also provides input to the overall strategic plan. The organization needs to be aware of future projections of demographics in the community in order to track potential changes in the work force. Also, any future projects planned in the community could have an impact on the business.

In addition to business concerns, today's human resources manager needs to be a good steward of the organization's resources. Being a good steward of the organization's resources begins with an evaluation of one's personal stewardship. The manager must ask if there are ways in which he or she could be more effective or efficient in his or her work. Is the manager giving satisfactory amounts of time, money, and energy to important personal relationship, community, and career priorities? To be a good steward for the organization requires maintaining an adequate life balance, in which all areas are appropriately attended to.

From the personal aspect, managers must then branch out to their staff and examine whether they are being challenged to the full extent of their capabilities or if there are additional contributions they would like to make but have not had the opportunity to. A major part of being a good organizational citizen is making contributions in an altruistic way to organizations in the community that improve the quality of life, regardless of whether there is any direct impact on the organization's business.[4]

MANAGING DIVERSITY

This is not a book of human resources practices. Indeed, there are many good books on the market that cover payment plans, health plans, hiring, and all of the other key factors we have mentioned. The one area that stands out for us as a clear opportunity for the human resources manager to take a leadership role is the management of diversity. Therefore, we devote most of our strategic discussion to this most important area of concern.

Anyone interested in the issue of diversity is already familiar with the demographics that are driving the concerns for the workplace. A simple reiteration of the population dynamics that are changing the work force is probably not useful or desirable. However, we believe it is useful to examine changes in population groupings in the United States from the perspective of the public schools. Those people coming through the public schools are most likely to be tomorrow's work force and provide the demographer with relatively accurate and ongoing snapshots of what that work force population will look like. Also, such an examination points out a factor that should be a strong driver for the institution of diversity programs. It is clearly in the best interests of the current power holders—the rapidly aging white middle class—to note that its retirement income will be generated by an increasingly nonwhite work force. Three primary demographic factors are influencing the diversity scenario: births, age, and family status.

Some groups have more children than others and, as a result, will be overrepresented in the next generations.

Group	Children per Female
Cubans	1.3
Whites	1.7
Puerto Ricans	2.1
Blacks	2.4
Mexican-Americans	2.9

A group needs about 2.1 children per female just to stay even. When one examines the birth rates, it becomes apparent that all these young people have to do is grow older, and we have the future.

A second factor is age. The census reveals that the average White in America is 31 years old; the average Black, 25; and the average Hispanic, only 22. It should be easy to see that age produces population momentum for minorities; as the typical Hispanic female is just moving into the peak childbearing years, the average White female is moving out of them. Currently, half the states have public-school populations that are more than 25 percent nonwhite, while all of our twenty-five largest city school systems have "minority majorities."

By the year 2020, most of the baby boom will be retired, its retirement income provided by the much smaller age groups that follow it. This is a demographic argument, not an economic one; but if larger numbers are taking out and much smaller numbers are putting in, the economics are rather clear. For example, in 1950, seventeen workers paid the benefits of each retiree. By 1992, only three workers provided the funds for each retiree, and one of the three workers was a minority.[5]

The final demographic factor, family status, also signals major changes. In 1955, 60 percent of the households in the United States consisted of a working father, a housewife mother, and two or more school-age children. By 1980, that family unit was only 11 percent of our homes; and by 1985, it was 7 percent—an astonishing change that is continuing. Of our 80 million households, almost 20 million consist of people living alone. Fifty-nine percent of the children born in 1983 will live with only one parent before reaching age 18. This now becomes the normal childhood experience. Of every 100 children born today:

- Twelve will be born out of wedlock.
- Forty will be born to parents who divorce before the child is 18.
- Five will be born to parents who separate.
- Two will be born to parents of whom one will die before the child reaches 18.
- Forty-one will reach age 18 within a traditional family structure.

We are also confronted with an epidemic of children born outside of marriage. Every day in America, forty teenage girls give birth to their third child.[6]

All of these factors are creating and will continue to create dynamic changes in the work force. Projections indicate that by the year 2020 we will be a nation of 44 million Blacks and 47 million Hispanics—even more if Hispanic immigration rates continue to increase.

The total U.S. population for 2020 will be about 265 million people, a very small increase from our current 248 million. Of that projected 265 million, more than 91 million will be minorities. In addition, Asian-Americans—who represented approximately 3.7 million in 1980—currently represent nearly 50 percent of all immigrants admitted to the United States; and, although classified as a group, their diversity is very great. When all of these factors are taken into account, it is clear to see that what is entering the work force and what is about to enter the work force is a group of people who will be poorer, more ethnically and linguistically diverse, and who will have more handicaps that will affect their ability to move ahead in traditional ways.

By the year 2020, America will be a nation in which one of every three of us will be nonwhite and minorities will cover a broader socioeconomic range than ever before, making simplistic treatment of their needs even less useful.

Diversity and Total Quality Management

The human resources manager who is serious about instigating diversity programs in his or her organization must find a way of fitting such a program within the concerns and strictures of Total Quality Management

(TQM) issues. If the target organization is not currently involved in some form of TQM it most probably will be soon.

It is beyond our purposes here to discuss why most major organizations are focusing on quality issues, but the fact is that whether the organization is truly rededicating itself to producing quality goods and services, viewing quality as a marketing strategy, using it as a guise to mask the true objective (such as downsizing), or all of these, it is unlikely that any major program initiative will receive the blessing of top management without some sort of quality hook. Fortunately, the connection is not difficult to make between TQM philosophy and the desire for managing diversity more effectively and productively. The basic tenet of TQM is to "treat your employees as you would have them treat your customers." There can be no question that companies are, to an increasing degree, dealing with a very diverse customer base both within the United States—or their home country, wherever it may be—and in their increasing contact with the world at large.

Another issue, if one is considering the institution of a diversity program at this time, is the expectation that downsizing and reorganization will continue. The concern about downsizing is twofold. First, any diversity program must take into account that resources could potentially diminish and that actual players could disappear at various stages of the project. Second, the survivor population will inevitably see diversity as a secondary issue, since it lies at a more abstract level of concern than their basic survival.

Also, not incidentally, downsizing has inadvertently worked against work force diversity by focusing the cuts on the middle-management level. Minorities, particularly blacks, who have been making their way with some success in the organization for the last two decades, have sustained an unequal share of the job loss, not as a result of racial discrimination but, rather, because they now find themselves occupying those very positions that are disappearing.

If a diversity program is to be successful, it must take into account the population it is trying to impact—the survivors. As we have pointed out, survivors feel a sense of distance between themselves and the company. They think more about personal security and less about corporate loyalty.[7]

The point is this: If the organization is not making concerted efforts to reintegrate and realign its survivors, any attempt to focus their attention on the issues of diversity is doomed to fail.

The Diversity Tangle

Most people who are sensitive to the diversity issue are aware that changes in race, gender, and culture are flooding the American work force. However, moving from this realization to implementing programs involves a paradox.[8] In our quest for equal treatment, companies desiring to provide equal employment opportunities have ended up replacing equality with sameness.

In efforts to manage diversity, companies run into the legal wall of the Equal Employment Opportunity Commission (EEOC), which requires companies not to treat people differently because of their race, sex, age, religion, or handicap. Interpretations of the antidiscrimination provisions of Title 7 of the Civil Rights Act of 1964 have led to the practice of avoiding disparate treatment of individuals. Although discriminatory intent must be proven in a disparate treatment case, that intent can be inferred from the actions themselves; so companies that institute diversity training, although having the best of intentions, still may find themselves guilty of discriminatory practice.

One method companies have used to address the diversity issue in the face of EEOC guidelines is to expand and broaden the criteria used to measure performance, so that particular groups are not disadvantaged merely because they are different from the dominant group. However, this broadening of criteria or standards potentially puts diversity initiatives in conflict with standards required by TQM initiatives.

Added to this is the problem created by the EEOC uniform guidelines on employee-selection procedures. These guidelines describe a goal system intended to produce fair representation of protected classes in all job groups. "Fair" is determined by the number of applicants from each protected class who desire to enter a job group. The system assumes that there are no skill differences between cultures or genders.

Diversity programs, on the other hand, capitalize on the strengths employees have that are inherent in their gender or cultural backgrounds. In fact, one of the goals of diversity is to help employees select those jobs or professions in which they feel comfortable and can perform well. Our legal climate may have to change in order to become a support for, rather than an impediment to, diversity issues.

Human resources must take the lead in communicating the need for managers and subordinates to face squarely the fact that they are creating a new order, that there is no going back to the past. Managers must believe and project that they have a clear vision of the future. They must be self-disclosive about their own anxieties and their own commitment to making diversity work for the organization. In short, the effective manager provides a model that others can see and emulate. Diversity must become part of the strategic thinking of the organization.

For managers who would say, "Why stir all of that up?" the response is that regardless of whether you stir it up, in a diverse environment these feelings already lie below the surface and are having a major impact on the productivity of the organization as well as the general quality of work life.

As a beginning, the organization must first identify the target groups within the organization that make it diverse. If not already available through human resources, data need to be collected to identify the demographics of the organization.

Once that is done, or simultaneously with the research component, it is useful for the organization to examine and reconstruct its mission statement to incorporate a strong position on diversity. In the early stages of implementation, this mission statement needs to be widely publicized.

Also, during the research component, qualitative data need to be collected on current attitudes toward and experiences with diversity issues in the organization. Answer the question, "What problems are we having with diversity?" These could range from concrete problems such as language difficulty and cultural orientation to the more abstract concerns of prejudice and discrimination. While paper-and-pencil surveys can be useful to get a sampling of attitudes, the value of the data from this source is highly dependent on how many people respond and who the respondents are. It is recommended, for the best results in collecting qualitative data, that focus groups be set up, consisting of both homogeneous and heterogeneous target groups in the organization. The focus groups are useful for several reasons. First, they send a signal to the population at large that the organization is serious about developing a diversity initiative. Second, assuming the focus groups are set up so as to represent an accurate sample of the total population, the participants can be pretested to establish a benchmark for measurement of the intervention effect.

This can be done in a number of ways. However, the most effective measure of qualitative data under these circumstances has proven to be a Q-sort of value statements. Focus groups also enable the discovery of opinion leaders from the target groups. These individuals can be approached to determine their willingness to be part of an ongoing resource group.

The next phase incorporates both a development component and a workshop component. Having identified members of the staff who are both opinion leaders and willing to serve as members of the resource group, the resource group is set up and begins to meet, with the charge to help with the development and presentation of diversity issues within the organization.

One innovative way to facilitate the collection of resource material would be for the organization to sponsor a conference or symposium on diversity. This conference could be done in house, with invited participants, or it could be done in association with some other institution, such as a local college or university. Such an event would enable the resource group, human resources staff, outside consultants, and any other parties involved in the development of this program to acquire a range of materials, including videotape for behavior modeling, which could later be used in the workshop component.

It is also important that corporate communications presents and positions the diversity initiative in an important and prominent way. Too often, programs of this sort appear on the back page of the newsletter after the announcement for the company picnic and the scores for the bowling league.

The workshops will vary with the size and character of the organization. They can range from half-day to full-day sessions. They can be stand-alone or be integrated as part of a broader training effort. The important thing is that they reach everyone in some way.

Content and methodology for these workshops will also vary. However, a successful workshop would include at least the following:

- A discussion and clarification of the organization's Equal Employment Opportunity (EEO) policy and its mission statement incorporating its commitment to diversity
- A presentation from members of the employee resource group
- Some behavior modeling, perhaps a video from the conference or symposium held as part of the development component
- Some training on communicating in a diverse workplace, focusing on such issues as the role of values in communication and language "bypassing"
- At least one activity that tasks the participants with developing an action plan for managing or working more effectively in a culturally diverse work environment

On the assumption that the acknowledgment and transition phases of the intervention have been successful, what the organization should have as a result is a more sensitive, better informed, and more trusting work force. With the diversity issue under control, the organization has a better opportunity to experience success with a total quality orientation.

During this phase, the resource group continues to function as a quality-monitoring group. Periodic focus groups should be convened to do posttest analysis of the progress being made with regard to attitude change.

Some have said that EEO and diversity are, at best, temporary issues. Within a short time, diversity will be the reality in the workplace. However, the basic underlying objectives—sensitivity, understanding differences, cooperation, and respect and trust for one another in the workplace—are what should exist with or without the issue of diversity. We spend much of our lives in the workplace, and if we subscribe to the basic tenet of quality—treat employees as you would have them treat the customers—this is a good place to start. It is the human resources manager who leads the charge.

CHAPTER 7

Motivating Survivors

Perhaps one of the manager's most difficult challenges within today's survivor organizations is motivating a survivor employee base. Before the current downsizing revolution, organizations and their managers could design intrinsically and extrinsically framed methods of employee motivation. This was largely because job security was dependent upon a person's ability to perform a job, as well as simply perform the tasks assigned. Workers perceived that those employees who showed up on time; performed their jobs well; and expressed some enthusiasm about their work, their companies, their bosses, and their colleagues generally got to keep their jobs as long as they wanted. In return, the unwritten employer–employee contract promised good pay, a secure job, health benefits, regular vacation and sick time, and a comfortable retirement plan.

Nowadays, managers operate in a strange new world where the game has radically changed, the playing field is full of land mines, and the previous rules no longer apply. When employees in a downsizing organization begin to see once-valuable and -productive workers let go, all reason flies out the window; and the ensuing earthquake produces aftershocks that never quite cease. Managers and their employees alike know that anyone's job security is, at best, precarious, and that traditional compacts of productive work for job security are no longer in force. To rebuild the downsized and restructured organization, we need those very survivor managers and employees to lead the new organization into a successful future. While loyalty to one's corporation or organization seems archaic and unrealistic, we must formulate new contracts of motivation with employees to revitalize a work force and reenergize an organization.

MOTIVATIONAL THEORIES WITHIN
ORGANIZATIONAL CONTEXTS

By taking a closer look at the continuum of motivational theories practiced in corporations and organizations in the twentieth century, we can begin to build contemporary models for employee motivation and productivity.

ABRAHAM MASLOW—HIERARCHY OF HUMAN NEEDS

Abraham Maslow's Hierarchy of Human Needs is perhaps the most widely known and studied theory of motivation and holds a primarily internal focus of needs satisfaction as it relates to individual fulfillment for both personal and professional needs. Maslow's emerging theory first took shape in the early 1940s with the publication of a seminal article, "A Theory of Human Motivation," in *Psychological Review* in 1943. His needs-based theory was further articulated and applied to both work and personal situations in subsequent works, including *Motivation and Personality* (1954), *Eupsychian Management* (1965), and *Toward a Psychology of Being* (1968).

Maslow's Hierarchy of Human Needs (see Figure 7.1) arranges five categories of needs in a pyramidal structure. Several assumptions are made concerning a person's relationship to these needs. First, Maslow infers that the fulfillment of human needs proceeds from basic, low-level needs up a vertical ladder to high-level wants and needs. Second, the hierarchy implies that once a need is satisfied, it no longer becomes a motivator. A person is then compelled to move up the ladder—he or she replaces a lower, satisfied need with a higher-level, unsatisfied need. Certainly, this hierarchy is a dynamic model of motivation, since, depending on life circumstances, a person can be at any level of the hierarchy.

The lower-level needs—physiological, security, and belongingness—are also referred to as deficiency needs. The two higher-level needs are also known as growth needs, and include esteem and self-actualization. The value of this hierarchy to a manager who is attempting to provide motivational factors for his or her employees rests in its use as a diagnostic tool for assessing the present levels of motivation.

Deficiency needs encompass those needs which must be satisfied to ensure the physical and psychological health of an employee. The first level, physiological needs, includes those factors which must be fulfilled in order to sustain life: air, water, food, sleep, rest, and relaxation. While in the past we could assert that a full-time job and its accompanying paycheck usually took care of a worker's physiological needs, today's precarious economic and business environment makes this a lesser certainty. For example, many well-paid middle managers have experienced downsizing and have found themselves out the doors of large corporations, despite their ability to do valuable work and "play by the rules." Suddenly, they

Figure 7.1
Maslow's Hierarchy of Needs

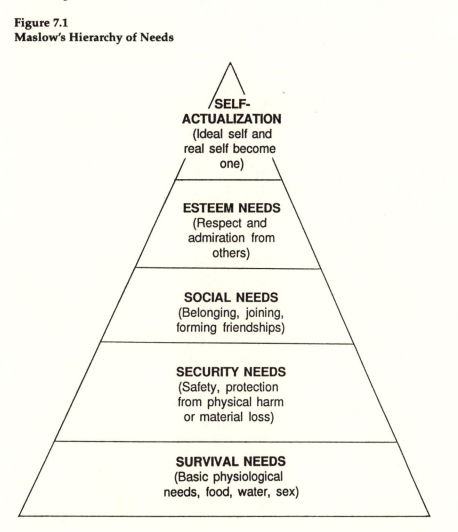

find themselves in a position where the need to put food on their tables becomes more than an abstract concern.

Security or safety needs include our desire for freedom from harm, financial security, and emotional security. The recent rash of workplace-violence incidents, sometimes perpetrated against management of a company which has laid off a disgruntled employee, makes this need a very real one, even for survivors and their managers who are well up the hierarchy and working on their growth needs.

Most employees in today's work force are particularly preoccupied with their financial and emotional security needs, since the employer–employee contract of long-term employment for a job well done becomes less of a viable model of motivation. The current trend for downsized professionals to resort to a variety of part-time consulting positions (often created by downsized companies who are outsourcing and reluctant to hire additional full-time employees) can markedly exacerbate the importance of having to fulfill basic security needs. A growing concern, particularly among working-class and middle-class people, which adds to the critical place of security needs in our current society is the decreasing availability of both health and retirement benefits for many employees in the work force. Once assumed as part of a full-time position, these necessary benefits are also eroding.

The last and highest level of deficiency needs, belongingness, includes the needs for love, affection, and friendship, and for approval, acceptance, and inclusiveness. Current workplace situations, which often dismantle entire departments and areas of previously tightly knit working groups, can have powerful negative effects on the satisfaction of belongingness needs for today's survivors. When a downsizing occurs, not only does the strength of belongingness and affiliation begin to fade among once-intact working groups; the survivor employee also begins to experience distrust and distance toward his or her employer. Any pride in being affiliated with a particular corporation or organization tends to disappear. It can be difficult, if not impossible, for a survivor to feel any sense of camaraderie; acceptance; and, most important, loyalty toward an employer who has been responsible for letting go productive and once-valuable employees.

The two higher-level growth needs include esteem and self-actualization. Esteem consists of two related groups of needs. These include achievement and independence, as well as recognition, rewards, prestige, and increased status. In a reorganized and reengineered working environment, it becomes critical for the survivors to rebuild their self-confidence and self-esteem both through successes in new organizational roles and through the ability to achieve tangible rewards for their efforts. Managers must pay close attention to these needs and provide many opportunities to fulfill these important needs for their survivors.

The apex of the hierarchy includes self-actualization needs, which refer to a person's continuing ability to strive to be the best in what he or she can be—both professionally and personally. Theoretically, once a person has fulfilled the four previous needs, he or she is free to pursue growth opportunities for increased achievement. Quests for new challenges, skills, knowledge, creativity, and innovation are all a part of the need for self-actualization. When a restructured and reorganized organization can provide its employees with opportunities for further education and training as well as with well-defined career paths within the organization, the fulfillment of survivors' self-actualization needs becomes a distinct and important reality, with many benefits to the health and success of that organization over the long term.

FREDERICK HERZBERG—TWO-FACTOR
THEORY OF MOTIVATION

In the 1959 book, *The Motivation to Work,* the Two-Factor Theory of Motivation was originally articulated. Based upon workplace research conducted with professionals, Herzberg and his colleagues noticed that those work factors which produced positive feelings and feedback were those related to job content. When people felt good about their jobs, it was because something had happened that showed that they were doing their jobs well or becoming more expert in their field. Negative feelings about their jobs were more often associated with external, or environmental, aspects at work. Herzberg categorized the job-content factors as *satisfiers;* he termed the external and environmental factors hygiene or maintenance factors, and these were labeled *dissatisfiers.* Table 7.1 summarizes the characteristics of Herzberg's Two-Factor Theory of Motivation.

The importance of Herzberg's theory begins to become apparent as we analyze the effect of both dissatisfiers and satisfiers on the satisfaction and productivity levels of employees. To maintain a well-motivated and

Table 7.1
Satisfaction and Dissatisfaction

Satisfiers (Job-Content Factors)	Dissatisfiers (External/Environmental Factors: Hygiene or Maintenance Factors)
Achievement	Company Policy and Administration
Recognition	Supervision
Work Itself	Salary
Responsibility	Interpersonal Relations
Advancement	Working Conditions
Growth	Status
	Job Security

healthy working environment, today's manager should pay close attention to fulfilling both satisfier and dissatisfier factors for his or her employees. However, only the presence of intrinsically focused satisfiers will contribute to increasing an employee's motivation and productivity. By satisfying acceptable levels of dissatisfiers, employers and managers are fulfilling important needs; research and practice show that the fulfillment of these factors has no direct correlation to the increase in an employee's motivational drive or productivity output. From another perspective, we can say that fulfilling dissatisfier needs is a short-term intervention to prevent dissatisfaction and unhappiness in the workplace. When we can contribute to fulfilling the satisfier needs of our employees, we initiate a long-term strategy of individual growth and achievement that will benefit both employee and organization within a broader context.

DAVID MCCLELLAND—NEED ACHIEVEMENT THEORY

Beginning in the early 1950s, David McClelland began to develop a theory of motivation in the workplace. Because, according to McClelland, our society places high values on achievement, power, and affiliation, an employee can be motivated by opportunities in the working environment that will enable him or her to fulfill these needs. With the application of the Need Achievement Theory, we are matching an employee's intrinsic motivators with extrinsic opportunities and rewards provided by an organization.

Need for Achievement

Employees who exhibit a high need for achievement are task oriented, goal driven, and prefer a considerable degree of autonomy. They often seek additional work and responsibilities and expect recognition and rewards for their efforts. Frequently, they display an entrepreneurial style in approaching their work and engage in considerable innovative behavior. McClelland's findings reveal that managers with a high need for achievement often practice a participative management style, encouraging openness and flexibility within their departments.

When managing and motivating survivors who exhibit a need for achievement, it is important to provide frequent challenges in their work as well as regular feedback and recognition for their accomplishments. If the work itself is perceived as interesting, challenging, and meaningful, a significant amount of motivation and productivity can result from those employees.

Need for Power

The need to control and influence others can reveal a strong need for power among some employees. Power is often exhibited by an employee's need to remain informed about organizational business and events, as well as his or her desire to influence the behavior of others. McClelland distinguishes between personalized and socialized power in the workplace. The personalization of power can result in damaging consequences in an organization, since self-aggrandizing and manipulative behavior toward other employees can be antithetical to achieving work goals in today's team-based environment. Socialized power can act as a catalyst for motivating employees toward success and goal completion.

When using socialized power, a participative style of management and teamwork is often practiced, and a synergy is formed among employees involved in their work efforts. By assisting teams in setting both challenging and achievable goals and by providing tangible and frequent recognition and rewards, managers in survivor organizations can utilize their need for power in order to achieve motivation among employees, all for the benefit of the larger organization.

Need for Affiliation

Employees and managers who exhibit high-affiliation needs emphasize the importance of close and friendly working relationships with their colleagues. While experiencing a downsizing or restructuring within their organizations, high-affiliation-need employees can frequently have heightened feelings of anxiety and survivor guilt, particularly as trusted coworkers and colleagues are let go.

Because the employee with a high need for affiliation has often spent considerable time building and maintaining good relations with his or her colleagues, the sudden breaking up of those relationships can be quite unsettling. Besides feeling guilty about not being let go, the survivor employee can experience resentment and anger toward the organization for eroding a previously well-functioning group of employees.

For survivor managers with a high-affiliation need, having to both lay off and reassign employees can also be most upsetting and traumatic. Because managers feel a good amount of loyalty to and investment in employees, severing all or part of those relationships can cause unproductive and resentful feeling toward the organization and the situation on the part of survivor managers. Loss of face with once-trusting employees can be a most difficult issue with survivor managers. It is no surprise that their relationships with their own managers can undergo upheavals and periods of mistrust and anger. It is critical that management responsible for orchestrating a downsizing or restructuring pay special attention to its managers and supervisors whose high need for affiliation might impede progress toward forming the new organization. These survivor managers need to be included as early as possible in collaborating with management on the process. They need to fully understand the reasons for the elimination or reassignment of certain employees, as well as have a solid sense of the vision and purpose of the new organization. By having a sense of control and understanding, not only can they make valuable contributions to management regarding appropriate downsizing decisions, but they can become critical allies who can lead the organization down a successful path.

CLAYTON P. ALDERFER—ERG THEORY

The ERG (Existence, Relatedness, and Growth) Theory of Motivation, initially proposed by the publication of Alderfer's *Existence, Relatedness and Growth* (1972), builds upon Maslow's needs-based theory yet disagrees with Maslow that human needs must be satisfied in a hierarchical order. Alderfer believes that people can have one, two, or three needs that require satisfaction simultaneously. Alderfer's needs include existence (which is very much like Maslow's physiological and safety needs), relatedness (parallel to Maslow's social and belongingness needs as well as McClelland's need for affiliation), and growth (which mirrors Maslow's top need for self-actualization). When employees are frustrated in realizing one of their needs, Alderfer posits that this intensifies the achievement of the other two ERG theory needs. For example, he believes that employees who feel a deficiency in satisfaction of growth needs within their organization will compensate for it by emphasizing the fulfillment of both existence needs and relatedness needs. They might spend a good deal of their time both cultivating interpersonal relationships with colleagues and managers and attempting to gain reassurance that their job and position are secure over the long term. When a change is occurring within the organization, managers and supervisors need to monitor the "needs pulse" of their employees and, where they know certain employees will be retained by the new organization, provide the support and encouragement to those employees to ensure a smooth transition for them. This prescription speaks equally well for management staff, who must be allies and catalysts for effecting the organizational change.

DOUGLAS M. MCGREGOR—THEORY X AND THEORY Y

McGregor's Theory X and Theory Y concepts of motivation, as initially proposed in *The Human Side of Enterprise* (1960), present us with a perceptual framework for shaping the fulfillment of human needs within an organization. For McGregor, how employees respond to their work and exhibit motivation and productivity is contingent upon the external conditions the organization and its management establish toward those employees.

While researching the often rocky relationships between management and labor in organizations, McGregor began to postulate that conflicting interpersonal relations are frequently caused by the perceptual framework sometimes enacted by management toward its labor-based work force. These observations led to the formulation of McGregor's Theory X.

Theory X

- The average human being has an inherent dislike of work and will avoid it if at all possible.
- Because of this human characteristic of dislike of work, most people must be coerced, controlled, directed, and threatened with punishment to get them to put forth adequate effort toward the achievement of organizational goals and objectives.
- The average human being prefers to be directed, wishes to avoid responsibility, has relatively little ambition, and wants security above all.

Theory X presupposes a highly coercive and punishing form of management and motivation where productivity is first and foremost and where workers' needs and ambitions are largely discounted. It is no wonder that an adversarial relationship between management and its workers is established in this type of working environment.

McGregor's research also found that a different perceptual framework could be developed between management and employees, which would not only improve productivity and goals achievement but would also foster individual needs satisfaction, increase good management–employee relationships, and build an organizational construct where both individual and organizational achievements could be met and recognized. This motivational theory is known as Theory Y.

Theory Y

- The expenditure of physical and mental effort in work is as natural for human beings as is play or rest.
- Human beings will exercise self-direction and self-control to achieve objectives to which they are committed.
- Commitment to objectives is dependent upon the satisfaction associated with their achievement.
- The average human being learns, under proper conditions, not only to accept but to seek responsibility.
- The capacity to exercise a relatively high degree of imagination, ingenuity, and creativity in the solution of organizational problems is widely, not narrowly, distributed in the general population.
- Under the conditions of modern industrial life, the intellectual potentialities of the average human being is only partially utilized.

Essentially, because today's American work force is historically the most educated and cognizant of the importance of working within an organization where both individual and organizational needs and goals are achieved, a Theory Y framework of motivation will enable both management and employees to realize a productive, harmonious, and adaptable working environment. By having a strong human relations base, an organization is often well-prepared to weather the storms of organizational change over the long term.

WILLIAM G. OUCHI—THEORY Z

With W. G. Ouchi's 1981 book, *Theory Z: How American Business Can Meet the Japanese Challenge*, we see the introduction of a new motivational paradigm, taking its initial cue from McGregor's Theory Y but expanding that model into a recommendation for organizational transformation. Based upon his study of Western (including American) businesses, Ouchi criticized the seemingly short-term, strongly hierarchical, and narrow-focused management style prevalent in many organizations. Because formulation of company policies and procedures, as well as strategic decision making and problem solving, was frequently occurring only at the executive levels of many Western organizations, not only did workers not always understand their importance in their contribution to organizational goals and objectives but management was losing key opportunities to gain worker expertise and loyalty. For Ouchi, the traditional Western style of management fostered specialized training, which perpetuated tunnel vision among workers, as well as a focus on short-term instead of long-term employment. It was, therefore, not surprising that Western management and its workers were often seen to be at odds with one another.

Theory Z introduces a participative, team-based style of management which emphasizes open, informal, and trusting relationships between management and its employees; frequent, broad-based training which produces generalists who are flexible in their job roles; employee participation in organizational decision making; a group orientation toward work; and empowerment of employees. As companies and organizations grapple with economic uncertainties and large-scale restructurings, a participative approach to managing change often enables a smoother transition into the new organization and can minimize widespread distrust and potential backlash.

VICTOR VROOM—EXPECTANCY/VALENCY THEORY

Victor Vroom's research on employee motivation, outlined in *Work and Motivation* (1964), proposes an expectancy (or goal-path) model for predicting employee expenditure of effort to achieve organizational goals and objectives. For Vroom, the behavior of an employee is largely dependent upon how well that employee perceives that conditions exist which make the achievement of goals and objectives possible; this produces an expectancy framework. Several characteristics define expectancy, including effort, which is the outlay of individual energy, and instrumentality, which is the probability that the expenditure of energy will yield the desirable outcomes. An additional dimension to Expectancy Theory is valence—the positive or negative values employees associate with behavior outcomes. The more positively employees view the work they perform, the more strongly they will be committed to successfully completing that work and receiving the perceived rewards of their efforts.

Certainly, a key component of increasing and maintaining employee motivation remains being able to provide tangible rewards, both nonmonetary and fiscally based, to excellent employees who achieve organizational objectives. Appreciation for an employee's output increases the likelihood not only that the employee will see a direct correlation between his or her effort and the final work product but also that the employee will be more likely to continue that behavior and exhibit a commitment to his or her work and the organization.

L. W. PORTER AND
EDWARD E. LAWLER—INTRINSIC/EXTRINSIC

L. W. Porter and E. E. Lawler provide an intrinsic as well as extrinsic motivational model for diagnosing individual outputs within organizations. With the publication of *Managerial Attitudes and Performance* (1968), they assert that employees exert energy and effort toward their work in direct correlation to the internal psychological benefits they perceive that they will receive, as well as to the external rewards to be gleaned from their organization for successful work completed. They believe that the more people are rewarded for their outputs, the greater the possibility that their work behaviors will be repeated. They also feel that these positive behaviors can often yield additional productive behaviors in employees. Three factors contribute to an employee's motivational level: the expected rewards as a result of expended energy and effort, the actual effort, and the actual reward. The reward must be in balance with the quality and quantity of the effort expended, and it presupposes that the employee must value both the reward and the effort it will take to achieve that reward.

As we have been emphasizing, employees today have strong needs to fulfill intrinsic motivational forces as well as to receive appropriate rewards from their organizations for their individual work efforts. The less internal motivation, external reinforcement, or both that people receive, the greater the likelihood that their commitment level will be significantly diminished. Particularly as a company or organization experiences major change, care must be taken to provide frequent feedback and reward mechanisms to maintain equilibrium and productivity.

HAROLD KELLEY AND JOHN THIBAUT—EQUITY THEORY

As a major influence on Social Exchange Theory, Harold Kelley and John Thibaut's *Interpersonal Relations: A Theory of Interdependence* (1978) examines how people conduct and evaluate their interpersonal relationships, particularly as they perceive an equity factor. Relationships between people can be viewed as economic transactions where the parties consider both the costs and rewards associated with those relationships.

Extending this concept into the workplace, we arrive at Equity Theory. Based upon social comparison, the theory states that if employees perceive a discrepancy between their output and their rewards and other employees' outputs and rewards, an inequity will be felt. Employees tend to focus on comparing themselves to similarly referenced other employees, in terms of work outputs, education, expertise, training, and so on. Not surprising, those employees who perceive that they are underrewarded in comparison to others not only feel that they are being treated unfairly but also will often expend less energy and exhibit less motivation in future work efforts unless that perceived inequity is taken care of.

From motivational, legal, and practical points of view, perceptions of equity and inequity among employees in the workplace need to be taken seriously. As companies and organizations make difficult choices and downsize certain employees, factors such as fair treatment, the actual value of an employee and his or her work efforts, the real potential for costly litigation in light of questionable downsizings, and the importance of providing a fair and equitable working environment are critical for any employer.

EDWIN LOCKE—GOAL-SETTING THEORY

Locke proposes that what essentially motivates employees, whether it is exhibited by perceptions of expected rewards or our perceived equity or inequity as compared to other employees, is generated by the goals and incentives that underlie the working relationship between employer and employee. The goals themselves must be specific, achievable, moderate in terms of difficulty level, and relevant to an employee's work and his or her value of individual efforts. Mutual goal setting and participation of employees in the process, as well as frequent feedback to employees, contribute to the successful completion of organizational goals and objectives.

Organizations that are able to provide specific indicators for successful job completion and include employee participation in the goal-setting process as well as provide rewards for their achievement can both increase individual motivation and productivity and improve organizational climate and profitability. As managers, we must provide realistic measures for successful workplace behavior, frequent feedback and rewards, and a sense of equity to motivate employees on a continuing basis.

BURRHUS F. SKINNER—REINFORCEMENT THEORY

From the approach of behavioral psychology, B. F. Skinner's Reinforcement Theory of motivation proposes that people produce and replicate certain behaviors in response to reinforcing conditions that are present in their working environment. The more a person is rewarded for a specific behavior, the greater the likelihood that the behavior will continue. Conversely, behavior which is not positively rewarded or reinforced and behavior which receives negative reinforcement will tend to diminish and possibly cease without the presence of external reinforcing conditions.

The importance of frequent communications, regular feedback, meaningful work, and tangible rewards between management and employees cannot be overemphasized, particularly within an organizational environment affected by internal and external change mechanisms.

DANIEL YANKELOVICH—DISCRETIONARY EFFORT

In 1983, Daniel Yankelovich, longtime researcher and significant contributor to motivation theory and its meaning to the American work force, published a report detailing an increasingly prevailing phenomenon influencing our self-motivation. *Putting the Work Ethic to Work: A Public Agenda Report on Restoring America's Competitive Vitality* outlines the importance of discretionary effort in determining motivation among workers. Discretionary effort refers to the effort and the quality of the effort that workers apply to their jobs. This effort is independent of what is expected of workers either by their employers, the actual nature of the work performed, or both.

Discretionary effort has to do with the work force's increasing independence in being able to control how and when to perform certain job tasks and responsibilities, how to pace their day-to-day work, how to solve problems, how to structure their day, and so on. While a higher proportion of high-skilled, white-collar workers report a substantial increase in their discretionary effort, this factor is rapidly becoming more prevalent among all types of workers and has become a way of life for those working within a virtual office environment.

While our traditional motivational theories would support the idea that, for high-skilled workers, in particular, an increase in the discretionary-effort factor should cause a correlative increase in motivation and productivity, Yankelovich found that this was not always the case. He found that a commitment gap existed between what workers were able to contribute to perform their job at a high-quality level and what their actual performance was. In fact, when 845 white-collar and blue-collar American workers were questioned, they themselves admitted their lagging motivation:

The Public Agenda found that fewer than one out of four jobholders (23%) say that they are currently working at their full potential. Nearly half of all jobholders (44%) say that they do not put much effort into their jobs over and above what is required to hold on to a job. The overwhelming majority (75%) say that they could be significantly more effective on their jobs than they are now.[1]

Although this report was researched and published more than a decade ago, we begin to make connections between the motivational needs and desires of the 1980s and 1990s worker. If anything, given the technological revolution which has transformed corporations and organizations, both white-collar and blue-collar workers have increased discretionary effort in the individual management of their jobs. In fact, the message put forth by organizations with more frequency these days advises employees that they alone are responsible for managing their jobs and their careers. The paternalistic view that companies take care of valued employees over the long term is no longer valid.

Yankelovich observed in 1983 that the primary reason for this commitment gap was that managers were failing to provide a positive motivational climate for their employees. He believed that organizations perpetuated outmoded motivational and reward systems which were not satisfying the needs, attitudes, and values of the contemporary work force.

With more than a passing nod to Frederick Herzberg, Yankelovich recommended that managers should focus on factors related more to motivational and job-achievement dimensions—such as interesting work, opportunity for growth and advancement, and the like—rather than solely on those factors which contributed to job satisfaction, that is, company policy and administration, good interpersonal relations, status, and so on. Managers also needed to recognize those employees who expend extra effort in the performance and completion of their work and should reward those employees on a regular basis.

Yankelovich also recommended that organizations and their managers pay closer attention to raising the standards of quality for both organizational and employee benefit and that the old hierarchical structure of organizing and implementing work should be discarded in favor of a flattened, horizontal organizational design. More than ten years ago, Yankelovich foresaw the transformation of the work force and workplace necessary to restore American corporations' competitiveness in an increasingly global economy.

As we take our motivational journey progressively through the turbulent 1990s and beyond, we begin to understand that while organizational and work force dynamics may continue to swirl in a vast sea of change, the needs and desires of people wishing to make a decent living as well as accomplish great things will not. The apparent reality that has shifted many working Americans' motivational perspectives is that workers are striving to accomplish their jobs in a successful manner but that the underlying commitment is now to themselves and their careers, not their current employers.

In the 1993 Families and Work Institute report, *The Changing Workforce: Highlights of the National Study*, 99 percent of the surveyed working respondents strongly agreed or agreed that they always try to perform their job well, regardless of what it takes; 97 percent of those same respondents asserted that, when required by their jobs, they commit to work very hard. However, when asked about how loyal they felt toward their employers, 27 percent answered extremely, 37 percent very, 29 percent somewhat, 4 percent not very, and 2 percent not at all.

Regarding specific motivators that indicate individual measures of success in work life, we see that the majority of workers desire those long-term factors which address internal ambitions and drives rather than factors which solely enhance job satisfaction. Of those surveyed, 52 percent indicated that workplace success means personal satisfaction from doing a good job; 30 percent cited that earning the respect or recognition of supervisors and peers was important; 22 percent cited getting ahead or advancing in job or career; 21 percent felt that making a good income was a measure of success; 12 percent stated that feeling that their work is important was critical; and 6 percent indicated that having control over their work content and schedule was a critical component in defining success for them in their jobs.[2]

While managers are also vulnerable to organizational change, and often more so than survivor employees, they can gain strength and perspective as well as a sense of stability throughout the course of change if they keep focused on and committed to their most important resource—the human spirit.

CHAPTER 8

Enabling Higher Levels
of Initiative

While Chapter 7 examined how survivor managers can positively motivate their work force from a macro perspective, this chapter provides
methods for establishing the kind of climate and relationships that lead to
increased motivation; productivity; renewed vitality; and, in short, the realignment of the survivor.

Much has been said so far about the survivor employee and about the
type of management necessary to deal with that survivor employee from
a conceptual perspective. However, before managers can lead effectively
or motivate, they must first define and understand their own significant
role in the achievement of business objectives. Managers also must apply
a series of tools to analyze their operation and to use nontraditional creative strategies for solving business problems.

MANAGEMENT DEFINED

No one has to tell today's manager that the job is changing. Someone
once defined *management* as "hanging wallpaper in a whirlwind." Managers today are finding that they are expected to do more with less and, of
course, with the highest quality. Presented with the type of responsibilities
demanded of management today, these are some of the questions that
managers are asking:

- How will my job change?
- What will happen to my current work relationships?
- I know I am good at my job, but how can I get others to work harder?

- How am I going to accomplish what I have to do if I cannot get my colleagues to be responsive to my needs?

There are many components that add up to effective management. Managing survivors adds a new wrinkle to the process; and over time, managers will develop more sophisticated techniques through experience, education, or some combination of the two. What we present in this chapter are practical strategies to provide some control and develop some momentum along the management track.

Successful managers need to develop their competence with task issues such as planning, staffing, and allocating resources and personnel, as well as with people issues such as delegation, motivation, influencing, and coaching (which will be discussed in detail in Chapter 10).

The term *management* derives from "mano," meaning "hand." In its early forms, *to manage* meant to handle or train horses by using a long rope and standing in the center while moving the horse around in a circle. This image of a person controlling the movement and pace of others while standing at a distance is a good one for a manager to keep in mind as he or she develops a perspective of what being a manager in a survivor environment means. Management is a dynamic process that is always in motion. It is in a constant state of development. The manager must also be in a constant state of development. The primary development issues for managers are:

- Staff development
- Organizational development
- Self-development

Table 8.1 illustrates several defined areas for management competency under each of these major headings. While it is our purpose to provide strategies and innovations for management at all levels, our key target is the new "middle manager" who has found himself or herself in the sometimes-unenviable position of doing more with less and trying to do it better. In addition to those mentioned in Table 8.1, there are three competencies which span all three major headings: using influence, consulting and contracting, and negotiating.

The flattening of organizational structures has not eliminated the need for middle management, but it has radically changed the character of the type of management occurring at that level. One of the first problems is to define where the middle is in an organization. We define a *middle manager* as an individual with management responsibility for people at supervisory levels and a reporting relationship to another manager below the company CEO.

Table 8.1
Managers' Development Issues

STAFF DEVELOPMENT	ORGANIZATIONAL DEVELOPMENT	SELF-DEVELOPMENT
Motivation	Strategic Planning	Stress Management
Delegation	Articulating a Vision	Time Management
Discipline	Finding Good People	Problem Solving
Managing Meetings	Keeping Good People	Decision Making
Appraisal	Building a Team	Communication
Coaching	Creative Problem Solving	Presentation
Counseling		Building a Support Group

We have already discussed several points highlighted in surveys by Yankelovich, the Families and Work Institute, and others that are underlying factors in our approach to managing survivors. Because technology, among other things, has increased the amount of discretion in the workplace, today's workers—and particularly the survivors—are resentful of authority and tend to demand greater autonomy. These are the underlying causes for the commitment gap and the erosion in work behaviors.

Despite the fact that the commitment gap is causing lags in productivity, there is still a broadly shared endorsement of the work ethic in all sectors of the American work force. Studies by Yankelovich and others show that a majority of the work force still describe themselves as having an inner need to do the very best job that they can, regardless of pay. Fewer than one-third of the work force polled reject the work ethic in favor of other motivations, such as work as a pure financial transaction. Nearly two-thirds say that they would prefer a boss who was demanding in the name of high-quality work.

One of the most striking findings of recent work force research concerns the effect of new cultural values. Many younger jobholders bring a new set of self-development and expressive values to their work. In the 1960s and 1970s, these values were not always translated into commitment in the workplace. Many of our best-educated young people sought to fulfill their values—desire for autonomy, inner growth, and a connection with na-ture—outside of the workplace through the pursuit of leisure. Now that affluence can no longer be taken for granted, younger, better-educated job-holders are discovering that the new values are in no way inconsistent with hard and effective work. In fact, expressive values actually reinforce and enhance the work ethic when people who focus on personal growth hold jobs that can serve as an outlet for self-expression and self-develop-ment. Opportunities for self-expression and self-development are, once again, key building blocks for realigning the survivors.

More than seven out of ten jobholders surveyed who endorse the new cultural values also subscribe to a strong work ethic. They feel an inner need to do the best job possible, regardless of pay. We are left with the fol-lowing questions then: If workers have an inner need to give their best to their jobs, and if increasingly they have a great deal of control over their level of effort on the job, what is preventing them from giving more to their work? Why do they hold back, and what steps can be taken to encourage them to give more?

Part of that answer is obvious and has already been discussed in detail: the loss of loyalty and the development of suspicion and cynicism toward the organization. In addition to the erosion of the traditional relationship, research findings suggest that the problem, in its simplest terms, arises from the fact that managerial skill and training have not kept pace with the changes that have affected the workplace. The trend toward greater dis-cretion on the job and the push for "empowerment" are outrunning present managerial practices.

Current managerial systems and incentives are out of sync with chang-ing values and attitudes. As a result, the actions of managers blunt rather than stimulate and reinforce the underlying work ethic.

Yankelovich and Immerwahr have drawn conclusions based on the dis-tinction between motivating factors and satisfying factors, discussed in the previous chapter. They claim that it helps to explain the somewhat ambiva-lent feelings that American jobholders have about their managers. Many people like and respect their managers. Based on their surveys, nearly seven out of ten workers, when asked, said that their managers were more interested in getting the job done than just bossing people around. Six out of ten said that morale in their place of work was good or excellent.

But the positive feelings that Americans have about their jobs and man-agers change dramatically when the focus shifts from satisfaction to pro-ductiveness. Three-fourths of the work force (75%) believe that the inability of managers to motivate the work force is a key reason why people are working less than they could.

A focus on job satisfaction, in other words, does not necessarily enhance work ethic values. If managers want to capitalize on the considerable human potential that already exists in the work force, they must focus on the key motivators that will realign workers in a productive way and not confuse those motivators with satisfiers which, although nice to have, do not necessarily yield more productivity.[1]

DEVELOPING A PERSPECTIVE AND GAINING OBJECTIVITY

It is our belief that all human progress begins with a self-inventory. The first thing a manager should do in assessing his or her situation is to ask himself or herself a few simple questions. The first question results in a short essay and addresses the changes being brought about in the survivor environment: How would I describe my tasks and responsibilities? The answer to that question should be stated in as behavioral a manner as possible. That is, what am I expected to do? How do I go about doing it? What am I responsible for? In the current work environment, rarely can a manager depend on being provided with a clear and accurate job description that tells him or her exactly how to handle the job. Asking this question provides a clear opportunity to interact with the human resources manager.

The second question to ask is this: What characteristics do I associate with good management? Developing this list of characteristics should point out that good management practices are not a mystery. Most managers, given an opportunity to examine the process, will come up with the same list, even though there may be variations in emphasis on various points.

The third question in the self-evaluation is perhaps the most difficult, since it asks the manager to examine some of his or her weaknesses: What knowledge, skill, or perception do I have to develop that would make a major difference in achieving my management objectives? One good approach to answering that question is to look at the list of characteristics associated with good management and divide them into those felt to be mastered already, those that could use some additional attention and development, and those for which there is little or no connection or comfort level.

The purpose of developing some sense of objectivity is to gain control. We believe that, in order to succeed, a manager must gain control in three areas:

1. Control of self
2. Control of tasks and responsibilities
3. Control of the people (below and above) with whom the manager interacts

The first step in controlling anything is to discover how it works. If you set out to control a machine, you would first learn as much as you could about it. You might read a manual, ask others who have had experience with it, and observe it on your own. People, however, do not come with manuals, so we must depend more on observation and on the experience of others to understand how they work. This concept of relying on observation and the experience of others is more difficult to apply to ourselves but is an important first step for developing good managerial behavior.

We recommend that a manager use the assessment process as part of survivor management. Admittedly, it takes some amount of courage to open up to criticism. However, managers who are unwilling to demonstrate their commitment to making changes by taking this kind of risk will find it very difficult to succeed in realigning their survivors.

The transition phase of survivor management can be greatly enhanced by a manager who initiates a 360-degree assessment. In this type of assessment, the manager evaluates himself or herself based on some list of competencies, has his or her subordinates make an evaluation based on the same list of competencies, and has his or her superior make the same evaluation.

There are several prepackaged 360-degree assessment instruments on the market. Some third party, either an outside consultant or the human resources manager, should be enlisted to conduct the assessment. This will help ensure confidentiality and, therefore, more honest responses from all of the parties involved.

One instrument we have used with great success is the *Manager Appraisal Profile (MAP)*, published by Education Research. The MAP, as it is called, quantifies 100 of the key managerial skills and behaviors by the frequency with which they are used. The end result is a composite performance appraisal, merging the three viewpoints: the manager's self-appraisal, the appraisal of the manager's superior, and the appraisal done by the manager's subordinates.

While all of the data from a 360-degree assessment are useful, perhaps the most important is the subordinate feedback. This adds a unique and helpful dimension to the manager's understanding of his or her own effectiveness. It provides a useful mirror of how others see and react to his or her skills and behavior. This critique becomes a springboard for change and helps to open communication.

This approach is particularly important in the survivor environment because it involves subordinates in a confidential and meaningful project. It also demonstrates that the manager is willing to become part of the change, not just the instigator of change. This willingness to be open to criticism and personal development fosters team building and participation, enhances morale, and contributes overall to a more healthy working climate.

The MAP divides the 100 management competencies into five basic categories:

1. Communications and interpersonal relations
2. Leadership, motivation, and supervision

3. Planning, time management, and administration
4. Problem solving and decision making
5. Training, development, and coaching

In addition to all of the positive outcomes already attributed to the 360-degree assessment, many managers will find both the categories and the competencies related to them helpful in defining management behavior. As an outgrowth of the self-assessment process, the manager is in a position to engage survivor employees in a future thinking and empowering exercise. Subordinates can now be asked to participate in the development of an ideal model of management competencies that, from their perspective, will best meet the needs and challenges of the organization.

We divide competencies into three dimensions: knowledge, skill, and perception. That is, there are certain behaviors that stand out—things that a manager must know about, skills that he or she must have, and intangibles and common-sense items that add up to perceptions.

Management competencies are also shaped by the particular requirements of the job tasks and responsibilities and by the environment of the organization. The purpose of a competency exercise is to formulate what the manager and his or her subordinates consider to be the ideal manager for their particular situation. The exercise is simple to do and can be conducted either as part of a group session or on an individual basis. Figure B.1 on page 201 is an example of a simple worksheet for management competencies.

Subordinates are asked to develop a list of competencies in each category by asking and answering the following questions:

1. What does a manager in our department need to *know* in order to accomplish the tasks and responsibilities of the job?
2. What does a manager in our department need to be able to *do* in order to accomplish the tasks and responsibilities of the job?
3. What does a manager in our department have to perceive *the need for*, be *intuitive about*, or be *sensitive to* in order to accomplish the tasks and responsibilities of the job?

Once these data are collected, it provides a fundamental view, from the survivor's perspective, of what the manager has to do (or become) in order to achieve the ideal.

The manager should engage in the exercise separately, listing what he or she feels are the primary competencies for the ideal manager. A simple comparison between the manager's version and the subordinates' version again provides a major opportunity for dialogue and subsequent understanding. Wherever possible, managers throughout the organization should engage in the same type of exercise so that a dialogue can be opened up across the organization at the management level as to what the necessary competencies are and to evaluate differences highlighted by conflicting ideals.

Communication-Behavior Checklist

The most visible part of a manager's behavior is the way he or she communicates with subordinates. All employees are sensitive to communication issues. However, survivors tend to be oversensitive; and, therefore, managers need to exercise particular care in the way they interact with their survivor subordinates.

The manager's communication behavior can either be punishing or rewarding. The following list of attributes provides a checklist for the manager to use in the self-assessment process. In order to ensure good communication, a manager should identify how many of these behaviors occur in the day-to-day patterns of working with others. The manager might also ask: To what extent do people voluntarily seek me out? To what extent do they contact me, share ideas and viewpoints with me, and include me in their personal and social activities?

Punishing behavior includes

- Monopolizing the conversation
- Interrupting
- Showing obvious disinterest
- Keeping a sour facial expression
- Withholding customary social cues such as greetings, nods, "uh-huh," and the like
- Throwing verbal barbs at others
- Using verbal put-downs
- Insulting or otherwise verbally abusing others
- Speaking dogmatically; not respecting others' opinions
- Complaining or whining excessively
- Criticizing excessively; fault finding
- Demanding one's way; refusing to negotiate or compromise
- Ridiculing others
- Patronizing or talking down to others
- Making others feel guilty
- Soliciting approval from others excessively
- Losing one's temper frequently or easily
- Playing "games" with people; manipulating or competing in subtle ways
- Throwing "gotcha's" at others; embarrassing or belittling others

- Telling lies; evading honest questions; refusing to level with others
- Overusing "should" language; pushing with words
- Displaying frustration frequently
- Making aggressive demands of others
- Diverting conversation capriciously; breaking others' train of thought
- Disagreeing routinely
- Restating others' ideas for them
- Asking loaded or accusing questions
- Overusing "why" questions
- Breaking confidences; failing to keep important promises
- Flattering others insincerely
- Joking at inappropriate times
- Bragging; showing off; talking only about self

Rewarding behavior includes

- Giving others a chance to express views or share information
- Listening attentively; hearing other person out
- Sharing one's self with others; smiling; greeting others
- Giving positive nonverbal messages of acceptance and respect for others
- Praising and complimenting others sincerely
- Expressing respect for values and opinions of others
- Giving suggestions constructively
- Compromising; negotiating; helping others succeed
- Talking positively and constructively
- Affirming feelings and needs of others
- Treating others as equals whenever possible
- Stating one's needs and desires honestly
- Delaying automatic reactions; not flying off the handle easily
- Leveling with others; sharing information and opinions openly and honestly
- Confronting others constructively on difficult issues
- Staying on the conversational topic until others have been heard
- Stating agreement with others when possible
- Questioning others openly and honestly; asking straightforward, nonloaded questions
- Keeping the confidence of others
- Giving one's word sparingly and keeping it
- Joking constructively and in good humor
- Expressing genuine interest in the other person

MANAGING GROUP PROCESS

It is one of the interesting factors in the current environment that, as the organization becomes flatter and employees become more involved cross-functionally, managers are still primarily responsible for defined territories. In the survivor environment, careful monitoring of the manager's own group is a management priority.

There are eight components of group process that astute managers can leverage for their success:

1. Involvement
2. Emotion
3. Affiliation
4. Opinion centers
5. Collaboration
6. Trust
7. Group maintenance
8. Commitment

Involvement

The involvement component relates to the number of people in the manager's charge and the intensity of their involvement in the work processes. Obviously, a high level of participation occurs when most of the group members are involved at an intense level. The involvement level is one of the easier process observations a manager can make—behaviors such as who talks to whom, how long they talk, general patterns of attendance, production levels, timing of deliverables, and so on.

Some things for the manager to watch for include the following:

- Who participates more than others?
- Who participates less?
- Are there any shifts in involvement (e.g., people who have been consistently involved suddenly becoming uninvolved, or vice versa)?
- How are those who appear to be uninvolved treated by the rest of their co-workers?
- How is their uninvolvement interpreted—consent, disagreement, disinterest, fear, and so on?
- What are the patterns of the relationships?
- Are there reasons for frequent interaction among the people who frequently interact?

Emotion

In the survivor environment, virtually every action or circumstance has an emotional envelope. Very strong feelings are frequently generated by interactions between survivors. Many of the topics surrounding the organization produce discomfort and a variety of individual emotional reactions, depending on how each person feels he or she either is or may be affected by what is going on.

The level of emotion is often betrayed through expressions, gestures, and many other forms of nonverbal cues that enable the manager to take the emotional temperature of his or her direct reports. Here are some things to monitor:

- Signs of anger, irritation, frustration, warmth, affection, excitement, boredom, defensiveness, or fear
- Attempts by members of the staff to block the expression of feelings, or a reluctance to discuss feelings when called upon to do so

Affiliation

Most survivors conduct themselves cautiously. They are not always certain that they want to be perceived as part of any particular group. Traditionally, individuals have a need to feel safe and secure in a group. Safety and security in the workplace are more psychological than physical. However, in the survivor environment, that safety and security has been removed by example. Any attempt to rally survivors to become an active part of a group may be met with initial resistance, which may be outspoken.

Survivors must make a conscious decision to realign themselves with the group before becoming comfortable as part of it. Once the decision is made, it becomes particularly important to ensure that all the survivors are included.

Survivors also have the need to feel effective and competent as part of the group. Insecurity about satisfying this need is at the root of many power struggles.

Managers must understand that in the survivor environment, employees are concerned about opening up and sharing personal values. While they are aware that working effectively requires that they get closer to each other, they are resistant to the idea of too much intimacy, particularly since either they or those with whom they interact may soon be gone.

When the needs of belonging, competency, and closeness are not being met, different patterns of behavior and issues will rise to the surface and prevent work from getting done. Here are some things to monitor:

- Do some people seem to be outside the group? Are some inside the group? How are those outside treated?
- Are subgroups forming, the members of which appear to support each other, or are several people in the department engaged in disagreements and opposition?
- Are people either saying or indicating that they are uncomfortable in the workplace?
- Do they say such things as, "I'm not sure what I'm supposed to do," as an indicator of effectiveness concerns?
- Do people appear to be overly polite and distant, as an indicator of intimacy concerns?

Opinion Centers

Opinion leaders can move the group forward or hold it back. Influence and participation are not the same. Some people may appear to be uninvolved, yet they capture the attention of the whole group. Others may appear to be deeply involved but generally are not listened to or followed by other people.

Factors that influence the way a manager's group behaves can come from a source that is outside of the group, such as a manager at a higher level or opinion leaders in different departments. Here are some things to monitor:

- Which members of your staff are high in influence, that is, when they talk, others seem to listen? What are their positions in the organization? What are their ages? Are they male or female? Other factors?
- Which members appear to be low in influence?
- Is there any shifting in influence, where some people appear to be influential at one time and not at other times?
- Is there any rivalry in the group? Is there a struggle for leadership? What effect is it having on other members of the group?
- What are potential power or influence sources outside of the immediate group?

Collaboration

Solving today's business problems requires that all of the people involved have a willingness to collaborate. The level of collaboration needs to be examined because it is a strong determinant of the group's performance.

Observation centers on how well the group works together. Although it is an intangible factor to observe, groups working well together exude a climate or atmosphere as they interact. Climates can be infused with hostility and defensiveness or cooperation and openness. In the latter, members can be observed sharing ideas and appearing to value each others' contributions.

As a general rule, collaboration occurs when the atmosphere is open and accepting, when conflicts over leadership have been resolved and the workers have defined their positions within the total group. A large part of accomplishing this type of atmosphere lies with the manager.

When the atmosphere is hostile and rejecting, survivors are not likely to take the risks needed to arrive at the best solutions. In the current environment, establishing an open and accepting atmosphere is no easy matter. It requires modeling and direction from the manager and the promotion of norms that legitimize risk-taking behavior. Here are some things to look for:

- Are suggestions and ideas for the solutions to business problems regularly forthcoming?
- Who seems to prefer an atmosphere of conflict and disagreement? Do any members of the team go out of their way to provoke or annoy others? Who among the direct reports presents an "I'd rather do it myself" attitude?
- Do people seem involved and interested? Are they eager?
- In both formal and informal settings, are certain topics avoided by the group? Or does the group tend to slant its attention off to topics not related to the immediate tasks?
- Do people seem to be enjoying themselves?

Trust

Trust is a factor that is easy to discuss and very hard to achieve. However, almost no one disagrees that a high level of interpersonal trust is required for a work team to achieve its goals. We might add that both the difficulty of achieving trust and the need for it has never been greater than in the current survivor environment.

Trust is required before collaboration can happen. There is a progression, like links in a chain. This progression mirrors the Survivor Management Model in that it begins with feelings, both good and bad, about the organization that hopefully will develop into a closeness after the feelings are dealt with. Subsequently, feeling closer to the overall group will develop the necessary trust as part of the final stage of the realignment process.

A low-trust-level group will avoid many issues and will appear cautious and wary. An air of formality may be present. Another indicator of a low-trust environment is humor in the form of negative wisecracking or cynical repartee. Here are some things to look for:

- Are risk-taking suggestions generally accepted or rejected by other members of the team?
- Do the direct reports appear eager and assertive or cautious and unwilling to commit themselves?
- What are the nonverbals? When interacting with each other and with the manager,

do members of the group use eye contact, touching, smiling? Do their body positions appear relaxed without being lethargic?

- Is there an aura of fear that permeates the group?

Group Maintenance

A group will not function effectively unless it occasionally examines its own actions. How much of a sense of belonging, group loyalty, or group cohesion exists in a department? A functioning group takes on a personality, much like an individual. As a group grows and matures, it takes on a life of its own and develops a set of needs. Much like an individual, the group needs to feel safe and is fearful of its disintegration.

In today's workplace, very few groups—departmental or otherwise—have survived intact. Some have been destroyed altogether, and the ripples from that destruction have washed over other groups in the organization. Any group has a basic instinct to survive, and its members will unconsciously resist attempts to close the group down. Also, there is a tendency for the group to want to stay together as a group.

Groups will resist the loss of members as well as the addition of new members. A mature, functioning group is cohesive. It has a pleasurable sense of itself as being together, and its members feel that they belong to something whole. Members of a mature group know that harmony is important and that too much hostility and frustration will destroy it.

Special roles arise, called maintenance roles: harmonizing, gatekeeping, compromising, encouraging. These have the effect of keeping the group together. While several members of any group may exhibit behaviors in these categories from time to time, a successful manager will be one who is able to promote and model these group-maintenance behaviors for his or her survivor population. Here are some things to look for:

- Are there attempts to reconcile disagreements, reduce tension, and get people to explore differences, thereby promoting a harmonious environment?
- Do members help to keep communication channels open, facilitate the participation of others in projects and meetings, and suggest and encourage procedures that ensure equal opportunities to present ideas?
- Is the general atmosphere friendly, warm, accepting of others, and responsive to others' contributions?
- Do members offer compromise when one's idea is in conflict with another's? Do they admit error and show willingness to sacrifice their own status in favor of group cohesiveness?

Commitment

When a manager achieves solid commitment from the people in his or her charge, realignment has been successful. A key factor in the development of commitment is that the mission and purpose of the group are effectively communicated to and understood by all of the members. If the mission is not clear, members may be confused about their purpose in the group and their role in any future actions that the group may take.

Survivors who do not either understand or buy into the organization's mission will begin to pursue disparate courses. If there is no common vision, the group has little chance of ever growing in a way that benefits all the members and, by extension, the organization.

Members of the organization whose goals do not conform to those of the group will ultimately be excluded from the growth process and, most likely, leave the organization. Here are some things to look for:

- Can each member of the group articulate the group's mission?
- Are suggestions or other comments being made that show confusion about the purpose of the group's work or direction?
- Is the group having unusual difficulty in getting organized around the tasks to be done?
- Does there appear to be frustration in the group that cannot be explained by other means?

To be successful in dealing with the eight components of group process, managers need to focus their attention on building good interpersonal relationships as never before. Managers in the survivor environment must rely on others for support in achieving goals to a degree not experienced at any other time in organizational life.

The more the manager commits to developing and maintaining respectful, productive relationships with the people he or she needs to accomplish the tasks and responsibilities of the job, the larger the payoff in terms of motivation, commitment, support; and ultimately, survivor realignment.

We discussed in some detail earlier in the chapter the need for a 360-degree assessment so that the manager can open up his or her own competencies for discussion and review. While we do not suggest a 360-degree survey of interpersonal relationships, the successful manager nonetheless needs to see himself or herself as others do.

Managers, in general, get little feedback about how they are perceived interpersonally. This is particularly true as managers move higher and higher in organizations. One way in which managers can receive feedback regarding interpersonal relationships with their own direct reports is by enlisting the aid of a colleague to play the role of conduit for this kind of feedback.

Regular and comprehensive performance-appraisal interviews, which are absolutely critical for realigning survivors, can also be used to encourage honest and direct feedback about relationships. By focusing some part of the performance-appraisal discussion on work style, direct reports can be encouraged to discuss differences in their perception of how the manager is coming across. Of course, more formalized 360-degree assessments are also available to collect data on the interpersonal aspects of a manager's performance.

Many managers are unaware that they are creating interpersonal problems. Sometimes enthusiasm for an idea or a particular project—or the effects of stress on the manager—can come across as abrasive, overbearing, or domineering. Behaviors that contribute to less-than-satisfactory interpersonal relations with subordinates involve frequent interruptions, restating opinions, frequent overforcefulness in presenting an idea, monopolizing discussion times at meetings and elsewhere, and being overly critical of others' ideas.

Under the best of conditions, subordinates are hypersensitive to criticism from their managers. However, survivors are particularly susceptible to what they perceive as negative reactions. The most successful manager with survivors will be one who is able to refrain from immediate judgments or criticisms and is able to deliver criticism in a way that demonstrates a sensitivity to the survivor's feelings. Chapter 10 details some of these behaviors in more concrete terms as part of coaching.

Managers must be particularly careful about being stress carriers. Adding unnecessary intensity or stress to an already-stressed environment is counterproductive. Managers who appear to be most effective in the survivor environment have a knack for being friendly and using humor that is not sarcastic or alienating.

Survivors, by nature, are highly attuned to inequities. Managers can make major strides in developing trust and gaining recommitment by ensuring that people are treated as fairly as possible. Because of the demands placed on managers as a result of diminishing resources, work assignments tend to be handed out in an unequal fashion. All managers gravitate toward those people who seem to be able to get tasks finished. However, this tendency may overlook the fact that both the employee who is being "dumped on" and others who feel underutilized are developing increasingly negative perceptions of the workplace.

It is the nature of management behavior in the best of times to lose track of the amount of work already handed out to individual employees. A good way to enhance the equitable treatment of employees is to conduct an audit of current work assignments and analyze the distribution of these assignments. Three questions to ask in the context of this audit are

1. How much work is assigned to each employee?
2. What proportion of the work can be categorized as interesting or challenging, as opposed to mundane or "grunt" work?
3. How much input do individual employees have regarding the assignment of work?

Some managers are just more personable than others. This is a fact that cannot be altered significantly. However, specific attempts to become more approachable, develop more effective working relationships, or take a personal interest in the workers will ultimately result in better interpersonal dynamics.

Besides being able to create a better climate and, ultimately, a better work force, managers who are approachable receive more feedback about what is going on. This serves to eliminate those surprises that create major problems for managers in the fast-paced competitive environment.

Managers need to make a point of being seen by their workers more frequently. In those cases where workers are at remote locations, special efforts need to be made to maintain lines of communication and contact. Scheduling regular blocks of time for discussion of employee concerns is also an effective technique.

With survivors, it is particularly important to demonstrate an interest in their personal as well as their work-related concerns. Showing a willingness to openly acknowledge and discuss their fears and anxieties in the changing environment will go a long way toward building trust and recommitment.

Managers who are effective at enhancing personal relationships find time for informal chats and are interested in the worker's family, hobbies, and goals. Self-disclosure is a powerful means of opening up discussion on personal matters. Employees will feel more comfortable discussing aspects of their personal lives if the manager is first willing to discuss aspects of his or her own personal life. Wherever possible and practical, social events should be scheduled to enable more personal interaction.

Another key factor in enhancing interpersonal relations with employees is a demonstration on the manager's part that he or she can and will maintain confidentiality about the employee's personal concerns.

DIVING IN

Perhaps the worst thing a manager can do is nothing. We have observed over the last several years, in a variety of organizations, a startling number of managers who "fiddle while Rome burns." Among this group of laissez-faire managers, the attitude appears to be, "I'll wait to see what this is going to be before I act."

This view of the current reality as transitory is dangerous for an organization. Managers who will succeed, both individually and for the organizations they represent, will be proactive and willing to dive in and do something. It is this willingness to do something, to put oneself into action, to take risks, model behaviors, and make mistakes, that ultimately captures the attention of the survivor employee.

Most people come to realize before very long that it is better to go down, if that is the result, because of something you did or an action that you took rather than because you took no action at all.

Survivor managers need to develop an action plan. First, collect all of the information that possibly can be derived about what is going on in the organization and, most specifically, in the department or work group. Examine all of the components of group process. Involve the survivor employees in the determination of what kind of leadership is necessary to succeed. Make sure that everybody participates in the creation of and, subsequently, the understanding of the vision or mission, goals and objectives of the organization and the department or work group.

Foster trust by being trustworthy. Promote openness by being open. Be realistic without being continually negative. Maintain objectivity and a sense of humor without being sarcastic. Ensure that all of the people receive the feedback that they need both to function and understand. Praise when praise is due (and in public, if appropriate), criticize constructively (and privately), and demonstrate a continual willingness to change.

CHAPTER 9

Reassessing Human Capital

Does this sound familiar? You're expendable. We don't want to fire you, but we will if we have to. Competition is brutal, so we must redesign the way we work to do more with less. Sorry; that's just the way it is. And one more thing—you're invaluable. Your devotion to our customers is the salvation of this company. We're depending on you to be innovative, risk-taking, and committed to our goals. OK?[1]

Most managers who find themselves still more or less in place during and after the process of reorganization have to face a few inescapable realities. One is that they will have to find ways to revitalize and recommit staff members who are left or who have been reassigned to their charges. Another reality is that a survivor manager ends up in one of two positions. The first is a situation in which the manager is now responsible for many additional people, some with cross-functional responsibilities. Because the ranks of management have thinned out, we might also note that these assignments are not always made based on logic. The second position finds a manager with less staff than before and either the same or more work. In the latter case, it is unlikely that the manager will have an opportunity to expand the number of staff members in the near future.

These are the questions that must be answered before any forward progress can be made:

- Who is now reporting to the manager?
- What are the individual employees' strengths and weaknesses?
- Who can be developed into the manager's successor?
- Who needs further training to best assist the manager in the challenges that lie ahead?

In Chapter 3, we discussed some of the needs for a new type of leadership, and in Chapter 8, we talked about how the manager can use a self-assessment as a springboard for enabling higher levels of initiative. Here, we place the focus on the survivors themselves. What are the jobs, tasks, or responsibilities that need to be accomplished? What competencies to meet these needs already exist in the current human capital? What competencies need to be developed to close the gap?

It will be very difficult to accomplish any goals and objectives without taking into account an additional facet of the survivor mentality. One of the most resilient attributes of organizational life is the expectation that one is situated on some sort of career track that is leading somewhere. Along with many other things in today's work environment, destinations along the track have become blurred and, in many cases, have disappeared altogether.

CAREER EXPECTATIONS

In the midst of all the drumming about teamwork and the need to follow Japanese models, we cannot forget that our society is characterized by its individualism, competitiveness, and compulsive commitment to upward mobility.

Embedded within our society are all sorts of signs and symbols that provide measures of success and external signs of achievement. Most of these achievement symbols are based on a linear career model. While far from extinct, one of the major considerations for managers going forward is that—along with everything else impacting today's work force—an increasing number of careers will be lived out in a nonlinear fashion.

The survivor manager needs to find ways to overcome the powerful attitudes that reinforce the linear status quo. The very language that we use to describe careers, by and large, works against our ability to alter linear perception and describe and reinforce nonlinear alternatives.

The linear career path that comes so naturally to most of us is based on a hierarchy supported by descriptive language that reinforces the hierarchy. We talk about "starting at the bottom" or "being at base level" and "working up the pyramid," "climbing the career ladder," or "following a particular route." All of these images project a progression, orderliness, or a rational approach to advancement based on skill, attainment, and competence. The notion of growth and achievement is as firmly embedded in a survivor's psyche as it ever was, and opportunities for growth and achievement continue to be perceived as primary motivators.

One of the by-products of this linear career focus is that it stifles innovative thinking about alternative career forms. Managers in the survivor environment need to see themselves as career counselors, in addition to everything else they must do. Uprooted from traditional thinking and traditional values surrounding organizational life, the survivor is grappling with some serious career issues. In the face of the new insecurity, the survivor is still left with the problem of making judgments about how he or she is doing in his or her career life. The traditional factors, such as the length of time in a position, the social desirability of the position's title, and the amount of power accorded a particular organizational role, are still the primary factors that, to the individual, specify his or her personal worth.

Survivors are also presented with several career paradoxes. On the one hand, they are being exhorted to downplay their individualism and become active members of self-directed teams. On the other hand, the society at large and the instruments of the society, such as the media, continue to celebrate winners who are recognized for their financial success, organizational perquisites, and achievements as individuals. People are continually described as winners and losers, leaders and followers, successful and unsuccessful.

The impact of the changes taking place in career orientation cannot be minimized. For a very long time, individuals have been defined personally and socially by their placement within the organizations they work for. Workers have granted an inordinate amount of power to the organizations for making decisions about their careers. Careers are directed and controlled by others with more power within the organization. Workers are regularly assessed and decisions made about their careers, and often the decisions that are made are neither accurate nor related to job performance.

Workers who reject an organization's decision about their careers, such as a job assignment or a relocation, take the serious risk that an alternative or additional opportunity may not be forthcoming. While, on the one hand, survivors adhere to the old notions of career—primarily because they have few cogent alternative models—they also now see through the structures that were built to perpetuate the old notions. For example, elaborate training and development programs have, for years, supported the notion that it was possible for anyone satisfying certain requirements to achieve the levels of aspiration survivors had within the organization. The events of the last ten years have clearly pointed out to the frontline worker that, if there is a logic or a rationale to who survives, it has nothing to do with following the formal path presented or keeping your nose clean and to the grindstone. Decisions about career, to the survivor, seem to be based on loose systems of executive interaction that are secretive and apply rules that are unknown outside of the inner circle.

Managers who continue to represent career tracking and advancement to their survivors—as J. E. Rosenbaum puts it in his writings, the "rags to riches," "Horatio Alger," and "late bloomer" myths—are bound to fail in attempting to motivate survivors toward realignment.[2]

Although it has always been the case, workers now perceive the true elusiveness of success based on the old model. We have all been taught that success is determined by the money, material possessions, and the position that a person holds; that, in America, it is available to everyone who works hard. In fact, according to Schaeffer, although 10 to 15 percent of organizational members may be earmarked as having high potential for external career success, less than 1 percent of an organization's employees (*prior* to the current reengineering environment) actually reached the highest levels.[3] Survivors recognize the absurdity of this system but are unable to toss aside these extrinsic success models because they are so thoroughly embedded in their psyches.

In his or her additional role as career counselor, the manager needs to help survivors reconceptualize the success model. However, in the process of doing so, it is necessary to avoid the trap of simply recreating the old linear career models in new forms. According to Buzzanell and Goldzwig, even "innovative career development and advancement programs such as career and family tracks and dual-career ladders simply recreate linear thinking. They also create the illusion of opportunity where little opportunity actually exists."[4]

NONALTERNATIVE ALTERNATIVES

Mommy Tracking

The fundamental problems, Buzzanell and Goldzwig claim, with mommy tracks and career primary tracks for women are that neither of these alternatives actually differs from linear corporate norms and that neither addresses the issue that all organizational members continue to be tracked in some way. Mommy tracks and the like then become another artificial division in the work force.

While providing an opportunity for women's careers to be put on hold in favor of life priorities, the mommy track reinforces the myth that women can remove themselves temporarily from the career race and still have the opportunity to rise to the top of the corporation. In the survivor environment it is becoming more clear that women who elect job sharing, shorter hours, or telecommuting from home find themselves in a professional limbo.

Dual-Career Ladder

As jobs continue to become more technical, it is more likely that a larger number of survivors come from the technical side of the organization. As an alternative, the dual ladder is not new. Dual-career models have existed for more than thirty years. They are primarily designed to provide a management track to individuals within the organization who are primarily technical specialists. The dual-ladder approach in managing survivors appears to be a very attractive option, the notion being to maintain the technical expertise of the survivor while motivating him or her through the potential of traditional rewards.

Employees are being told that they have options to move from the technical to the managerial ladder. Buzzanell and Goldzwig tell us that, as conceived, dual-career ladders should result in a satisfied, motivated, and technically oriented work force. However, in practice, this approach often fails miserably. It fails because dual-ladder plans tend to stereotype technical professionals, who are not perceived as truly being on a management track and, in fact, are often perceived as having failed in management but still making a necessary contribution to the organization. For many, this results in lesser wages and perquisites and the denial of decision-making power, even on technical issues.[5]

Because of their essential role as technicians, survivors in this category are often "rewarded" with assignments as project managers, which, in and of themselves, hold neither power nor prestige. Surveys of individuals involved in dual-career ladders show that this approach is perceived as a myth created by the organization to recruit and retain necessary technical personnel. Respondents, consisting of engineers and engineering managers participating in a career-development program of Purdue University's Krannert Graduate School of Management, Executive Education Division, indicate that they do not believe there can be equality between managerial and technical career tracks.

The limitations of this approach are based on the fact that advancement still appears to be the primary arbiter of success. Promoting technical personnel from within is supposed to signal the worth of these competencies. However, higher dual-career positions often do not carry increased decision-making power or perquisites and potentially represent another disappointment for the already-cynical and wary survivor.

What this all adds up to is that when you are assessing your human capital, part of that assessment involves an understanding of attitudes, values, beliefs, and expectations that the survivor drags from the past and continues, somewhat unwittingly, to carry into the future.

SURVIVOR ASSESSMENT

One of the major mistakes that managers make after a reorganization is to apply guesswork and wishful thinking to the assignment of tasks and responsibilities to the remaining survivors. An important first step in analyzing and assessing human capital is to consider what kind of an organization is needed to meet the objectives. The way a manager structures his or her territory plays a large part in determining both his or her success and the success of the department or group.

In many cases managers have only limited opportunities to restructure. However, even in those instances, informal structural arrangements can be made that will help to work through, over, or around roadblocks created by administrative mistakes made at a higher level.

Structure, either formal or informal, will have a direct effect on productivity, quality, customer satisfaction, and the general morale of the survivors. The manager should think of structure as an extension of leadership initiatives. Setting up a good structure begins with the mission or vision that needs to be accomplished. A flowchart should be created that depicts the operations performed by the department. The next important activity calls for the development of an organization chart. It is always useful, particularly after a downsizing, to examine the old chart in light of the new situation to determine which job categories, tasks, and responsibilities need to be shifted to other workers. There also may be ways to consolidate functions in such a way as not to overload remaining staff.

A major problem looms when downsizings leave whole areas of competence lacking. Obviously, if and when this happens, interventions to manage that problem must take priority. Retraining could be an option, but it is potentially too slow. Other individuals may be identified who have the necessary competencies. Another alternative is outsourcing, at least for the short term, the tasks and responsibilities of the uncovered needs.

When a new chart has been drafted, look for areas where there may be duplication of effort. Also, there may be people working on tasks that do not directly impact the department's goals or objectives.

The *Successful Manager's Handbook* lists some key questions to answer as part of developing an effective structure:[6]

- Does the work unit lack technical expertise that would help it attain its goals?
- Does the department possess technical expertise it no longer needs?
- Do individuals in the work unit have ready access to the information, expertise, or other resources needed to perform their functions?
- Are too many or too few individuals available to carry the work load for any step of the process?

It is always a good idea to research how other managers in the organization are dealing with organization issues. Once the organizational plan has been drafted, attention should be returned to the survivors themselves.

The beginning of a sincere effort to realign survivor employees includes a complete and objective assessment of who they are, what they are, and what they can do. A useful construct for approaching this process is derived from selection interviewing—that is, if no people were left and the manager was charged with the responsibility of hiring individuals to fit the tasks and responsibilities in his or her charge, what characteristics would those people need to have?

Most practitioners and writers in the field of personnel selection and interviewing subscribe to a scheme to categorize candidates' characteristics that contains four separate dimensions. The first dimension identifies intellectual characteristics. The second considers knowledge, skill, and experience with the job under consideration. The third catalogs personality variables, and the fourth considers motivation and aspiration.[7] Table 9.1 provides a checklist of attributes to consider in each of these dimensions.

In many current scenarios, managers find themselves with entirely new or an additional group of direct reports. In that case, an effort should be made as soon as possible to interview each direct report to determine what characteristics, skills, personality factors, and motivation he or she is

Table 9.1
Survivor Assessment Checklist

Intellectual Characteristics	Motivations and Aspirations
Level of intelligence	Motivation level
Analytic ability	Health
Ability to diagnose client needs	Ambition
Creativity/innovativeness	Willingness to take risks
Pragmatism	Interests compatible with organization's expectations
Intellectual flexibility	Initiative/resourcefulness
Oral communications skills	Perseverance
Written communications skills	Track record
Education	
Preferred work style	
Knowledge/Skill	**Personality**
Technical expertise	Interpersonal flexibility
Time with the organization	Assertiveness
Different jobs held	Team player/loner
Level of responsibility	Enthusiasm
Knowledge and skill outside of immediate area	Empathy
Administrative abilities	Leadership
	Self-objectivity
	Independence
	Standards of performance
	A "doer"
	Emotional maturity/stability/resilience

bringing to the party. A significant by-product of this activity is the opening of lines of communication between the manager and the survivor that will start the process of realignment.

As part of any discussion, managers need to collect input from the survivor on how he or she views the job. In order to make the most effective deployment of existing staff, managers need to know how each survivor views the purpose of his or her job and whether that purpose is clear.

Survivors are also generally confused about areas of responsibility. If, as a result of restructuring, the survivor has also been assigned to any number of cross-functional work teams, he or she is probably also confused about which manager has priority demands on his or her time.

Survivors also vary in their feelings about the level of authority they have to carry out the tasks and responsibilities assigned to them. They are confused about the meaning of empowerment and have seen colleagues punished for taking actions without going through "normal channels."

THE TASK AND RESPONSIBILITY AUDIT

To collect basic information to assess each of the survivors, we use an instrument we call the Task and Responsibility Audit (TARA). A complete copy of the TARA is included in Appendix B. However, it is summarized here.

The TARA collects personal data and work history. Survivors are asked to discuss how they originally came to the company and their background and previous experience, including training and other job-related skills picked up while working elsewhere.

The work history is particularly important because it provides an opportunity to uncover competencies that may be available but are currently not being tapped within an existing group.

From there, the TARA provides an opportunity for individual workers to describe their tasks and responsibilities in competency terms. They are asked what a person needs to know in order to do the job; what a person needs to be able to do; and what intangibles are associated with doing the job well. They have an opportunity to discuss areas where they feel they are strongest and areas where they feel they need additional development, as well as to speculate on what knowledge, skill, and perception they may need based on their understanding of changes coming down the line.

The TARA then looks into job-related attitudes, values, and beliefs. Survivors are asked to respond to how they feel about the changes in general and how those changes will affect them specifically. They are encouraged to talk about whether changes were needed; how they describe themselves on the job; what they like about the current working conditions, about the job, and about the company; and their working relationships and the general level of communication. They are asked to express their concerns and what they would change if they had the opportunity.

In the last part of this section of the interview, survivors are asked for their wish list of resources, manpower, or direction that would enable them to do their jobs more effectively.

The final parts of the instrument focus on motivation, intellectual, and personality data, based on questions about current projects, the survivors' goals, outside interests, problem-solving style, and the like. The manager should be able to make some judgments regarding the individual's ability and willingness to cope with the new situation.

SETTING TRAINING AND DEVELOPMENT OBJECTIVES

On the assumption that the manager has written detailed behavioral specifications for the primary jobs in his or her charge, the task of matching people as closely as possible to the right jobs becomes somewhat simplified. In addition, when the characteristics of the people available are compared to or matched with the behavioral specifications of the available tasks and responsibilities, it becomes immediately clear where there are gaps and where action such as training and redistribution needs to be taken.

Figure 9.1 provides a model for maximizing training efforts. Application of the model is a simple matter of subtraction. Once you understand the competencies needed to do the jobs and the competencies available within your existing human resources, it should become clear which competencies are weak or lacking. This is the area where training efforts must be focused. It should also be apparent that it is both wasteful and time consuming to try to apply off-the-shelf packaged training interventions to meet these needs. In most cases, customized programs can be developed in-house or with the help of an outside instructional designer for significantly less cost and a higher degree of effectiveness.

Figure 9.2 provides a list of options that the manager can select from to meet his or her training needs.

A NEW DEAL FOR SURVIVORS

Creating a new contract to structure the working relationship with survivors is no easy matter. Burdened with the old linear ideas of success and the new reality of perpetual insecurity, the survivor is wary of making any deals at all.

Patricia Braus, writing for *American Demographics*, points out that not too long ago, everyone who might be considered for a job would apply. In this climate however, with increasing frequency, you hear people saying, "I don't want that job. The price you have to pay is too great." This perception is balanced off by the fact that everyone is working longer hours and many are grateful to have any kind of job at all.

Figure 9.1
Manager's Model for Training and Development

Assess the Jobs

Accomplishments
Requirements
Measures
Standards

▼

Assess the Competencies
Needed for the Jobs

| Knowledge | Skill | Perception |

▼

Assess the Competencies
of the Workers

| Knowledge | Skill | Perception |

▼

Focus Training on
Missing Competencies

Many companies are making efforts to assist their survivors in balancing their lives by providing such things as flexible schedules and part-time jobs for employees with families. "Understanding the changing goals of workers is the key to attracting the best candidates, keeping the best employees, and removing barriers to greater productivity."[8]

If they have not rediscovered the fact already, most employers will soon return to the basic understanding that the cost of pleasing and keeping

Figure 9.2
Resources for Training and Development

Manager/Supervisor

Another Staff Member

Organizational Resources

- Training Department
- Other Departments

Resources outside the Organization

- Formal Education
- Seminars, Workshops
- Professional Meetings and Associations

Self-Development

- Reading
- Observation

people is less than the cost of eventually replacing them. While each situation will require variations in approach, based on the composition of the work force, some generalizations are worth making.

Many workers, in addition to their other concerns, are finding it necessary to spend more work time on personal chores such as running errands, talking to family members on the phone, or going to the doctor. Managers who are able to approach this situation with a more flexible attitude will have a better chance of gaining more discretionary effort. As Braus suggests, if you are half of a dual-income couple, some of your personal chores need to be handled during working hours, and most married-couple households headed by a person in the working years, are dual-income households.[9]

A very basic management rule holds true in this case: Manage results, not activity. Workers who are finding it necessary to take longer breaks during the day make up for it by working after hours, in the evenings, and on weekends. The fact is that, eventually, workers will be able to find more of what they want, whether in their current organizations or elsewhere.

There is always a period after a contract is broken when people will try to adhere to the old rules and continue to work hard.[10] However, workers are beginning to say to management, "I have choices now. If the new relationship being suggested is not one that I like, I can decide if I want to stay or go elsewhere."

Brian O'Reilly, in his article for *Fortune*, provides an example of what he calls "the new contract in its most naked form."[11] The contract claims that there will never be job security. Instead, the worker will be employed as long as he or she adds value to the organization, and the responsibility for adding value lies with the worker. In exchange for that, the worker has the right to demand interesting and important work, the freedom and resources to perform it, pay that reflects the level of his or her contribution, and the experience and training needed to be employable for new or additional jobs in the present organization or elsewhere.

With the old rules no longer in force, survivors are rapidly becoming far more responsible for their own work and careers. They no longer trust nor want the child-parent relationship of old and wish to be treated like adults.

One paradox that arises out of this new scheme for the worker is that there is a need to be constantly learning. Even when opportunities for this learning are provided, both inside and outside of the organization, the time it takes to do the actual work leaves relatively little time to pursue the learning necessary to be able to maintain the competencies to keep the jobs they have.

New technologies that support individualized learning are beginning to play a major role in the quest for lifelong learning. We have been working with large companies in the throes of reorganization to develop innovative and cost-effective ways of delivering individualized instruction to a large and geographically dispersed population. One major insurer is currently operating what is, arguably, the largest-distance learning network in the world, reaching interactively over 17,000 field representatives located in all fifty states. Representatives, using the network, can receive training and be tested on competency any day of the week, any time of the day, at the office, in their homes using their own television sets, or anywhere they can carry a laptop personal computer.

In addition to being a powerful training resource, the technology has become a central part of the new contract between employers and their suvivors. This is because it offers what the survivors need in order to succeed more quickly and continuously as they develop in their careers.

Despite the drawbacks and the insecurity associated with the new contract that is developing between organizations and their workers, survivors who have effectively realigned themselves with the new reality have begun to realize that they are freer, in many ways, than they ever were before. As one employee puts it, "The old days could be obnoxious. You had to kiss ass and dress right to get ahead. Now, none of that matters any more. If you work hard, you'll find a place."[12]

In their attempts to build new contracts, managers need to consider these most important factors:

- Be open and candid with employees, even when the news is not good.
- Be willing to provide the opportunity and resources for survivors to be able to engage in self-development and learning.
- Base all attempts at contracting with employees on an understanding of what employees value in their jobs and tailor rewards to these values.
- Clearly explain to survivors what the standards of job performance are.
- Develop clear connections between performance and rewards.
- Commit to and provide regular and frequent performance evaluations.
- Commit to their own self-development as managers, particularly in the areas of communication and appraisal skills.

DEVELOPING NONLINEAR CAREER MODELS

We began our discussion in this chapter by pointing to factors that exacerbate transition problems for the survivor. The traditional or linear career model is all that they know and understand; therefore, they peer with even greater uncertainty into a future that does not seem to hold the same opportunities.

If alternatives to the linear model are to be considered, the notion of a career needs to be redefined. One such redefinition is provided by the work of Arthur, Hall, and Lawrence. They redefined career as "the evolving sequence of a person's work experiences over time."[13]

In this definition, success becomes an internal construct; and internal success is determined by personal evaluations, adaptability, and personal identity. It becomes a process which the person, not the organization, manages and controls. The focus is not on the external trappings of traditional success, but on self-fulfillment. This type of career is shaped by the individual's needs and values rather than by the organization. It emphasizes growth, self-knowledge, fulfillment, freedom of choice, and psychological success.

Individuals in nontraditional career tracks still may be externally rewarded through salary increases and promotion, but the key difference is that the focus is on the individual rather than the organization. Workers in nontraditional careers break free of the presumption that the organization knows what is best. They fully reclaim responsibility for their own careers and relinquish little or no control to the organization. Emphasis is placed on enhancing opportunities for personal growth rather than trying to get ahead.

One alternative, termed the *"steady-state" career*, already exists in many occupations where individuals remain in the same position for their entire working lives. In terms of a linear model, these people would be described as plateaued, stuck, or dead-ended. In spite of this, many such people are fulfilled by the work itself and may be very effective at specific-task accomplishment.

We used to marvel at workers at all levels, from the factory floor through middle management, who balked at the notion of promotion simply because they were perfectly happy doing exactly what they were doing. Such workers find alternative status hierarchies, such as expert knowledge in particular areas.

Survivors in the process of assessing their own career options may discover, or be led to discover, that because traditional upward mobility is not available to them in the current work environment, they need to shift their focus to increasing skill attainment and broadening their expertise to encompass all of the tasks and responsibilities in their occupational area.

Another model, termed the *"spiral"* or *"multichannel" career*, sets a course for the individual that enables (or requires) a major career change at several intervals during his or her life. While there may be upward or linear achievement in each of the separate careers, the emphasis for the individual is placed on knowledge acquisition, personal development, and freedom of choice. Empowered with the notion that he or she will only commit five or ten years to a single career option, the survivor is freer to act in his or her own behalf and to pick and choose more-fulfilling or interesting or self-developing work at the cost of less-fulfilling assignments that may ultimately provide the opportunity to rise higher in that temporary career choice.

Needless to say, the application of such a career model requires a concept of self on the part of the employee that is open to continual change and can incorporate multiple views of self.

As intellectually attractive as some of these options are, if any meaningful change is to be made in our concepts of a career, we must also change our concepts of the organization. As time goes on, this may not be as difficult as it first appears, since organizations as a whole are facing the same kind of rapidly changing environments in their relationships with the external world that their workers are facing in their relationships with the internal world of the organization.

As systems theories take hold in organizations, it is not too farfetched to envision companies that are in a continuous state of redesign and actually come to value impermanence. The members of this type of organization will have a constant need to review themselves and their evolution to meet dynamic environments and create opportunities.[14]

Once this prospective is achieved, these self-designing organizations will, by nature, focus on skills, processes, and competencies that individuals must acquire to deal with change rather than merely attending to jobs and outcomes.

Changes of this magnitude will not occur overnight. At the start of the day, managers are still left with the problem of explaining some kind of contract to their survivors in order to develop a reasonable reciprocal agreement. Short of creating a revolution, today's managers still have several opportunities to enhance the realignment process.

In order to accomplish this, managers must first recognize that they will need to relinquish some control over the people who work for them. Survivors must be kept informed as to career-development opportunities, and the career opportunities provided must be continually updated. No longer can managers afford to hide the training department's catalog in the bottom drawer for fear that employees will take time off of work to go to training.

In addition, managers will have to openly discuss career objectives with each employee and give fair and accurate assessments of the employee's potential within the organization and without. Survivors would be offered assistance in creating a balance in their lives between workplace, home, and self-fulfillment. Wherever possible, managers can replace many of the traditional signs of success by providing opportunities for stimulation, flexibility, and decision-making power.

CHAPTER 10

Managing for Performance

One point that constantly reasserts itself is that all of the best efforts to realign and motivate survivors will fail without the application of exceptional skill sets on the part of the managers charged with this task. One thing working in the manager's favor is that, even in the survivor environment, most people do not get up in the morning, look at themselves in the mirror and say, "I'm really going to get out there and fail today." Whether the employee is pulling for himself or herself, for the organization, or some combination of the two, there is still a need to achieve, grow, and be left with the feeling that something worthwhile has been accomplished.

Survivors are more sensitive to the need to constantly look for ways to improve their skills. Every individual needs to believe that he or she can always get better at his or her profession. One of the most important aspects of skill improvement is receiving accurate feedback about performance. Game tapes, speeches, and medical and legal procedures are routinely analyzed to help professionals improve their performance. Likewise, the careful monitoring, coaching, and reviewing of learning and job performance is critical to the development of the people you manage.

It is difficult to improve your performance if you do not know your strengths or where your performance needs improving. The survivor manager's primary focus is to help others see specific ways that they can improve, to ensure they are part of the future—whether with this organization or another. We have already discussed the need for the manager to be something of a career counselor. He or she also must be a "coach." To be an effective coach, the manager needs to be comfortable with specific coaching guidelines to help identify survivors' strengths and development needs and be able to present the feedback in a constructive manner.

Effective coaching can be quick, frequent, and informal or thorough, structured, and in depth. It can also be done one on one or in small groups.

Whatever the situation, the skills and guidelines that follow can help the manager become a more effective coach of all direct reports, including new hires as well as survivors. Good coaching behavior helps keep survivors on track, even after they have recommitted themselves.

GAINING OBJECTIVITY

"What do I do now, coach?"

"Back up ten yards and punt!"

Is there anyone who has not either heard this little expression or found themselves actually saying these words? The humor—if we find it funny—is that a person with some immediate need, in this case a player on a football team, seeks advice from his coach to get out of a predicament. Instead of deep, insightful, focused directions, the player is told to beat a "strategic retreat" and pass the problem (in this case the ball) to the other team.

That is not to say that in some circumstances—as with a fourth-down-and-fifteen situation on your own ten-yard line—punting is not the answer. The problem is that many times, when you are approached for advice, and having discovered that a particular action is useful or correct in one situation or for one individual, you assume that that action will be the same for a wide range of situations or a wide variety of individuals. It is the coach, not the player, who needs the objectivity provided by backing up ten yards and the involvement, collaboration, and empowerment inherent in allowing the person being coached to decide what to do with the ball.

INITIATING AND PLANNING A COACHING SESSION

A man walking down the street is approached by a stranger who asks if he knows where Main Street is. The man points it out to the stranger and says, "Straight down and to your left." Assured that he has been understood, the man walks on, but he notices that the stranger is walking in the wrong direction. "Sir," he says, "you're going in the wrong direction." "I know," replies the stranger. "I'm not ready to go to Main Street yet."

As individuals we are unique, and what we discover is that we can best help others by enabling them to do what they themselves really want to do. The stranger had asked the man for directions; the man had given directions to the best of his ability. The stranger had understood, but was "not ready" to go in the direction in which he was pointed.

Sometimes, managers want to move others, like their survivors, too quickly along the path. At what point is there danger of helping too much? At what point is the manager interfering where he or she is neither wanted nor needed? There are many elements that shape the coaching session. A good starting point is to ask what the factors are that influence the preparation for and the beginning of a coaching session.

INITIATING

Initiating contact involves meeting, greeting, and gaining control of the coaching process. Initiating also takes place when a transition is made or a new idea is introduced. The main focus here is on making the initial contact with an employee because, in a coaching framework, this is extremely critical. It can make the difference between a motivated realigned developing employee for the organization or another statistic following an exit interview. The process begins with three simple steps:

1. Opening dialogue
2. Demonstrating interest and concern
3. Orienting to the session's objectives

OPENING DIALOGUE

This process of meeting, greeting, and gaining control is similar regardless of where you encounter a coaching opportunity—on the phone, in the office, or in the field. There are some factors, however, that influence the outcome of each situation.

On the phone, people can only respond to what they hear in your voice. Your courtesy and concern must quickly show. Regardless of how busy you are, you cannot sound rushed or impatient.

When you are face to face with your direct reports, they can see you and you can see them. This provides an opportunity for common courtesies, such as greeting in a friendly manner, smiling, and using other body language to indicate your eagerness to be of assistance.

One of the most important lessons you will ever learn about coaching is that there is no one in the situation but the person needing help and you. Two people working together to meet a need—that is the basis of the helping relationship.

The first coaching session with an employee begins with a degree of uncertainty. Although you have undoubtedly held coaching sessions before, an initial session makes you all the more conscious of the process. Remember: Even if you initiated the session, since the person has come for a specific purpose, he or she may know best how you can help.

Coaching sessions occur for one of two reasons: because they are initiated by the employee, or because they are initiated by you. Experience tells us that most coaching sessions are initiated by the manager. However, this is not an absolute; in fact, many opportunities for coaching are lost because the manager did not identify the staff member's request or concern as a potential coaching opportunity.

Because of these two possible ways in which the coaching session is initiated, the process of meeting, greeting, and gaining control can vary with the situation.

When the Employee Initiates

When a staff member asks to see you, the most sensible thing to do is to let him or her state what led to the need for the meeting. This is not always easy to do. You may feel that you should know what the issue is, so you might say, "So, I guess you're having problems with what's happening in your area." This may or may not be correct. If it is, you gain nothing except perhaps a sense of pride in guessing right. If it is not correct, the employee may be put in an awkward position. He or she may feel that this is what the meeting should be about and so, not wishing to contradict, may agree even though the real issue was something else entirely.

A better approach is to let him or her state why the meeting was requested. Once the formalities of greeting and being seated are over, the most useful thing you can do is listen as best as possible to what the person has to say. If you must say something, it ought to be brief and neutral:

"Please tell me what you wanted to see me about."

"I'm glad we have this chance to talk."

"I understand you wanted to see me."

"What's on your mind?"

Here are some things to remember about the initial coaching session with survivors that may also be true for subsequent sessions:

- The survivor does not always know what help may be available.
- The survivor may know but not be immediately able to verbalize it.
- The survivor may know but hesitate to state it bluntly so soon.
- The survivor may not like the idea of having to come for help.
- Our culture is so permeated with, "May I help you?" when the intent is clearly something else that it is probably best to try to provide help as much as possible without using the word.

Perhaps the key point to remember when an employee initiates the session is that he or she has a genuine interest in this meeting, and as long as you do not get in the way, he or she will begin to talk.

When the Manager Initiates

When you initiate a coaching session, it starts off with a different tone. After the initial greetings and perhaps some brief "small talk," you move directly to orientation. In this process there is both a rule and a concern.

The rule is simple. You state at the outset exactly why you asked the person to come and see you. The great danger in the manager-initiated session is the possibility that it will turn into a monologue, a lecture, or a combination of the two. You can avoid this danger if you stop talking after you have indicated what the purpose of the coaching session will be and have furnished the information, if any, you intended to give. Your survivors will usually have a great deal to say if they feel you are ready and willing to listen to them.

There are also some don'ts for manager-initiated coaching sessions:

- Don't say, "I suppose you know why I asked you to come in."
- Don't say, "We both know why you are here."
- Don't say, "Can you guess why I asked you to stop by?"

These openings are usually perceived as threatening. Employees may not know and yet fear that you will not believe they do not know. They may think they know and not wish to tell, or they may imagine several reasons why you asked them to come in—including that they are being fired—and become confused. This approach may be perceived as a challenge and reacted to in kind. Depending on their style, some people may decide to resist rather than cooperate. In short, it is very doubtful that this sort of opening will bring two people together.

Under the best of conditions, the person being coached is entitled to know immediately your purpose in calling him or her in for a discussion. In the survivor environment, it is critical. The more honest and open you are, the more honest and open the other party can be. You need to demonstrate at the outset that your purpose is to provide assistance and not to make judgments.

DEMONSTRATING INTEREST AND CONCERN

Trust is a critical factor in the success of a coaching session. One way of building trust and demonstrating interest is to ask questions. These initial questions must be open ended, friendly, and nonthreatening. Plan and practice your questions so that they are natural and effective. Your survivors will judge you by your skill at asking questions and your attentiveness to their answers.

Another way of building trust is self-disclosure. Self-disclosure is any revelation about yourself that is not readily apparent through observation or prior knowledge. Self-disclosure should not be irrelevant or too intimate. Used with care and discretion, self-disclosure can be an effective tool for establishing rapport and encouraging the exchange of information. People do not like dealing with strangers. You might say, "Let's see. This is the way I was feeling after my first six months."

Responses to relevant self-disclosures are usually positive. This happens because, when you reveal information about yourself, you appear trustworthy. Self-disclosure also encourages others to disclose and reduces the initial defensiveness in a new relationship.

Demonstrating interest and concern may be a distinctly separate element or integrated with the greeting. It can range from nonrelated personal comments to asking a survivor about his or her interest in the company or the current project. The purpose is to indicate that you are interested in the survivor as a person as well as an employee. When interest and concern have been exchanged, both you and the employee will more easily discuss the issues at hand. Expressions of interest and concern tend to build trust. Trust is the most important component for stimulating the free flow of information.

ORIENTING TO THE SESSION'S OBJECTIVES

Orientation establishes the parameters of the coaching session. It tells the person what will occur when the conversation goes beyond the greeting stage. Orientation answers these questions:

1. What do I need to do?
2. How long will it take?
3. What obligations will I have at the end?

In most cases, you will tell the person explicitly how much of your time is available for this session. This provides an important framework for the coaching session. "Sally, I want you to understand up front that I have a meeting in 20 minutes that I must attend. However, if we are not finished with our discussion by then, we will make another date to continue this meeting."

BEFORE BEGINNING A COACHING SESSION

1. Coaching, to be effective, should be an ongoing process, not a rare and isolated event. Coaching should be expected and accepted as an ongoing "part of the game."
2. Coaching sessions should be conducted in a reasonably private environment so that others in the immediate area are not aware of the specific feedback you may be providing. Praise in public; criticize in private.
3. Let the person know that you are going to be conducting a coaching session. When you schedule a session to discuss the feedback, you should let him or her know what performance you will be using as a basis for your feedback.
4. Before you can coach a person to improve, he or she must have a clear understanding of your goals for him or her and an opportunity to perform. Without goals and baseline performance measures, coaching becomes subjective and general.
5. Accurate feedback about how a person is performing, based on specific goals and standards, is the essence of the coaching session.

6. Always try to arrange a coaching session with as positive an expectation as possible. "I'd like to discuss with you some ways that will make you more effective on the telephone. I also want to point out some things that you are doing very well."

THE COACHING ENVIRONMENT

Make sure that the conditions created for the coaching session help the process. First, recognize that you are part of the coaching environment. Ask yourself a couple of questions:

- How do I feel about being a coach?
- How do I feel about coaching this particular individual?
- What would I like the outcome to be?
- What do I anticipate the outcome will be?
- If there is a discrepancy between my expected and desired outcomes, what would be the causes for that?
- How do I think the other person feels about being coached?
- What can I do to make this coaching session as helpful to this person as possible?

Of course, opportunities to praise or constructively criticize workers occur outside the structured coaching session. Alert managers take advantage of these opportunities to enhance or modify behavior. However, survivors need the structure, focus, and attention provided by a scheduled session.

The external and internal conditions you create for the survivor before his or her arrival and during the time the coaching session is taking place are of major significance. The atmosphere that will result if you succeed in your purpose will be intangible and yet will be felt by the survivor during the coaching session itself—or, if not then, will possibly be sensed some time after the session.

External Factors

External conditions such as the room where the coaching session takes place are difficult to specify, since they are both a matter of individual taste and the limitations dictated by the spaces available in the existing offices. Of course, a coaching session can be carried out almost anywhere, but it would be preferable for other external reasons that it occur in a room. The room can be any room you normally use for work. As long as the atmosphere is not threatening, noisy, or distracting, the person being coached will adjust to it. Under ordinary circumstances, nothing that is part of a manager's usual work material needs to be hidden away. You will probably want to put aside files on other employees in your charge, customer files, the remains of a late lunch, or any other items that would detract from the professional atmosphere of the room.

The question of how to arrange chairs often arises. In most coaching sessions, no more than two people are involved, and usually you decide where you and the employee will sit. There is no definitive answer as to a right or wrong arrangement. Some managers like to sit behind a desk facing the other person; others feel best when facing the other person without a desk between them. Still others prefer two equally comfortable chairs placed close to each other at a 90-degree angle, with a small table nearby.

An additional external consideration is minimizing the possibility of interruptions. A coaching session is demanding of both partners. The coach must concentrate as completely as possible on what is going on right there and then, thus establishing rapport and building trust. Phone calls, knocks on the door, people who want "just a word," secretaries who must have you sign this document at once may well destroy in seconds what you and your survivor have tried hard to build over a considerable length of time.

The coaching session is personal and deserves and needs the respect you wish to show the survivor. Once you appreciate this fact, you will find a way to achieve the necessary cooperation from your associates.

Internal Factors

The internal factors are perhaps more important to the person being coached than all of the external conditions put together. There are three primary internal conditions that are relevant to the successful coaching session:

1. Being ourselves—desiring to help
2. Knowing ourselves—trusting our ideas
3. Being honest—listening and absorbing

Being Ourselves—Desiring to Help

Two internal conditions are basic to the desire to help:

- Bringing to the coaching process just as much of your own knowledge, skill, and personal experience as is needed, stopping at the point where this may hinder the process or deny the survivor the help he or she needs
- Feeling within yourself that you wish to help this person as much as possible and that there is nothing at the moment more important to us

The fact that you hold this attitude will enable the person being coached to sense your sincerity. These are ideals you may seldom realize entirely, but when the person who is the object of your coaching perceives that you are doing the best you can, this will go a long way to hold down defensiveness and remove barriers to potential solutions.

It has been a successful coaching session if the survivor being coached takes away from the session the feeling that you may be trusted as a person and that he or she is respected by you as a person, knows what to improve, and has a plan to accomplish the necessary improvement.

You cannot accomplish an atmosphere of trust and respect by simply saying, "I can be trusted" or "I respect you." On the other hand, if mutual trust and respect are clearly present in the coaching session, they will not require words. The establishment of trust and respect in interpersonal relationships is what we generally speak of as "making contact" or "developing good rapport" or "establishing a relationship."

A manager sometimes makes the mistake of assuming that he or she is the most important person in the session. The atmosphere you create is determined most by the interest you express in what the other person is saying. You communicate this interest in many subtle ways. You must try to see yourself as the survivor sees you:

- Facial expressions
- Bodily gestures
- Tone of voice

To conduct a successful coaching session, you must bring your professional competence and a sincere concern for and support of the success of this person.

Knowing Ourselves—Trusting Our Ideas

The more you know about yourself and the better you can understand, evaluate, and control your behavior, the better you can understand and appreciate the behavior of others.

While it is certainly easier to say than to do, there is a clear relationship between how tolerant and comfortable you become with the things you both like and dislike in yourself and how effective you will ultimately be at helping others.

In addition, if you are at ease in your role as a coach, you will be in a better position to understand the other person during the coaching session. This ability to focus on the other person will help the other person trust you. If you do not feel the need to hide behind a mask, the survivor you are coaching will, in turn, hide less.

The more you can be free from a preoccupation with your own behavior, the better you will be able to concentrate wholeheartedly on the person being coached: listening to understand, trying to find out what it is like to feel the way the other person does, demonstrating genuine interest in the other person's problems.

Of course, you are expected to have ideas, suggestions, and solutions of your own. Because of the relative positions of authority, your ideas and feelings strongly influence the outcome of a coaching session. To minimize the tendency to accept your point of view in such situations, you must present your ideas as expressions of opinion that are not binding (except in cases where they are policy). The person being coached should feel that he or she will continue to receive your respect, no matter how he or she responds to your expressed feelings and ideas.

Ideally, the survivor will arrive at a plan of action that enables him or her to accept both the responsibility and ownership of the result and, at the same time, is acceptable to you. While this is the ideal, it often becomes necessary for you, particularly in performance-problem situations, to be more assertive about the necessary actions toward a solution.

Being Honest—Listening and Absorbing

The good coaching manager is honest with himself or herself so that he or she may be honest with the person being coached. If something was not heard or understood, or if focus was lost for a moment and listening was not taking place, it is far better to say so than to act as if, or pretend that, you understood.

Most subordinates feel best with managers whom they perceive as human beings with failings. This makes it easier for them both to reveal and discuss their own fallibility.

Being honest in the coaching session might involve telling the survivor that you do not have the solution to the problem. Instead of creating inhibitions, this frankness may encourage the survivor to confront the situation more energetically. To do this, you must not feel the need to appear to others as all-wise, all-knowing, or near-perfect.

Sometimes, managers are so concerned with what *they* are going to say next that they find it difficult to listen to and absorb what is going on. In the coaching situation, what you have to say is generally much less important than you think it is. Be careful that your own enthusiasm does not get in the way. Remember that it is the other person who needs the help. You do not need to prove how confident you are.

Both manager and subordinate bring something of themselves to the coaching session. It is best to act in such a way that you do not impose your needs and concerns on the other person. You cannot confuse your needs and concerns with his or hers. Behave in a manner that will let the survivor explore his or her own needs and concerns because of your presence and not in spite of it. Sensing trust and respect, he or she may be able to discover personal solutions, understandings, and energies that will help ensure his or her success.

PLANNING

Timing for coaching is an important element. To be most effective, the coaching session should be timed to occur very close to the performance you want to coach. If too much time passes between the behavior and the coaching session, important, specific information may be lost. In conducting a coaching session there are some general points to keep in mind from the beginning. These points form the basis of your coaching plan.

1. *Prepare for the session* by writing down some specific—even if rough—notes and an outline or agenda. The more specific you can be, the more helpful your feedback will be. Preferably, the individual whose progress or performance you will be discussing will be able to prepare some notes or discussion items from his or her perspective as well.

2. *Create a positive environment.* During the session, try to remain as positive and optimistic as possible regarding the individual's ability to improve the performance you plan to work on. Confidence and positive expectations are important to a person's motivation to improve.

3. *Specific observations are critical to good coaching.* Do not attempt to identify every "glitch" in the individual's performance. Rather, focus on the most significant aspect or two which can be improved. Write down the issues you will focus on before the meeting rather than trying to do it while one or both of you are talking.

4. *Avoid personality issues or generalizing performance.* A criticism such as "You really don't seem to care," all by itself, is not very helpful. The words or data you use to draw that conclusion are important. You will be able to discuss the information openly with the individual if you have set a positive environment and have made clear your interest is in helping him or her improve.

5. *Avoid setting yourself up as the perfect example of adaptability.* To be an effective coach does not require that you be better than each person. It does require that you be perceived as wanting to help, having valid observations, and being able to offer good ideas for improvement.

6. *Demonstrate good coaching skills* throughout the coaching session. For example, you should not interrogate an individual with a series of closed-ended questions and then tell him or her he or she needs to ask more open-ended questions. Rather, you should probe and ask open-ended coaching questions which cause the individual to gain insight into his or her performance and other concerns.

7. *Demonstrate your understanding of the individual's point of view* by empathizing—summarizing both the facts and feelings he or she provides. It is an excellent way to build trust and rapport. You should look for opportunities to describe appropriate benefits for him or her as a result of improving performance based on your coaching suggestions.

8. *Close on commitments* at the end of the coaching session. This is critical to confirming your, as well as the individual's, understanding of what is expected as a result of the coaching session.

QUESTIONING TO IDENTIFY SURVIVORS' NEEDS

When we think of what coaches do, we generally get an image of the traditional locker-room setting. It is halftime; the coach is pacing back and forth between the benches and the bowed heads, ranting, raving, and exhorting his troops to return to the field and render defeat, destruction, and humiliation to the evil forces that oppose them in the adjoining locker room.

In this context, it may be hard to believe that the most important tool for a coach is the questions he or she asks. The best coaches are those who ask questions rather than make presentations—those who listen more than they talk.

Your success as a coach depends on knowing your people. Questions are your means of collecting information about what the person you are coaching really needs. Without them, you are dependent on assumptions and whatever information the person is willing to volunteer. In addition, questions are your means of controlling the conversation. This is because your questions have a very powerful influence on the other person's behavior.

The following is a checklist that highlights potential problems. If your questioning behavior is not adequate:

- Did you help the survivor open up his or her perception of the problem as much as possible?
- Was he or she able to look at things the way they appear to him or her rather than the way they seem to you or someone else?
- Was the survivor free to look squarely at what he or she sees as the concern and to express it, or did he or she perceive the concern through the eyes of someone else?
- Did the survivor find his or her own problem or find a problem he or she thought should be found?
- Did your attitude or approach prevent the survivor from exploring his or her own experience, unhampered by external influences?
- Did you help the survivor move toward action and away from inaction with regard to his or her needs?
- Did you help the survivor explore and express what he or she found as a need rather than respond to your preconceived idea about what the need is?
- Did you let the survivor tell you how he or she genuinely feels about a problem, or how things truly look to him or her?
- Did you let the survivor explore his or her concerns in his or her own way, or did you lead him or her in a direction you chose?
- Did your behavior truly indicate the absence of threat?
- Did you really want to listen to the survivor, or did you want the survivor to listen to you because you already had the answer to the problem, because you were anxious to scold or correct, or because you really did not want to hear anything you did not know how to manage?

It is only through your questioning that a survivor will understand how your resources as manager and the resources of the organization can meet the needs you help identify. Research has demonstrated that the way a question is worded can significantly influence the response received, the completeness of the answer provided, and the impact the question has in terms of creating credibility and trust.

If you do not ask questions, you must make assumptions about the survivor's needs. Making assumptions is a dangerous strategy and often will cause you to go off in directions inappropriate for the survivor or create additional obstacles to overcome. However, it is important to know where to draw the line. Sometimes you can lead the survivor in a desired direction by the way you frame and ask your questions. When you overdo this, you do not allow the survivor to fully express himself or herself.

Some people require leading and like to be questioned, but they usually expect you to solve their problems for them rather than help them arrive at their own solutions. When you do this, there is no growth; and the survivor does not develop the ability to deal with future situations.

QUESTION CAUTIONS

A problem could develop if, by asking questions and getting answers, then asking more questions and getting more answers, you set up a pattern that neither you nor the other person can get out of. The person being coached should not perceive that the coaching situation is one in which you ask the questions and he or she answers. Even though the survivor already knows who the boss is, the question–answer pattern emphasizes the fact that you are the authority and that you know what is important and relevant.

Another difficulty arises from this pattern. The survivor expects you to come up with the solution. If you do not have a solution, or if you cannot offer help after the long third degree, what right had you to ask? Having asked the questions and obtained the answers, you will feel obligated to formulate a solution to provide *the* answer; to pronounce *your* verdict.

The suggestion here is that the question–answer pattern does not create an atmosphere in which a positive working relationship can develop. Be careful that your questioning does not get in the way of the survivor's ability to discover more about himself or herself, strengths and weaknesses, and an opportunity to grow and thrive in the new environment. The ultimate test of a question is this: Will the question I am about to ask be helpful to the person I am coaching?

ACTIVE LISTENING

To understand the concept of active listening, you first need to understand something about defensiveness. Among the factors that hinder communication between two people, defensiveness ranks at the top of the list. The less defensive you can become, the more you will be able to help the survivor discard his or her defenses. Communication between you will improve as a consequence.

Whenever a manager says, directly or indirectly, to the survivor, "You shouldn't say this," he or she is using his or her value system to block communication. Whenever a manager states or implies, "I can't listen to this," he or she is telling the survivor not to communicate—to be ashamed of what he or she just said and to keep silent.

If the manager in a coaching situation will not listen, who will? If the survivor is thinking, "I can't speak out on this issue," or "The manager doesn't want to hear this," major obstacles to good communication exist. Good communication in the coaching session becomes possible when the survivor can say, "I know the manager won't like hearing this, but I also know he or she can take it."

NONDEFENSIVE LISTENING

You can never be certain just how the survivor perceives you. The only choice you have is to be as genuinely yourself as possible and to behave as nondefensively as possible in the hope that eventually you will be seen as you really are.

The psychologist Carl Rogers has pointed out that our own need to evaluate, to confirm, or to deny constitutes a major obstacle to good communication. Some managers use authority as a defense. When confronted by a façade of superiority, the survivor puts up a defense. In this case, there are two major obstacles to good communication: your use of authority and the survivor's use of weapons to combat it.

The alternative is an atmosphere in which a sense of equality prevails—equality of worth and dignity, with each person fully respecting the other. In such an atmosphere, the defensive shields are down. Both parties have no alternative but to be flexible and to look at and respond to all aspects of a given situation. You may help the survivor reach a decision—in some cases, even make the decision for the survivor—but whatever happens, it will be done *with* the survivor, not *to* the survivor.

If you tend to talk as much, or even more, than the person you are coaching, chances are that you are blocking communication. You may be lecturing and not becoming sufficiently aware of the survivor's needs and frame of reference. On the other hand, you can also talk too little. Coaching sessions with many pauses, awkward silences, and tenseness between both parties might suggest that you need to become a more active participant in the process.

The concept of active listening, as discussed in this chapter, is based on a test devised by Carl Rogers that is frequently used in human relations training. In the test, two or more people are asked to discuss a topic on which they hold differing views. Each is allowed to say whatever he or she likes, under one condition: Before voicing his or her point of view, each person must restate the ideas and feelings expressed by the person who spoke immediately before and do so to that person's satisfaction. The assumption is that if I can tell you what you said and felt, then I heard and understood you. If I cannot, either I placed obstacles in the way, or you did not make yourself sufficiently clear.

In the coaching session, you may not always want to restate the thoughts and feelings expressed by the survivor, but if you are able to recapture the content in this manner, it will show that communication lines are open between you. In other words, you are listening actively when you can demonstrate that you have heard, understood, and accepted the ideas and feelings of the survivor you are coaching.

This approach minimizes obstacles to communication, and in this atmosphere, the survivor will be receptive to the ideas and feelings that you communicate. The result will be a genuine coaching experience.

EMPATHIZING

Empathizing is the most powerful active listening skill. Like paraphrasing, it summarizes and reflects back to the survivor the content of what he or she has been saying. However, it goes one step further and demonstrates your understanding of the facts and how the person is feeling about the topic or issue. Understanding the concern, emotion, or motivational intent of what a survivor is saying is critical to understanding his or her feelings and concerns. Empathizing can be used very effectively to

- Clarify feelings
- Demonstrate a sense of concern
- Increase the credibility of the coach
- Build additional trust
- Increase the survivor's desire to seek solutions to problems

It is important that you reflect the survivor's opinion or concern—not your own feelings or opinions. It is virtually impossible to empathize if you have not asked sufficient questions to elicit feelings.

One way to improve the focus on the survivor rather than on you is to watch for responses that begin with the word "I"; for example, "I understand your concern." This is sympathy, not empathy. A simple strategy for focusing on the survivor in a more empathetic fashion is to start your summary or paraphrase with the word "you"; for example, "You're concerned about being let go if there is a new round of cutbacks." In this second example, the manager is reflecting concern from the survivor's point of view.

Note that the empathetic reflection does not suggest or imply that the manager agrees with the survivor's perspective but simply reflects understanding of the concern.

DEALING WITH CONFLICT

In one sense, we could say that the activities involved in active listening are responsive. You are communicating to the survivor that you both understand the facts of his or her situation and can articulate the associated feelings. However, you now have come to the point in the coaching session where you and the survivor have to get down to cases. That is, it is time to move toward a plan of action that is going to resolve what is perceived as a coaching issue and move the survivor toward realignment.

In the perfect world, survivors in a coaching session would understand and reveal all of their needs and concerns. They would immediately see the wisdom of your suggestions and would never disagree.

We do not live in the perfect world. Therefore, you will often find it necessary to address some issue, disagreement, previously hidden concern, or unacceptable idea generated from the discussion that may cause the survivor to withhold commitment to a plan of action.

The first thing to understand about conflict is that it is inevitable. Virtually all relationships include disagreements and misunderstandings. The manager–subordinate relationship is no exception.

While it is unrealistic to expect to avoid conflict completely, it is not unrealistic to believe that you can create and sustain working relationships in which conflict is almost always dealt with in positive and productive ways. When you experience conflict in a coaching session, you can choose to react to it in a number of possible ways:

- Ignore it.
- Actively deny its existence.
- Run away.
- Attack the other person.
- Give in.
- Agree to meet the other person halfway.
- Postpone the confrontation.
- Work through the problem until you resolve the differences.

How you will respond is influenced by a number of factors, including your style of dealing with conflict. For example, you and the survivor you are coaching exist within a power relationship. Power is usually defined as the ability of one person to provide something another person wants and cannot readily get anywhere else. The survivor wants to succeed and feels that he or she can only succeed with your help. This is the basis of the power that you, the manager, have over your survivors.

Conflict over a power relationship can arise when the manager disagrees with the survivor's expectations of what the manager should be able to do to ensure the survivor's success. The survivor may be thinking, "Why can't you get me additional help?" "Why can't you give some of my projects to someone else?" "Why can't you guarantee that there won't be any more layoffs?" The manager is thinking, "You need to develop as an independent businessperson and find creative solutions." "It's *your* job to resource your projects so you can meet the objectives." "There aren't any guarantees." Especially when the stakes are high, disagreements over power relationships can be very difficult to handle.

Conflicts can also arise from the opposite condition; that is, the survivor may feel that the manager is exerting too much power over the decision-making process. Conflicts often arise when a survivor perceives the structure and directives provided by the manager as interfering with his or her right to decide how to proceed and what experiences are meaningful to his or her own development.

When you handle an objection, disagreement, or misunderstanding badly, it is usually because you become angry. While anger may have a place in the manager–survivor relationship, in most cases the manager who controls anger at a disagreement will be more effective. There is no situation in which anger is the only possible response. If you respond with anger, it is because you have chosen to respond with anger.

A good coach takes responsibility for his or her own feelings. Following is a list of don'ts when responding to objections:

- Don't respond to conflict with commands, accusations, or judgments.
- Don't describe anyone's feelings but your own.
- Don't use generalizations, accusations, inferences, or other kinds of evaluation as a substitute for specific descriptions of events, behavior, or feelings.

While staying in touch and managing your responses, it is also necessary to deal directly with the subject matter of your disagreement. Here are three suggestions that help focus your attention on the process of handling objections:

1. *Limit your disagreement to one issue at a time.* Make sure the specific issue of the disagreement is mutually understood. Be sure that you and the person involved agree about the focus of your disagreement. Restrict the argument to topics that actually mean something to both of you. Avoid making mountains out of molehills.
2. *Remember to be tentative in your evaluation of ideas.* Control your need to fight or win at the expense of the other person. Realize that you do not have to prove the other person 100-percent wrong; there may be a way both you and the survivor

can win by finding an alternative solution. Be careful about making assertions or arguments until you are sure you understand the survivor's point of view clearly. The objection or disagreement might be based on a misunderstanding. Keep your active listening skills working to stay in touch with any changes in the context of the disagreement. You may find yourself continuing to argue a point that the survivor has already conceded.

3. *Be prepared to offer and explain alternative actions or ideas.* If you are prepared to criticize a position or an idea, you must also be prepared to offer and explain an alternative point of view. Your main goal may be to change a course of action that your survivor is taking, but a disagreement involves not just stopping one kind of action but also starting a different one. Be ready with suggested alternatives and, even more important, be willing to work mutually with the survivor to reach a choice that both of you find acceptable.

Sometimes a conflict, obstacle, or objection appears as if it cannot be resolved. It is helpful to remember that most conflicts look unresolvable at some point. People tend to take exaggerated positions that they are actually willing to move away from. As a manager, you need to create an opportunity for the survivor to have the freedom to change.

If you have examined the context, used descriptions in place of evaluation, shared your feelings about the conflict, kept the conflict on a specific issue, and offered positive suggestions for a solution, and the conflict still has not been resolved, call a time-out. You may need to let an hour, a day, even several days or a week pass to give all persons involved time to think and feel things through. Do not wait so long that the issue gets ignored or forgotten. However, you will need to build in some breathing space—some time to put things into perspective.

Remember that there is nothing inherently destructive or threatening about conflict. The important thing is how you set about handling objections, obstacles, or uncertainties. Resolving conflict between yourself and your survivors is much easier when you listen responsively, empathize, and, at all times, work to diminish defensiveness.

COMMITTING TO ACTION

Gaining commitment during the coaching session is in many ways similar to initiating contact, except it operates in reverse. Like gaining commitment for a sale, completing any kind of interpersonal interaction can be difficult for some people. The manager may be afraid that he or she will make the survivor feel pushed out. Also, since there are always schedules to keep, the manager may not be prepared to end but must bring this session to a close. There are two basic factors in preparing to end the session:

1. Both the manager and the survivor should be aware that the session is ending and accept this fact.

2. During the commitment phase, no new material should be introduced. Commitment concerns issues that have already been discussed. If there are new or additional issues, another coaching session should be scheduled.

It is your responsibility to deal with these two factors as effectively as possible. Unless the survivor is a veteran of many coaching sessions, he or she will not always know how much time is remaining in the session. You can help by indicating, at some point before the end, that there are only a few minutes left, using phrases like "Well, our time is just about up," "Is there anything else we need to discuss before we summarize where we are?," or "My sense is that neither of us has anything else to add at this point. Well then, let's see where we are."

There are several very good reasons for avoiding new issues during the commitment stage. Having dealt with the issue at hand and beginning to think about the next problem of the day, you will not be as concerned or listening as closely as you should to the new material. What often happens is that you find yourself becoming angry at the survivor for bringing up new material that might have been introduced previously. The situation is unfair to both of you, since you cannot provide your undivided attention and the survivor will probably not get what he or she needs. To end, in spite of the presentation of new issues, is easier when both of you know that another meeting is scheduled.

Coaching sessions are not inflexible, mechanical meetings with the manager keeping one eye on the clock. However, being conscious of the time limits can help most coaching sessions. Both parties involved accept and work within the time structure and, therefore, maximize the time that they have. It promotes the notion that working together in this manner has limitations and that, beyond the coaching session, both you and the survivor are persons with professional and private obligations that must be respected.

The final step in the coaching session is to obtain a commitment from the survivor to proceed with an appropriate action. This step comes naturally and logically if specific needs have been identified and appropriate and relevant suggestions have been presented.

During the coaching session, the survivor's receptivity to your ideas and suggestions will vary. After he or she has indicated an interest in a suggestion that you have presented, it is appropriate for you to confirm the acceptance of your suggestion. To do this you should

1. Confirm the needs as you understand them.
2. Summarize the specific actions agreed to, including resources, time frames, and the like.
3. Ask the survivor to confirm his or her commitment to the agreed-upon actions.
4. Provide a solid statement of support.

In Step 1, you refocus survivors on what is important to them. In Step 2, you summarize the specific actions. There should be commitments to action from both parties. What is the survivor going to do? What are you going to do to support and monitor the actions? How will you both know the actions are succeeding? In Step 3, you request that the survivor confirm his or her commitment. This ensures that both parties understand and agree to the actions. The confirmation becomes a contract and should be noted either informally or in a follow-up memo.

In Step 4, you provide a solid statement of support. Remember that being criticized or asked for a commitment is not a comfortable situation for most of us. Even when it is well meaning and constructive, the fact that you are coaching your survivor about a performance issue or other survivor manifestations suggests that he or she has failed in some way. It is extremely important, at the end of each coaching session, that you make a statement that reinforces your belief in the future success of that survivor.

CHAPTER 11

Action Plan for
Survivor Transition

Any programs or interventions designed to realign survivors will take somewhat different shapes depending on the nature of the organization, its size, the configuration of its work force, its culture, and other factors.

All of the possible variables cannot be accounted for in one case model. However, we have found that using the Survivor Management Model as a development tool sets the stage for asking the right questions and developing a progression that will work in most situations.

While we acknowledge the part that differences play in developing programs, it is also important to know the similarities. The similarities in the survivor environment provide the impetus for action.

There are three key actions that need to be taken in a survivor realignment program: Action 1 we call "Management Appraisal"; Action 2, "Understanding Functions, Roles, and Responsibilities"; and Action 3, "Strategic Planning and Future Thinking."

ACTION 1—MANAGEMENT APPRAISAL

As our earlier discussion of the Survivor Management Model indicates, there is a strong tendency on the part of line managers to become focused on technical-, cultural-, and political-resistant forces. Without the full involvement of the line managers, it is difficult if not impossible to expect any meaningful change to take place in the survivor workers.

A vehicle is needed to capture the managers' attention and clearly focus it on the future rather than on the past. We have found that the best way to put the manager into play, as well as send a strong signal to the survivors that the organization is making a serious effort, is to begin with an assessment profile. By putting himself or herself on the line as part of what must potentially change, the manager puts himself or herself into play as an integral part of the change process.

We recommend a multidimensional assessment be conducted with all of the appropriate line managers. This should be a 360-degree assessment, incorporating input from the manager, the manager's superior, and the manager's subordinates. A more detailed discussion of 360-degree assessments is provided in Chapter 8.

ACTION 2—UNDERSTANDING FUNCTIONS, ROLES, AND RESPONSIBILITIES

In order for workers to begin to function less like individual survivors and more like part of a group or a team, they must have a clear understanding of the tasks, responsibilities, and expectations that they are facing in the new organization. Discussion groups, coaching and counseling sessions, and formal workshops need to be developed to ensure that individual survivors understand the differences between where they were and where they are now with regard to tasks, responsibilities, reporting relationships, and the like, and also to ensure that they have the appropriate organizational support to develop the necessary competencies to meet these objectives.

As an important part of the survivor management process, the workshops, discussion groups, and one-on-one sessions provide an opportunity for survivors to express their anger, concern, and fears, and thereby begin the transition process.

Since most of the focus following a downsizing is placed on how to re-apportion work, and given the current organizational thrust toward more team activity, at least some workshop attention must be placed on understanding the differences between work groups, teams, and other group processes available for problem-solving and decision-making activities.

ACTION 3—STRATEGIC PLANNING AND FUTURE THINKING

Depending on the identified objectives of the organization, the interventions at this stage consist of a combination of seminars, strategic planning sessions, and facilitated department meetings.

In order for an organization to successfully work through the transition from its current state to a realigned and recommitted team of workers, it is critical that all staff actively participate in problem solving, team bonding, and the generation of action plans and new objectives.

Survivors must accept the precept that they will be primarily responsible not only for their own success but for their own professional development. Every effort must be made at this stage to ensure that all survivors have involvement in the strategic-planning issues. In a successful realignment, all workers feel that, individually and collectively, they own a piece of the future.

CASE MODEL FOR SURVIVOR TRANSITION

In May 1991, an international news and information corporation was in the process of downsizing and reorganizing their major departments, particularly the sales and marketing groups. As the consultants to assist the transition, we entered into a discussion with the vice president of sales and marketing of a key information-intensive and revenue-producing group. She had been tasked with the assignment of reorganizing her management team—which represented sales, marketing, development, and administrative functions—to increase revenue over a short, six-month time frame; to reconfigure geographic territories and distribution of work (since staff were scattered throughout the United States and Canada); and to build a cohesive, committed team of professionals who could lead this division into economic stability and continued growth. By our definition, both the managers and their direct reports were survivors.

The process began with several discussions with the vice president. From her perspective, the group was suffering from a morale problem that was impacting productivity. She also felt that there was little effective communication taking place between the functional units. We set two primary goals: to open lines of communication, and to assist the group toward working together more effectively.

Using the Survivor Management Model, we began to focus on organizational transformation and realignment and the reestablishment of individual loyalty, commitment and innovation. Following is a description of the organizational intervention which was implemented for this department in the three phases outlined in the model: Assessment–Acknowledgment, Implementation–Transition, and Follow-Up and Evaluation–Realignment.

ASSESSMENT–ACKNOWLEDGMENT

When the vice president of sales and marketing, as representative of the organization, contracted with us as consultants, there was a sense that, because of the tumultuous changes, downsizings, and reorganizations which were occurring, the current department structure could not fully support the increasing demands facing it at that time and beyond. In addition to the need for an organizational intervention to address a decline in group productivity and revenue and a growing morale problem, the vice president wanted to create an organizational climate where concerted teamwork and collaborative communication systems were in place.

As might be expected, there were strong resistant forces on both the cultural and economic fronts: low morale, negativity, and cynicism were becoming accepted behavior within the organization. This period was clearly a difficult one for any company but particularly for one with its major clients in the financial services and banking communities that were still trying to recover from serious reversals.

Initial interviews were conducted with all of the managers to discover their points of view, ideas, and special problems and to assess their willingness to "buy in" to the organizational development initiative. These were followed by interviews with key staff members in each functional area.

The vice president and the consultants were encouraged by the reactions of individual managers and staff within the department. They were predictably frustrated and disoriented, but they had collectively reached the Acknowledgment phase of the Survivor Management Model, where staff typically will express and demonstrate manifestations of anxiety, guilt, disorientation, disengagement, and what Daniel Yankelovich and John Immerwahr refer to as the "commitment gap," described in their survey report, *Putting the Work Ethic to Work*. The information-management industry provides a good example of the "discretionary effort" concept. In the information-management industry (and other places where technology is playing an increasing role), the composition of the work force has been undergoing a complex set of changes. Besides being survivors, today's workers are better educated, resent authority for authority's sake, and demand greater autonomy in the workplace. Because of the nature of their work, they have greater discretion over how hard they will perform. This combination of technology, discretion, and the desire for autonomy creates what Yankelovich and Immerwahr call a "commitment gap." "Because of a widespread 'commitment gap,' many high-discretion jobholders are, by their own admission, holding back effort from their jobs, giving less than they are capable of giving, and less than they are, in principle, willing to give."[1]

It was determined that the managers had the greatest need and the potential for the greatest impact. The first task was to develop objectives that everyone would accept and that would serve to accomplish the goals. We secured a commitment from management to implement and participate fully in all interventions.

We began again with the vice president, who was asked to detail both the critical issues to be addressed and goals and objectives to be achieved. While the end goal was to increase sales revenue through the reorganization of this department into a cohesive, collaborative team, five key objectives were developed, which were to be addressed through the organizational development interventions in this program:

1. To clarify the organization's cultural issues, department goals and objectives, and pressures experienced by each group

2. To identify leadership and motivational techniques, such as coaching and counseling strategies, constructive criticism, handling performance problems, and providing recognition, for improving staff performance and productivity

3. To effectively delegate and delineate tasks, responsibilities, and authority

4. To use influencing and negotiation skills for increasing team collaboration

5. To create, assess, and implement specific team-building and work group–building strategies

The participants in the resulting program included the vice president and fourteen of her key management staff, representing sales, marketing, development, and administration.

After program goals and objectives were solidified, we moved into the individual assessment component of this phase, where a management communications and feedback tool, the Manager Appraisal Profile (MAP), as described in Chapter 8, was used to collect critical, objective information on the strengths and development areas of each participant. With the MAP, each participant received a blueprint of feedback from three distinct sources: the manager, the subordinates, and himself or herself. Each source was asked to rate the participant on the strengths of five management performance areas:

1. Communications and Interpersonal Relations

2. Leadership, Motivation, and Supervision

3. Planning, Time Management, and Administration

4. Problem Solving and Decision Making

5. Training, Development, and Coaching

Each of the fifteen participants, including the vice president, was administered a MAP. The information gathered was then quantified and analyzed by the consultants.

IMPLEMENTATION–TRANSITION

For the implementation–transition phase, it was determined that the best vehicle for impacting some of the objectives was focused training. There were two activities:

- Individual interviews with staff, including review of results codified from the MAP
- Department Training and Development Program

Individual Interviews

The purpose of the Implementation–Transition phase is to take survivors and their organizations beyond the Acknowledgment phase of expressing feelings and concerns. It is during transition that confrontation and mobilization are used to guide the survivors and the organization through this difficult phase so that realignment and recommitment may be achieved. In the first activity—which consisted of one-on-one strategic interviews with department participants—questioning; evaluating; sharing; and, to a certain extent, confronting expressions of anger and concern were exhibited by the staff. Feedback from his or her manager, subordinates, and himself or herself was discussed with each participant, confirming positive managerial behaviors with some and confronting weak managerial behavior areas with others. According to the MAP, when there is more than a ten-point differential between feedback perceptions (e.g., if a manager and his or her boss differ ten points or more in their feedback scale or if there is a wide discrepancy with staff feedback), this indicates areas of development for the manager and suggests that he or she needs to initiate a dialogue in one or more of his or her working relationships.

The consultants also tried to ensure that individual concerns and objectives would be addressed in the larger Training and Development Program. From a systemic viewpoint, we also were examining individual attributes, personalities, and perceived and real relationships among department members, since both content and process were critical to achieving objectives within the Training and Development Program.

Training and Development Program

The second part of the Implementation–Transition phase occurred with the rollout of the two-day Training and Development Program, entitled "Successful Management Strategies." It was here where all participants came to terms with the need to take the impotent feelings of anger, guilt, disappointment, disorientation, and disengagement and transform them into positive, action-oriented collective behaviors, such as questioning, evaluating and monitoring, sharing, bonding, planning, and future thinking, in order to transform the department and organization into a thriving, realigned and recommitted, dynamic force.

For an organization or department to work through the transition phase successfully with a goal toward realignment, it is critical that all the staff actively participate in a common activity or series of activities where problem solving, team bonding, and generation of action plans and new objectives are practiced. For the duration of the two-day Successful Management Strategies program, all managers and their vice president committed themselves to finding new and collaborative methods of working with one another. By the time the program had begun, there was strong evidence that team members were committed to the revitalization of their department. They were eager to be moved along a continuum of discovery and realignment. While there may have been some concern or skepticism about the outcome, the fact that some major action was taking place was itself very reinforcing.

The Training and Development Program took the form of an experiential, facilitator-guided workshop; methodology included group discussions, behavior models, individual exercises, and small-group problem-solving workshops. On Day 1, the vice president introduced the program, both articulating the critical need for this intervention and committing herself and the group to two days of confronting, collaborating, and future thinking. It was clear that the group had put its trust and its direction in the hands of the process. After eliciting participant objectives and articulating program objectives, the first group activity was introduced, "Gaining Perspective—Empathy Exercise." The participants were given instructions that required each person to assume the role and perspective of someone in another functional area, yet in their same department. Specifically, small groups were set up; and each person was given a hat labeled sales, marketing, development, or administration, making sure that the hat assigned differed from their usual job function. Each small group was then given the task of constructing a presentation on a new company product. During the group presentations, each person was asked to react as he or she believes someone from the area represented by his or her hat would.

The exercise proved to be both a lighthearted and a thought-provoking insight into the way we are often compelled to react as a result of a particular function. Certainly, being able to view "objectively" how one might be coming across to a group, as an outsider, can assist one in quickly changing unknowingly obstacle-producing behavior into more collaborative team-building behavior. This exercise also provided the group with an icebreaking, sharing experience that increased trust and openness.

To address the objective of increasing leadership and motivation among staff, the participants were put into small groups and provided with a list of job factors such as good pay, challenging job, working with people I like, and the like and were asked to rank these factors as they believe their staff would rank them. The results were then processed in several ways. First, they were compared to ratings derived from research done by The Public Agenda. Then the factors were divided into Frederick Herzberg's classification of motivators and satisfiers. Participants then discussed the distinction between motivators and satisfiers and how managers create ambivalence in their workers by emphasizing satisfiers over motivators. Further discussion then pointed out changes in the current work force and organizational life and emphasized the need to recapture a larger measure of the "discretionary effort" available in the work force. The participants were able to construct specific motivational plans for their staff as a result of this exercise.

The afternoon of the first day focused on the process of communication among team members; since, geographically, individuals are not located in one area and since, because this particular organization is linked with an E-mail system, actual written and verbal communications need to be examined. The exercise required participants to pass information along to others using a chain-network configuration. Participants were given specific roles of director, manager, and employee, with certain hierarchal guidelines set (i.e., the proper chain of command must be followed for any communication, employees must wait for a directive from their manager before any action can take place, etc.). Group discussion following the simulation centered on both exploring and exploding certain organizational communication practices which were no longer valuable and on constructing the best methods and combinations of methods for communicating with each other better as a team.

Since the larger organization in which this department functions operates largely within a matrix framework, the ability to get work from other people in other departments depends on using influence as a primary method of communication. Participants took an Influencing Style Assessment instrument, which classified their preferential influencing style as Assertive–Persuasive, Reward and Punishment, Participation and Trust, or Common Vision. Specific behaviors associated with each of the styles were identified. The participants were then provided with role-play scenarios that required the use of the various influencing behaviors. They were next grouped into triads, with each person having the opportunity to play the role of the person who influences, the person who is being influenced, and the observer. As a result of this exercise, participants were able to identify and demonstrate specific behaviors which can increase their communicative effectiveness both inside and outside of the department.

The final activity of Day 1 consisted of Action Planning, where participants related the day's activities to their specific problem issues and discussed actions that could be taken to enhance the performance of the group as a whole. Participants were assigned the *Harvard Business Review* article "Managing Your Boss,"[2] by John J. Gabarro and John P. Kotter, for evening reading.

Day 2 of the Successful Management Strategies program began with an in-depth discussion of the highlights of the "Managing Your Boss" article. The participants then individually completed an exercise that required them to examine their strengths and weaknesses, their work styles, their bosses' work styles, and other factors that influence the boss–subordinate relationship. Group members were then placed into small groups. Each group was asked to generate three key questions the group needed answered by or for the vice president (style, communication, interaction, future plans, etc.) in order to manage the team's relationship with her more effectively. The vice president responded to the questions in as forthright, honest, and candid a manner as was possible. The time allotted for this exercise was extended to accommodate the positive discussion on improvement of intergroup relationships. It was here where the vice president truly achieved a bonding with the team, with an assertion for proaction, commitment, and empowerment among her people.

The next exercise picked up on the solidification of the group and was entitled "Space Tower–Building and Maintaining a High-Performance Team." Participants were divided into two teams, and were required to plan and construct a Tinker Toy structure (Space Tower) that met specific criteria. The two teams competed with each other to see who met the criteria best. The discussion that followed pointed out the need for planning in group work, the clear definition of roles, capitalization on special abilities of team members, seeking and valuing the input of all team members, and demonstrating the overt superiority of a good working team versus individual effort. The participants then made specific application to implementing new team-building techniques for their work groups as a result of this exercise.

Last, as both a closing ritual and a sharing mechanism, the group, which was now functioning as a high-performing team in reality, participated in "Team-Talk." A list of team-building questions (such as "What can I do to make your job easier?" and "One question I've always wanted to ask you is . . .") previously posted provided the questions for this exercise. Participants were arranged in a circle and provided with a ball. Each person got the opportunity to ask at least one question and tossed the ball to someone he or she wanted to answer that question. A general discussion of the program followed, where it became apparent that the group was near completion of the transition phase. They were ready to go back to the job with their energies refocused, with goals and objectives clarified, with the promotion of a common vision, and with the implementation of specific action plans.

FOLLOW-UP AND EVALUATION–REALIGNMENT

Subsequent follow-up sessions confirmed the continuation of the realignment phase. Discussions with the vice president indicated that, individually, staff had become more productive, more clearly refocused, possessing clearer professional and personal objectives, and that there had been an increase of trust and loyalty among group members. What the group collectively needs more of is a sense of innovation, where the group enters a more mature phase which is less leader focused and more team driven.

To date, five additional departments have worked though similar interventions. While it is impossible to link cause and effect directly in this case, the company continues to enjoy significant growth; and its stock has risen more than 30 percent since the beginning of the realignment program.

Appendixes

Survivor Climate Assessment

Debates about what constitutes effective teams and work groups can be endless, but most well-working organizations seem to exhibit a set of nine common characteristics:

1. Clear objectives and agreed-upon goals
2. Openness and confrontation
3. Participation and trust
4. Cooperation and conflict
5. Workable procedures
6. Leadership
7. Benchmarking and review
8. Personal development
9. Good intergroup relations

The following instrument is an effective tool for assessing your survivor environment. It also helps initiate the process of realignment by providing the survivors with both an outlet for their frustration and a focus on key issues to work on.

SURVIVOR CLIMATE QUESTIONNAIRE

This simple questionnaire has been developed as an aid to discovering which of the nine characteristics could be most useful to your group. It is a collection of statements that members might be heard to making about their group. The more people in the group who complete it, the more accurate the results will be.

Instructions for Completion

Turn to the answer grid on page 189. Work through the statements in numerical order, marking an "x" on the appropriate square of the grid if you think a statement about *your* group is broadly true. If you think a statement is not broadly true, leave the square blank. Do not spend a great deal of time considering each statement; a few seconds should be long enough.

Remember that the results will be worthwhile only if you are truthful.

1. We are forced to accept decisions by others.
2. People are not encouraged to speak out.
3. Because of the current climate, it is every man for himself.
4. The general level of communication needs improving.
5. Decisions are made at the wrong level.
6. Some of the managers are not trustworthy.
7. We seldom question the content or usefulness of our meetings.
8. Insufficient development opportunities are available.
9. We are frequently at war with other departments.
10. No one is really clear where we are going.
11. People do not say what they really think.
12. People have an "I'm all right, Jack" attitude.
13. Conflict is destructive rather than stimulating in this group.
14. There is inadequate information upon which to base decisions.
15. Our managers do not tell us the truth.
16. We do not learn from our mistakes.
17. Managers do not help subordinates to learn.
18. Relationships with other groups are not cordial.
19. We are all very busy but we do not seem to get anywhere.
20. Issues are brushed under the carpet.
21. It would help if people were more willing to admit their mistakes.
22. There is mistrust and hostility.
23. People are uncommitted to the decisions.
24. There is little loyalty.
25. Outside opinions are unwelcome.
26. There should be more job sharing.
27. We seldom work effectively with other groups or departments.
28. We do not spend adequate time planning for the future.
29. Delicate issues are avoided.
30. People get "stabbed in the back."

31. We do not really work together.
32. Inappropriate people make the decisions.
33. Managers are weak and not prepared to stand up and be counted.
34. I do not receive sufficient feedback.
35. The wrong kinds of skills are valued.
36. Help is not forthcoming from other parts of the organization.
37. We do not have a clear view of what is expected of us.
38. Honesty is not a feature of our group.
39. I do not feel strengthened by my colleagues.
40. Skills and information are not shared sufficiently.
41. It is the strong personalities that get their own way.
42. Dignity is not afforded to people.
43. We should spend more time questioning the way we operate.
44. Managers do not take personal development seriously.
45. The rest of the organization does not understand us.
46. The way an individual is valued has little to do with what he or she achieves.
47. There are too many secrets.
48. Conflicts are avoided.
49. Disagreements fester.
50. Commitment to decisions is low.
51. Our manager(s) believe(s) that tighter supervision produces increased results.
52. There are too many taboos in this group.
53. There are much better opportunities in other departments.
54. We put a lot of energy into defending our boundaries.
55. Priorities are unclear.
56. People are not involved sufficiently in decision making.
57. There are too many recriminations.
58. There is not enough listening.
59. We do not utilize the skills we have available.
60. Managers believe that people are inherently lazy.
61. We spend too much time doing and not enough thinking.
62. Individuals are not encouraged to grow.
63. We do not try to understand the views of other groups.
64. We do not understand what other departments are aiming at.
65. There is a general tendency to back down if challenged.
66. Generally, there is low trust here.

67. People are unwilling to take the views of others into account.
68. We do not consider alternative solutions sufficiently.
69. Yesterday's approaches and attitudes prevail with our management.
70. The accepted order is rarely challenged.
71. Our manager(s) lack(s) the skills to develop others.
72. We have too little influence on the rest of the organization.
73. Managers do not plan for the future together.
74. In this group, it pays to keep your mouth shut.
75. A lot of time is spent "defining" territory.
76. There are too many fights.
77. People feel frustrated because they are not consulted.
78. Management does not care whether people are happy in their work.
79. We seldom change our working procedures or organization.
80. We should spend more time growing our own senior people.
81. We do not reach out to help other groups.
82. Different parts of the organization are pulling in different directions.
83. People are not prepared to put their true beliefs on the table.
84. People are not really helped to develop.
85. Everyone seems to be continually engaged in a battle.
86. There is a need for more participation in decisions.
87. Managers take little action to make employees' jobs interesting and meaningful.
88. Delicate issues are not raised.
89. Many people trained by the company later join competitors.
90. Ideas from outside the group are not used.
91. Our aims are not democratically agreed on.
92. Team members do not get sufficient honest feedback.
93. People should stand on their own feet more.
94. We should discuss our differences more.
95. Team members are not sufficiently involved in making decisions.
96. Our leader does not make the best use of us.
97. We should seriously consider the relevance of our meetings.
98. Individual development is stifled by the group.
99. Information does not flow freely enough between groups.
100. We should place more emphasis on results.
101. People "hear what they want to hear" rather than the truth.
102. More time should be devoted to discussing fundamental values.

103. We do not get down to the root of our differences.
104. Decisions are taken at the wrong level.
105. Our leader is not true to his or her own beliefs.
106. We should take more account of how others see us.
107. People are discouraged from being authentic.
108. The organization as a whole is not a happy place to work in.

ANSWER GRID

Follow the instructions given at the beginning of the questionnaire. In the grid there are 108 squares, each one numbered to correspond to a question. Mark an "x" through the square if you think a statement about your organization is broadly true. If you think a statement is not broadly true, leave this square blank. Fill in the top line first, working from left to right. Then fill in the second and subsequent lines. Be careful not to miss a question.

A	B	C	D	E	F	G	H	I
1	2	3	4	5	6	7	8	9
10	11	12	13	14	15	16	17	18
19	20	21	22	23	24	25	26	27
28	29	30	31	32	33	34	35	36
37	38	39	40	41	42	43	44	45
46	47	48	49	50	51	52	53	54
55	56	57	58	59	60	61	62	63
64	65	66	67	68	69	70	71	72
73	74	75	76	77	78	79	80	81
82	83	84	85	86	87	88	89	90
91	92	93	94	95	96	97	98	99
100	101	102	103	104	105	106	107	108

TOTALS

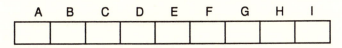

A	B	C	D	E	F	G	H	I

Write the scores for each column here.

A _____ Clear Objectives and Agreed-Upon Goals

B _____ Openness and Confrontation

C _____ Participation and Trust

D _____ Cooperation and Conflict

E _____ Workable Procedures

F _____ Leadership

G _____ Benchmarking and Review

H _____ Personal Development

I _____ Good Intergroup Relations

Graph your scores by entering dots representing the above scores on the chart below and connecting the dots with lines.

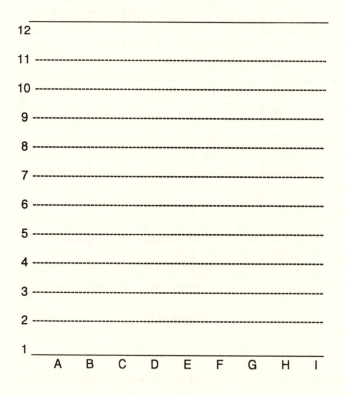

DEFINING THE CHARACTERISTICS

Having identified the areas in need of attention, you need a definition of what they are.

Clear Objectives and Agreed-Upon Goals

All organizations exist for a purpose, yet so often the way they operate demonstrates that the purpose is unclear. No group of people is likely to be effective unless it knows what it wants to achieve, but having clear objectives and agreed-upon goals is more than just knowing the intended outcomes.

People are most likely to be committed to objectives if they also feel some identity with and ownership for them. Even where the objectives are understood and agreed upon, a gap often exists between organizational and personal objectives. One of the chief indicators of effective realignment is that this gap has been narrowed as much as possible. Effective organizations must recognize both personal and group needs. Here are some pointers for setting objectives:

- To motivate people, objectives must be democratically conceived.
- Managers, teams, and individuals must be involved in determining their own areas of responsibility and their own objectives.
- The emphasis should be on "results to be achieved" rather than "things to do."
- Managers and subordinates must agree on results required, methods of measuring them, and a timetable for review.
- The changing environment must be kept in mind throughout.
- Objectives should, as far as possible, be (a) specific, (b) time bounded, and (c) measurable.
- Organizational, team, and individual objectives need to change as circumstances change.

Openness and Confrontation

Two of the hallmarks of a good work environment are openness and confrontation. In most organizations, these characteristics are slow to appear and difficult to teach; but managers willing to take the risks can develop them. Openness and confrontation improve as the following circumstances come about:

- *Improve Communication Feedback.* Real communication is candid and honest. It means a genuine understanding or sharing of feelings and experiences and actively listening to others' points of view.

- *Increase Self-Knowledge*. As individuals work together in teams, and as part of strategic planning, they begin to know themselves and their colleagues better. They find that openness and confrontation also develop. A person with honest self-knowledge recognizes true weaknesses and strengths and admits them to others so that help can be offered and obtained. Requesting and obtaining help increases mutual understanding and respect among team members and fosters genuine openness.

- *Constructive Use of Conflict*. Conflict, properly managed and constructively employed, leads to greater understanding among members of any group. Positive conflict, which deals in facts and is intended to help individuals or the group to improve by talking through problems until sound understanding is reached, encourages both openness and trust. Negative conflict, which relies on rumor and opinion and is intended to wound and divide, breeds mistrust and hostility.

Participation and Trust

Participation and trust can best be achieved when individual team members

- Do not feel they have to protect their territory or function
- Feel able to talk straight to other team members about both nice and unpleasant things

With trust, people can talk freely about their fears and problems and receive from others the help which they need to be effective. People, whether in a family or a firm, will never be able to feel frank and open unless they also feel that other members are equally frank and open. Conflict avoided in the name of being participative will not build relationships.

When a manager participates actively in the process, it is possible to create a supportive climate in which survivors can begin to move toward agreed objectives and participate with each other in constructive criticism; mutual confidence building; and frank, direct communications. When survivors really trust each other, true participation can be experienced.

Cooperation and Conflict

Cooperation means working together—or, as defined by one dictionary, "working together to share the profits." Perhaps this is the essence of teamwork—that people put the team's objectives before their own and share both the financial and psychological rewards of their efforts.

Cooperation implies that individuals are committed and willing to be involved in the work they do, and that they are ready to share their skills and information with the rest of the team, knowing that the others will reciprocate. It also implies that individuals trust their team members' ability to consider their interests equally with their own and are willing for people to undertake assignments that contribute to the group's objectives. People are less suspicious of individuals' motives in carrying out important assignments.

Cooperation encourages high morale; individuals accept each others' strengths and weaknesses and contribute from their pool of knowledge and skills. All abilities, knowledge, and experience are fully used by the team; individuals are not afraid to draw upon other people's abilities to help with their problems.

With true cooperation comes a degree of conflict. The effective team works through issues of conflict and uses the result to achieve objectives. Conflict is often seen as the opposite of cooperation, but it is inevitable in the survivor environment. A certain amount of conflict prevents the organization from becoming complacent and is often the source of new ideas. The management of conflict should be an aid to cooperation.

Constructive, healthy conflict has a problem-solving base. Those involved in solving the problems are willing to sublimate personality differences, to listen to others' views, to be open and candid with each other, and to be supportive and helpful. Subsequent interaction becomes more effective, and cooperation improves.

Workable Procedures

The effective organization thinks results first and methods second but also realizes that sound working methods and decision making lead to achievement of objectives. Clarifying objectives is essential, as it can prevent all the misunderstandings and defensive arguments that result from some people not knowing what is happening. In making decisions, good groups develop the ability to collect information quickly and then discuss the alternatives openly. They then become committed to their decisions, and ensure that action ensues quickly. Critical issues to consider are as follows:

1. How is decision making accomplished?
   - Is it mainly formal or informal?
   - At what levels are decisions taken?
   - Are people who will be affected really involved?
   - Is information collected properly and by the proper people?
   - Do people have the right information?
   - Is gossip used?
   - Do power groups operate? If so, are they harmful?
2. How are decisions implemented?
   - Do those who make decisions give the necessary authority for others to implement them?

- Are decisions communicated effectively?
- Are the right resources available and present?
- Are resources coordinated?
- Are people resistant to change? If so, how should we overcome this?
3. How are decisions reviewed?
   - Who carries out the review?

Leadership

Whether led or managed continually by the same person or by a variety of people, we all have views about the way in which we should be managed. Successful managers the world over differ in what they regard as good management, but what all agree on is that

- the group that is dissatisfied with the way in which it is led will operate below maximum effectiveness
- the way people lead and manage others is a product of the attitudes and assumptions they have about them

The survivor environment demands a management or leadership style which is both flexible and appropriate.

Decision making is a critical aspect of leadership, yet it is often badly done—at the wrong level, with incomplete information, or remote from the people who must carry it out. To arrive at good decisions, a flexible and explicit working procedure must exist which all members understand and accept.

Benchmarking and Review

Reviewing allows the group to learn from experience and to improve consciously. The numerous ways of reviewing essentially focus on survivors receiving feedback about their performance as individuals and about the performance of the group as a whole.

Review can often be carried out during and after the completion of a task. The skills needed include both openness and trust in ample quantities if the exercise is to be realistic. Stress the positive contribution which regular review can make.

Another method is called "process review," and it involves someone or several people outside the group observing and reporting what happens. These people could be colleagues, customers, or consultants. Information can be collected by report, focus group, survey, or other methods.

This approach is in line with the application of TQM principles. Setting realistic goals for continuous improvement will help keep the group in a future-thinking mode.

Personal Development

While the effectiveness of the group can be greater than the sum of its parts, the development of personal skills is also important. One obvious fact about teams, departments, or work groups is that they are a collection of individuals; and their effectiveness must, in part, be a function of individual ability.

The work world is full of countless examples of people who seem to have all the right skills and knowledge and yet never seem to achieve worthwhile results. We also meet many people who have had little training and, on the surface, appear deficient in the accepted managerial skills yet have created immensely successful careers and seem to have the knack of always succeeding.

In practice, success is not simply a question of skills and textbook knowledge; it is about seeing opportunities, seizing them, and making them happen—and some people seem able to do that continually. Observers have noticed that the most and least effective persons almost invariably display two different sets of characteristics (see Table A.1).

Usually, no one displays either one or the other set of characteristics exclusively. It is a question of degree, and personal development is essentially about which set of characteristics we move toward and which we move away from. The two sets of characteristics, when placed side by side, become stark alternatives—choices which we are able to make about ourselves, our approach to life, and our approach to work.

Often those individuals who predominantly exhibit the high-effectiveness characteristics are uncomfortable people to work with; their drive and dynamism at first sight appear to inhibit the common good of the group. Very effective groups, however, learn to capitalize on these qualities and encourage their less-effective members to move toward them.

The survivor climate has served to push low-effectiveness people further in the hole (or out of the organization) and has also dampened the spirits of many naturally high-effectiveness people.

Good Intergroup Relations

Organizational success will be hindered without good relations among the groups or individuals within the organization. The cohesive group often appears threatening to other groups, who perceive that they are less effective. Just as teamwork means individuals working well together, so effective organizational life means groups interacting well together. Thus,

Table A.1
Summary of High- and Low-Effectiveness Characteristics

High-Effectiveness Characteristics	Low-Effectiveness Characteristics
1. Active	1. Passive
2. Seek challenge	2. Avoid challenge
3. Seek insight into themselves	3. Avoid self-knowledge
4. See and use time and energy as valuable resources	4. Misuse time and energy
5. In touch with their feelings	5. Out of touch with their feelings
6. Show concern for others	6. Do not care for others' feelings
7. Relaxed	7. Tense
8. Open and honest	8. Use manipulation
9. Stretch themselves	9. Avoid stretching experiences
10. Clear personal values	10. Programmed by the views of others
11. Set high standards	11. Set low standards
12. Welcome feedback	12. Avoid feedback
13. See things through	13. Opt out
14. Tolerate and use opposing views	14. Intolerant of others' views
15. Use conflict constructively	15. Avoid conflict
16. Give freedom	16. Restrain freedom
17. Are happy about life	17. Are unhappy about life

the highly effective group constantly reaches out to others to ensure that its efforts are well received, supported, and assisted. To ensure effective external relationships:

- The actions and decisions of the group must be communicated clearly.
- Although groups are not the same, they can still work together well.
- Try to understand the other group's point of view, their strengths, and weaknesses; lend a helping hand when needed.
- Do not be too rigid in defending group boundaries.
- Recognize that group boundaries and responsibilities will need to be reviewed and amended from time to time.
- Anticipate and eliminate potential intergroup problems before they arise.

- Really try to listen to others, and do all that is possible to help them listen to you.
- Use others as a source of ideas and comparison.
- Understand and use differences in people.

Once achieved, effective intergroup relationships bring numerous advantages, including greater ability to influence the organization; more available help; easier flow of information; better problem solving; less anxiety; and happier, more enjoyable working lives.

Task and Responsibility Audit

NAME: _____

JOB TITLE: _____   LENGTH OF SERVICE: _____

REPORTS TO: _____

PERSONAL DATA

How did you come to this company?

WORK HISTORY

Knowledge/Skill/Perception Data

What does a person need to know in order to do your current job?

What does a person need to be able to do in order to effectively accomplish the tasks and responsibilities of your job?

What are the intangibles associated with doing your job well?

What instincts must a person have?

What must a person perceive a need for?

What do you feel are your strongest points?

What areas within yourself would you like to develop further?

Assuming that additional changes are coming, how do you perceive that your job will change?

The knowledge you will need? Skill? Perception?

How do you spend your time on any given day?

What parts of the job command the most time?

Where would you rather spend more of your time?

Figure B.1
Management Competency Worksheet

KNOWLEDGE	SKILL	PERCEPTION

<u>Job-Related Attitudes, Values, Beliefs</u>

What do you know about projected changes?

How will they affect you?

Are the changes needed?

How do you describe yourself on the job? (What do you tell others you do?)

What do you like:

About your current working conditions?

About the job?

(What do you like:)

       About the company?

       About your working relationships?

       About the general levels of communication?

What general concerns do you have?

What would you change?

What is good about the current output of this group?

What do you need to do the job better? Resources? Manpower? Planning?
Direction?

<u>Motivation Data</u>

Interests

High_____Low

Aspirations

High_____Low

Energy

High_____Low

From among your projects, tasks, and/or responsibilities, which one (or ones) do you enjoy most? Why?

Where would you like to be in five years? Why have you selected that (those) goals?

<u>Intellectual Data</u>

Organized_____Disorganized

Logical_____Illogical

Skilled   Unskilled
Communicator_____Communicator

Concise_____Tangential

Reflective_____Impulsive

Nonverbal   Nonverbal
Agreement_____Conflict

What are your outside interests?

What was the biggest problem you have had on this job?

      How did you solve it?

How would you describe yourself as a problem solver? Action-oriented? Detail-oriented? Other?

<u>Personality Data</u> (Interpersonal Skill/Coping Behavior)

Outgoing_____Open_____Withdrawn

Aggressive_____Assertive_____Passive

Confident_____Restrained_____Self-Defeating

Cooperative_____Judicious_____Defensive

Enthusiastic_____Accepting_____Bitter

Leading_____Conforming_____Dependent

Appendix C

Motivators and Satisfiers Exercise

For each of the job factors in the list that follows below, indicate if it primarily enhances job satisfaction or primarily enhances productivity.

S = satisfaction   P = productivity

_____ Fair treatment in work load

_____ Good chance for advancement

_____ Pay tied to performance

_____ Good fringe benefits

_____ Flexible working hours

_____ Good pay

_____ Flexible workplace

_____ Recognition for good work

_____ Being informed about what goes on

_____ Challenging job

_____ Working with people I like

_____ Job allows me to think for myself

_____ A great deal of responsibility

_____ Convenient location

_____ Job enables me to develop abilities

_____ Get along well with supervisor

_____ Workplace free from dirt, noise, and pollution

_____ Interesting work

_____ A job without too much rush and stress

_____ Job requires creativity

Factors that Enhance Productivity

Good chance for advancement
Pay tied to performance
Good pay
Recognition for good work
Challenging job
Job allows me to think for myself
A great deal of responsibility
Job enables me to develop abilities
Interesting work
Job requires creativity

Factors that Enhance Satisfaction

Fair treatment in work load
Good fringe benefits
Flexible working hours
Flexible workplace
Being informed about what goes on
Working with people I like
Convenient location
Get along with supervisor
Workplace free of dirt, noise, and pollution
A job without too much rush and stress

Managers need to distinguish between motivators and satisfiers in order to ensure that they are placing their emphasis on those issues that will most directly affect productivity. See Chapter 8 for a more complete discussion of the research behind motivators and satisfiers.

APPENDIX D

Managing the Relationship with Your Manager

Survivor managers have an additional obligation. They are charged with managing the relationship with their managers. This inventory helps the survivor manager discover areas that need work in his or her relationship with superiors.

The inventory can also be used by managers who want to open a dialogue with their direct reports. By having subordinates respond to the following questions, managers can get a clear picture of how effectively the communication channels are working:

What are your manager's goals and objectives?

_____

_____

_____

What factors are creating pressures or placing major restrictions on him or her?

_____

_____

_____

_____

What are your manager's strengths?

_____

_____

_____

What are your manager's weaknesses?

_____

_____

_____

Describe your manager's preferred work style.

_____

_____

_____

What are your strengths?

_____

_____

_____

What are your weaknesses?

_____

_____

_____

What is your preferred work style?

_____

_____

_____

An action plan for managing your manager: What can you do to reconcile work styles? Develop mutual expectations? Keep your manager informed? Enhance dependability and honesty? Make the best use of your manager's time and resources?

_____

_____

_____

_____

_____

_____

_____

Notes

CHAPTER 1

1. John Greenwald, "The Great American Layoffs," *Time*, 20 July 1992.
2. Steve Malanga, "N.Y. Job Losses Show Modest Rebound in '93," *Crain's New York Business*, 29 June 1992.
3. "Big Blue's Blues," *New York Times*, 4 October 1992.
4. Michael J. Mandel, Stephanie Anderson Forest, and Gary McWilliams, "No Help Wanted: Ongoing Layoffs Are Hobbling the Recovery," *Business Week*, 21 September 1992.
5. Sarah Lubman and Joseph B. White, "GM's Hughes Aircraft Write-Off of $749.4 Million," *The Wall Street Journal*, 1 July 1992.
6. Greenwald, "Great American Layoffs."
7. Steven V. Roberts, "Tears and Fears in America's New Civil War," *U.S. News and World Report*, 9 March 1992.
8. Mandel, Forest, and McWilliams, "No Help Wanted."
9. Bruce Nussbaum, "The End of Corporate Loyalty," *Business Week*, 4 August 1986.
10. Perri Capell, "Downsizing Doldrums," *National Business Employment Weekly*, 18–24 September 1992.
11. Bruno Bettelheim, *Surviving and Other Essays* (New York: Alfred A. Knopf, 1979).
12. Ibid.
13. "Eye on the Future," *The Wall Street Journal*, 25 May 1994.
14. Ibid.
15. Leonard Greenhalgh and Todd D. Jick, "Survivor Sense Making and Reactions to Organizational Decline: Effects of Individual Differences," *Management Communication Quarterly* 2 (3; February 1989).
16. Ibid.

17. Bruce Nussbaum, "I'm Worried about My Job: A Career Survival Kit for the '90s," *Business Week*, 7 October 1991.

18. John Naisbitt and Patricia Aburdene, *Megatrends 2000: Ten New Directions for the 1990's* (New York: William Morrow 1990).

19. Ibid.

20. Ibid.

21. Ibid.

22. Noel M. Tichy and David O. Ulrich, "The Leadership Challenge—A Call for the Transformational Leader," *Sloan Management Review*, Fall, 1984.

23. Ibid.

24. Ibid.

CHAPTER 2

1. Edmund L. Andrews, "A.T.&T. Cutting up to 15,000 Jobs to Trim Costs," *New York Times*, 11 February 1994.

2. Louis Uchitelle, "Male, Educated and Falling Behind," *New York Times*, 11 February 1994.

3. Juliet B. Schor, *The Overworked American: The Unexpected Decline of Leisure* (New York: Basic Books, HarperCollins, 1993).

4. Daniel Yankelovich, *New Rules: Searching for Self-Fulfillment in a World Turned Upside Down* (New York: Bantam Books, 1982).

5. Ibid.

6. Jaclyn Fireman, "Are Companies Less Family Friendly?" *Fortune*, 21 March 1994.

7. Ibid.

8. Schor, *Overworked American*.

9. Ibid.

10. Ellen Galinsky, James T. Bond, and Dana E. Friedman, *The Changing Workforce: Highlights of the National Study* (New York: Families and Work Institute, 1993).

CHAPTER 3

1. "IBM Exec Quit under Pressure: Experts Say Layoffs Not Quick Enough," *The Times Herald-Record*, Middletown, N.Y., 29 April 1994, reprinted from *The Wall Street Journal*, n.d.

2. Robert G. Eccles and Nitin Nohria, *Beyond the Hype* (Boston: Harvard Business School Press, 1992).

3. J. R. P. French and B. Raven, "The Bases of Social Power," in *Studies in Social Power*, ed. D. Cartwright (Ann Arbor: University of Michigan Press, 1959).

4. Brian Dumaine, "America's Toughest Bosses," *Fortune*, 18 October 1993.

5. Lee Smith, "Burned-Out Bosses," *Fortune*, 25 July 1994.

6. John A. Byrne, "The Survivor: Staying Power Has Rewards—And a Price Tag," *Business Week*, 9 May 1994, a subarticle of idem, "The Pain of Downsizing: What It's Really Like to Live through the Struggle to Remake a Company," *Business Week*, 4 April 1994.

7. Brian O'Reilly, "The New Deal: What Companies and Employees Owe One Another," *Fortune*, 13 June 1994.

8. Ibid.

9. Myron Magnet, "Let's Go for Growth," *Fortune*, 7 March 1994.

10. Louis S. Richman, "How to Get Ahead in America," *Fortune*, 16 May 1994.

11. Ibid.

12. Peter M. Senge, *The Fifth Discipline* (New York: Doubleday/Currency, 1990).

13. Brian Dumaine, "America's Smart Young Entrepreneurs," *Fortune*, 21 March 1994.

14. Jon R. Katzenbach and Douglas K. Smith, "The Discipline of Teams," *Harvard Business Review*, March-April, 1993.

15. Jack Gordon, "The Team Troubles That Won't Go Away," *Training Magazine*, August, 1994.

16. Robert H. Waterman, Jr., Judith A. Waterman, and Betsy A. Collard, "Toward a Career-Resilient Workforce," *Harvard Business Review*, July-August, 1994.

CHAPTER 4

1. Mary Parker Follett, *Dynamic Administration: The Collected Papers of Mary Parker Follett*, ed. Henry C. Metcalf and L. Urwick (London: Sir Isaac Pitman & Sons, 1941).

2. Robert Eccles and Nitin Nohria, *Beyond the Hype* (Boston: Harvard Business School Press, 1992).

3. Frederick W. Taylor, *Scientific Management* (New York: Harper, 1911).

4. Michael Hammer and James Champy, *Reengineering the Corporation* (New York: HarperBusiness, 1993).

5. Tom Peters, *The Tom Peters Seminar: Crazy Times Call for Crazy Organizations* (New York: Vintage Books, 1994).

6. William Bridges, "The End of the Job," *Fortune*, 19 September 1994.

7. Keith H. Hammonds, Kevin Kelly, and Karen Thurston, "The New World of Work," *Business Week*, 17 October 1994.

8. Michael J. Mandel, "Business Rolls the Dice," *Business Week*, 17 October 1994.

CHAPTER 5

1. Kenneth Labich, "Why Companies Fail," *Fortune*, 14 November 1994.

2. H. Wayland Cummings, Larry W. Long, and Michael L. Lewis, *Managing Communication in Organizations: An Introduction*, 2nd ed. (Scottsdale, Ariz.: Gorsuch Scarisbrick, 1987).

3. Thomas E. Harris, *Applied Organizational Communication: Perspectives, Principles and Pragmatics* (Hillsdale, N.J.: Lawrence Erlbaum Associates, 1993).

4. Ram Charan, "How Networks Reshape Organizations for Results," *Harvard Business Review*, September-October, 1991.

5. Ibid.

6. Ibid.

7. Thomas A. Stewart, "Managing in a Wired Company," *Fortune*, 11 July 1994.

8. Ibid.

CHAPTER 6

1. George Milkovich and William Glueck, *Personnel/Human Resource Management: A Diagnostic Approach*, 4th ed. (Plano, Tex.: Business Publications, Inc., 1985).
2. Ibid.
3. Brian L. Davis, Carol J. Skube, Lowell W. Hellervik, Susan H. Gebelein, and James L. Sheard, *Successful Manager's Handbook* (Minneapolis: Personnel Decisions, Inc., 1992).
4. Ibid.
5. Harold L. Hodgkinson, *All One System: Demographics of Education—Kindergarten through Graduate School* (New York: Institute for Educational Leadership, 1989).
6. Ibid.
7. Bruce Nussbaum, "The End of Corporate Loyalty," *Business Week,* 4 August 1986.
8. Chris Chen, "The Diversity Paradox," *Personnel Journal,* January, 1992.

CHAPTER 7

1. Daniel Yankelovich and John Immerwahr, *Putting the Work Ethic to Work: A Public Agenda Report on Restoring America's Competitive Vitality* (New York: The Public Agenda Foundation, 1983).
2. Ellen Galinsky, James T. Bond, and Dana E. Friedman, *The Changing Workforce: Highlights of the National Study* (New York: Families and Work Institute, 1993).

CHAPTER 8

1. Daniel Yankelovich and John Immerwahr, *Putting the Work Ethic to Work: A Public Agenda Report on Restoring America's Competitive Vitality* (New York: The Public Agenda Foundation, 1983).

CHAPTER 9

1. Brian O'Reilly, "The New Deal: What Companies and Employees Owe One Another," *Fortune,* 13 June 1994.
2. J. E. Rosenbaum, "Organization, Career Systems, and Employee Misperceptions," in *Handbook of Career Theory*, ed. M. B. Arthur, D. T. Hall, and B. S. Lawrence (New York: Cambridge University Press, 1989).
3. R. G. Schaeffer, *Staffing Systems: Managerial and Professional Jobs* (New York: New York Conference Board, 1972).
4. Patrice M. Buzzanell and Steven R. Goldzwig, "Linear and Nonlinear Career Models: Metaphors, Paradigms, and Ideologies," *Management Communication Quarterly,* May, 1991.
5. Ibid.
6. Brian L. Davis, Carol J. Skube, Lowell W. Hellervik, Susan H. Gebelein, and James L. Sheard, *Successful Manager's Handbook* (Minneapolis: Personnel Decisions, Inc., 1992).

7. Bradford D. Smart, *Selection Interviewing: A Management Psychologist's Recommended Approach* (New York: John Wiley & Sons, 1983), and John D. Drake, *Interviewing for Managers: A Complete Guide to Employment Interviewing* (New York: Amacom, 1982).

8. Patricia Braus, "What Workers Want," *American Demographics*, August, 1992.

9. Ibid.

10. O'Reilly, "New Deal."

11. Ibid.

12. Ibid.

13. M. B. Arthur, D. T. Hall, and B. S. Lawrence, eds., "Generating New Directions in Career Theory: The Case for a Trans-Disciplinary Approach," in *Handbook of Career Theory* (Cambridge, Mass.: Harvard University Press, 1989).

14. Buzzanell and Goldzwig, "Linear and Nonlinear Career Models."

CHAPTER 11

1. Daniel Yankelovich and John Immerwahr, *Putting the Work Ethic to Work: A Public Agenda Report on Restoring America's Competitive Vitality* (New York: The Public Agenda Foundation, 1983).

2. John J. Gabarro and John P. Kotter, "Managing Your Boss," *Harvard Business Review*, January-February, 1980.

Bibliography

BOOKS

Alderfer, Clayton P. 1972. *Existence, Relatedness and Growth*. New York: Free Press.

Argyris, C. 1960. *Understanding Organizational Behavior*. Homewood, Ill.: Dorsey.

Arthur, M. B., D. T. Hall, and B. S. Lawrence, eds. 1989. "Generating New Directions in Career Theory: The Case for a Trans-Disciplinary Approach." In *Handbook of Career Theory*. New York: Cambridge University Press.

Barnard, C. I. 1938. *The Functions of the Executive*. Cambridge, Mass.: Harvard University Press.

Bettelheim, Bruno. 1979. *Surviving and Other Essays*. New York: Alfred A. Knopf.

Cummings, H. Wayland, Larry W. Long, and Michael L. Lewis. 1987. *Managing Communication in Organizations: An Introduction*. 2nd ed. Scottsdale, Ariz.: Gorsuch Scarisbrick.

Davis, Brian L., Carol J. Skube, Lowell W. Hellervik, Susan H. Gebelein, and James L. Sheard. 1992. *Successful Manager's Handbook*. Minneapolis: Personnel Decisions, Inc.

Drake, John D. 1982. *Interviewing for Managers: A Complete Guide to Employment Interviewing*. New York: Amacom.

Eccles, Robert, and Nitin Nohria. 1992. *Beyond the Hype*. Boston: Harvard Business School Press.

Follett, Mary Parker. 1941. *Dynamic Administration: The Collected Papers of Mary Parker Follett*. Ed. Henry C. Metcalf and L. Urwick. London: Sir Isaac Pitman & Sons.

French, J. R. P., and B. Raven. 1959. "The Bases of Social Power." In *Studies in Social Power*, ed. D. Cartwright. Ann Arbor: University of Michigan Press.

Galinsky, Ellen, James T. Bond, and Dana E. Friedman. 1993. *The Changing Workforce: Highlights of the National Study*. New York: Families and Work Institute.

Hammer, Michael, and James Champy. 1993. *Reengineering the Corporation.* New York: HarperBusiness.

Harris, Thomas E. 1993. *Applied Organizational Communication: Perspectives, Principles and Pragmatics.* Hillsdale, N.J.: Lawrence Erlbaum Associates.

Herzberg, Frederick. 1966. *Work and the Nature of Man.* Cleveland: World.

Herzberg, Frederick, B. Mausner, and B. B. Snyderman. 1959. *The Motivation to Work.* New York: John Wiley.

Hodgkinson, Harold L. 1989. *All One System: Demographics of Education—Kindergarten through Graduate School.* New York: Institute for Educational Leadership.

Katz, Daniel, and Robert Kahn. 1978. *The Social Psychology of Organizations.* New York: John Wiley.

Kelley, Harold, and John Thibaut. 1978. *Interpersonal Relations: A Theory of Interdependence.* New York: John Wiley.

Likert, Rensis. 1961. *New Patterns of Management.* New York: McGraw Hill.

Maslow, Abraham H. 1954. *Motivation and Personality.* New York: Harper & Row.

———. 1965. *Eupsychian Management.* Homewood, Ill.: Irwin.

———. 1968. *Toward a Psychology of Being.* 2nd ed. New York: Van Nostrand.

Mayo, Elton. 1933. *The Human Problems of an Industrial Civilization.* New York: Macmillan.

McClelland, David C. 1953. *The Achievement Motive.* New York: Appleton-Century-Crofts.

———. 1961. *Achieving Society.* Princeton: Van Nostrand.

———. 1975. *Power: The Inner Experience.* New York: Irvington.

McClelland, David C., and D. G. Winter. 1969. *Motivating Economic Achievement.* New York: Free Press.

McGregor, D. M. 1960. *The Human Side of Enterprise.* New York: McGraw Hill.

Milkovich, George, and William Glueck. 1985. *Personnel/Human Resource Management: A Diagnostic Approach.* 4th ed. Plano, Tex.: Business Publications, Inc.

Naisbitt, John, and Patricia Aburdene. 1990. *Megatrends 2000: Ten New Directions for the 1990's.* New York: William Morrow.

Ouchi, W. G. 1981. *Theory Z: How American Business Can Meet the Japanese Challenge.* New York: Avon.

Peters, Tom. 1994. *The Tom Peters Seminar: Crazy Times Call for Crazy Organizations.* New York: Vintage Books.

Porter, L. W., and E. E. Lawler. 1968. *Managerial Attitudes and Performance.* Homewood, Ill.: Dorsey Press.

Pritchett, Price. 1994. *The Employee Handbook of New Work Habits for a Radically Changing World.* Dallas: Pritchett and Associates.

Pritchett, Price, and Ron Pound. 1992. *The Employee Handbook for Organizational Change.* Dallas: Pritchett.

Rosenbaum, J. E. 1989. "Organization, Career Systems, and Employee Misperceptions." In *Handbook of Career Theory,* ed. M. B. Arthur, D. T. Hall, and B. S. Lawrence. New York: Cambridge University Press.

Schaeffer, R. G. 1972. *Staffing Systems: Managerial and Professional Jobs.* New York: New York Conference Board.

Schor, Juliet B. 1993. *The Overworked American: The Unexpected Decline of Leisure.* New York: Basic Books, HarperCollins.

Senge, Peter. 1990. *The Fifth Discipline.* New York: Doubleday/Currency.

Simon, Herbert A. 1958. *Administrative Behavior*. New York: Macmillan.

Skinner, B. F. 1957. *Verbal Behavior*. New York: Appleton-Century-Crofts.

———. 1975. *Beyond Freedom and Dignity*. New York: Bantam.

Smart, Bradford D. 1983. *Selection Interviewing: A Management Psychologist's Recommended Approach*. New York: John Wiley & Sons.

Taylor, Frederick W. 1911. *Scientific Management*. New York: Harper.

Thompson, J. D. 1976. *Organizations in Action*. New York: McGraw Hill.

Vroom, Victor. 1964. *Work and Motivation*. New York: John Wiley.

Vroom, Victor, and P. W. Yetton. 1973. *Leadership Decision-Making*. Pittsburgh: University of Pittsburgh Press.

Weber, Max. 1947. *The Theory of Social and Economic Organizations*. Trans. A. M. Henderson and T. Parsons. New York: Free Press.

Woodward, Joan. 1965. *Industrial Organization: Theory and Practice*. London: Oxford University Press.

Yankelovich, Daniel. 1982. *New Rules: Searching for Self-Fulfillment in a World Turned Upside Down*. New York: Bantam Books.

Yankelovich, Daniel, and John Immerwahr. 1983. *Putting the Work Ethic to Work: A Public Agenda Report on Restoring America's Competitive Vitality*. New York: The Public Agenda Foundation.

JOURNALS, MAGAZINES, AND NEWSPAPERS

Andrews, Edmund L. 1994. A.T.&T. Cutting up to 15,000 Jobs to Trim Costs. *New York Times*, 11 February, D1.

Barnes, Sue, and Leonore M. Greller. 1994. Computer-Mediated Communication in the Organization. *Communication Education* (April): 129–142.

Big Blue's Blues. 1992. *New York Times*, 4 October, B2.

Braus, Patricia. 1992. What Workers Want. *American Demographics* (August): 30–37.

Bridges, William. 1994. The End of the Job. *Fortune* (19 September): 62–74.

———. 1994. Seven Rules to Break in a De-Jobbed World. *Fortune* (19 September): 72.

Buzzanell, Patrice M., and Steven R. Goldzwig. 1991. Linear and Nonlinear Career Models: Metaphors, Paradigms, and Ideologies. *Management Communication Quarterly* (May): 466–505.

Byrne, John A. 1993. Congratulations. You're Moving to a New Pepperoni. *Business Week* (20 December): 80–81.

———. 1993. The Horizontal Corporation. *Business Week* (20 December): 76–81.

———. 1994. The Cost-Cutter: He's Gutsy, Brilliant and Carries an Ax. *Business Week* (4 April): 62–63.

———. 1994. Dream Jobs All Over: The Market for Top Executives Is Perking Up. *Business Week* (4 April): 34–36.

———. 1994. The Pain of Downsizing: What It's Really Like to Live through the Struggle to Remake a Company. *Business Week* (4 April): 60–68.

———. 1994. The Survivor: Staying Power Has Rewards—And a Price Tag. *Business Week* (9 May): 67.

Caminiti, Susan. 1994. What Happens to Laid-Off Managers. *Fortune* (13 June): 68–78.

Capell, Perri. 1992. Downsizing Doldrums. *National Business Employment Weekly* (18–24 September): 16.

Charan, Ram. 1991. How Networks Reshape Organizations for Results. *Harvard Business Review* (September-October): 104–108.

Chen, Chris. 1992. The Diversity Paradox. *Personnel Journal* (January): 32–33.

Davenport, Thomas H. 1994. Saving IT's Soul: Human-Centered Information Management. *Harvard Business Review* (March-April): 119–131.

Drucker, Peter F. 1988. The Coming of the New Organization. *Harvard Business Review* (January-February): 45–53.

Dumaine, Brian. 1993a. America's Toughest Bosses. *Fortune* (18 October): 39–48.

———. 1993b. Payoff from the New Management. *Fortune* (13 December): 103–110.

———. 1994. America's Smart Young Entrepreneurs. *Fortune* (21 March): 34–48.

Eye on the Future. 1994. *The Wall Street Journal*, 25 May, p. 1.

Fireman, Jaclyn. 1994. Are Companies Less Family Friendly? *Fortune* (21 March): 64–67.

Gabarro, John J., and John P. Kotter. 1980. Managing Your Boss. *Harvard Business Review* (January-February): 92–100.

Gordon, Jack. 1994. The Team Troubles That Won't Go Away. *Training Magazine* (August): 27.

Greenhalgh, Leonard, and Todd D. Jick. 1989. Survivor Sense Making and Reactions to Organizational Decline: Effects of Individual Differences. *Management Communication Quarterly* 2 (3; February): 318.

Greenwald, John. 1992. The Great American Layoffs. *Time* (20 July): 64.

Hall, Gene, Jim Rosenthal, and Judy Wade. 1993. How to Make Re-Engineering Really Work. *Harvard Business Review* (November-December): 119–131.

Hammonds, Keith H., Kevin Kelly, and Karen Thurston. 1994. The New World of Work. *Business Week* (17 October): 76–87.

Henkoff, Ronald. 1994. Getting beyond Downsizing. *Fortune* (10 January): 58–64.

IBM Exec Quit under Pressure: Experts Say Layoffs Not Quick Enough. 1994. *The Times Herald-Record*, Middletown, N.Y., 29 April, reprinted from *The Wall Street Journal* (n.d.).

It's a Job: Guaranteed. 1994. *The Times Herald-Record*, Middletown, N.Y., 27 June, 10B.

Jaffe, Betsy. 1988. Power Failure: The Rise of Influence. *New York Metro ASTD Lamplighter* (February): 9–10.

Katzenbach, Jon R., and Douglas K. Smith. 1993. The Discipline of Teams. *Harvard Business Review* (March-April): 111–120.

Krackhardt, David, and Jeffrey R. Hanson. 1993. Informal Networks: The Company behind the Chart. *Harvard Business Review* (July-August): 104–111.

Labich, Kenneth. 1994. Why Companies Fail. *Fortune* (14 November): 52–68.

Locke, Edwin. 1968. Toward a Theory of Task Motivation and Incentives. *Organizational Behavior and Human Performance* 3: 152–189.

———. 1978. The Ubiquity of the Technique of Goal Setting in Theories and Approaches to Employee Motivation. *Academy of Management Review* 3: 594–601.

Lubman, Sarah, and Joseph B. White. 1992. GM's Hughes Aircraft Write-Off of $749.4 Million. *The Wall Street Journal*, 1 July, A1.

Magnet, Myron. 1994. Let's Go for Growth. *Fortune* (7 March): 60–72.

Malanga, Steve. 1992. N.Y. Job Losses Show Modest Rebound in '93. *Crain's New York Business* (29 June): 1.

Mandel, Michael J. 1994. Business Rolls the Dice. *Business Week* (17 October): 88–90.

Mandel, Michael J., Stephanie Anderson Forest, and Gary McWilliams. 1992. No Help Wanted: Ongoing Layoffs Are Hobbling the Recovery. *Business Week* (21 September): 26.

Maslow, Abraham H. 1943. A Theory of Human Motivation. *Psychological Review* 50: 370–396.

Noer, David M. 1993. Leadership in an Age of Layoffs. *Issues and Observations* (Greensboro, N.C.: Center for Creative Leadership), pp. 1–6.

Nussbaum, Bruce. 1986. The End of Corporate Loyalty. *Business Week* (4 August): 42.

———. 1991. I'm Worried about My Job: A Carreer Survival Kit for the '90s. *Business Week* (7 October): 94–104.

O'Reilly, Brian. 1994. The New Deal: What Companies and Employees Owe One Another. *Fortune* (13 June): 44–52.

Patterson, Jack. 1994. Welcome to the Company That Isn't There. *Business Week* (17 October): 86–87.

Reich, Robert B. 1993. Companies Are Cutting Their Hearts Out. *The New York Times Magazine* (19 December): 54–55.

Richman, Louis S. 1994. How to Get Ahead in America. *Fortune* (16 May): 46–54.

Roberts, Steven V. 1992. Tears and Fears in America's New Civil War. *U.S. News and World Report* (9 March): 8.

Sasseen, Jane, Robert Neff, Shekar Hattangadi, and Silvia Sansoni. 1994. The Winds of Change Blow Everywhere. *Business Week* (17 October): 92–93.

Sherman, Stratford. 1993. Are You as Good as the Best in the World? *Fortune* (13 December): 95–96.

———. 1993. A Master Class in Radical Change. *Fortune* (13 December): 82–90.

Smart, Tim. 1994. A Day of Reckoning for Bean Counters. *Business Week* (14 March): 75–76.

Smith, Geoffrey, Wendy Zellner, Russell Mitchell, Susan Chandler, Nancy Peacock, and David Greising. 1994. The Rules of the Game in the New World of Work. *Business Week* (17 October): 94–102.

Smith, Lee. 1994a. Burned-Out Bosses. *Fortune* (25 July): 44–52.

———. 1994b. Landing That First Real Job. *Fortune* (6 May): 58–60.

Stewart, Thomas A. 1993. Reengineering: The Hot New Management Tool. *Fortune* (23 August): 40–48.

———. 1994a. Managing in a Wired Company. *Fortune* (11 July): 44–47.

———. 1994b. Rate Your Readiness to Change. *Fortune* (7 February): 106–110.

Tichy, Noel M. 1993. Revolutionize Your Company. *Fortune* (13 December): 114–118.

Tichy, Noel M., and David O. Ulrich. 1984. The Leadership Challenge—A Call for the Transformational Leader. *Sloan Management Review* (Fall): 59.

Trist, Eric, and K. W. Bamforth. 1951. Some Social and Psychological Consequences of the Long-Wall Method of Coal-Getting. *Human Relations* 4: 3–38.

Uchitelle, Louis. 1994. Male, Educated and Falling Behind. *New York Times*, 11 February, D1.

Waterman, Robert H., Jr., Judith A. Waterman, and Betsy A. Collard. 1994. Toward a Career-Resilient Workforce. *Harvard Business Review* (July-August): 87–95.

Index

ABOUT THE AUTHORS

MARVIN R. GOTTLIEB is Associate Professor of Communication at Lehman College (CUNY), and president of the Communication Project, Inc. Gottlieb has over fifteen years of experience as a consultant, management development specialist, and trainer for manufacturing, travel, banking, financial services, and advertising companies. Major clients include American Express, Bankers Trust, Thomas Cook Travel, Ogilvy & Mather, Transilwrap Company, Reuters, Marriott Corporation, and the Prudential. He is the author of *Oral Interpretation* (1980), *Interview* (1986), and with William Healy *Making Deals: The Business of Negotiating* (1990). He is also a member of the Commercial Panel of the American Arbitration Association.

LORI CONKLING is Director of Continuing Education and Community Development at Orange County Community College–SUNY. She was formerly Manager of Management Training at Reuters America. She also initiated and established the Management Development Institute, a consulting organization within Long Island University, where she managed major grants from the New Jersey Department of Human Services, the U.S. Department of Agriculture, and the U.S. Department of Treasury.